VAULT COMICS

PUBLISHER
DAMIAN A. WASSEL
EDITOR-IN-CHIEF
ADRIAN F. WASSEL
ART DIRECTOR
NATHAN C. GOODEN
EVP BRANDING & DESIGN
TIM DANIEL
DIRECTOR OF PR & RETAILER RELATIONS
DAVID DISSANAYAKE
OPERATIONS MANAGER
IAN BALDESSARI
PRINCIPAL
DAMIAN A. WASSEL, SR.

WRITTEN & CREATED BY
ELIOT RAHAL

ILLUSTRATED BY
FELIPE CUNHA

COLORED BY
DEE CUNNIFFE & ELLIE WRIGHT

LETTERED BY
TAYLOR ESPOSITO

COVER BY
IRENE KOH

RIP G. RAVES DESIGNED BY

JOHN BIVENS

SPECIAL THANKS TO

GRACE THOMAS

CULT CLASSIC

RETURN TO WHISPER

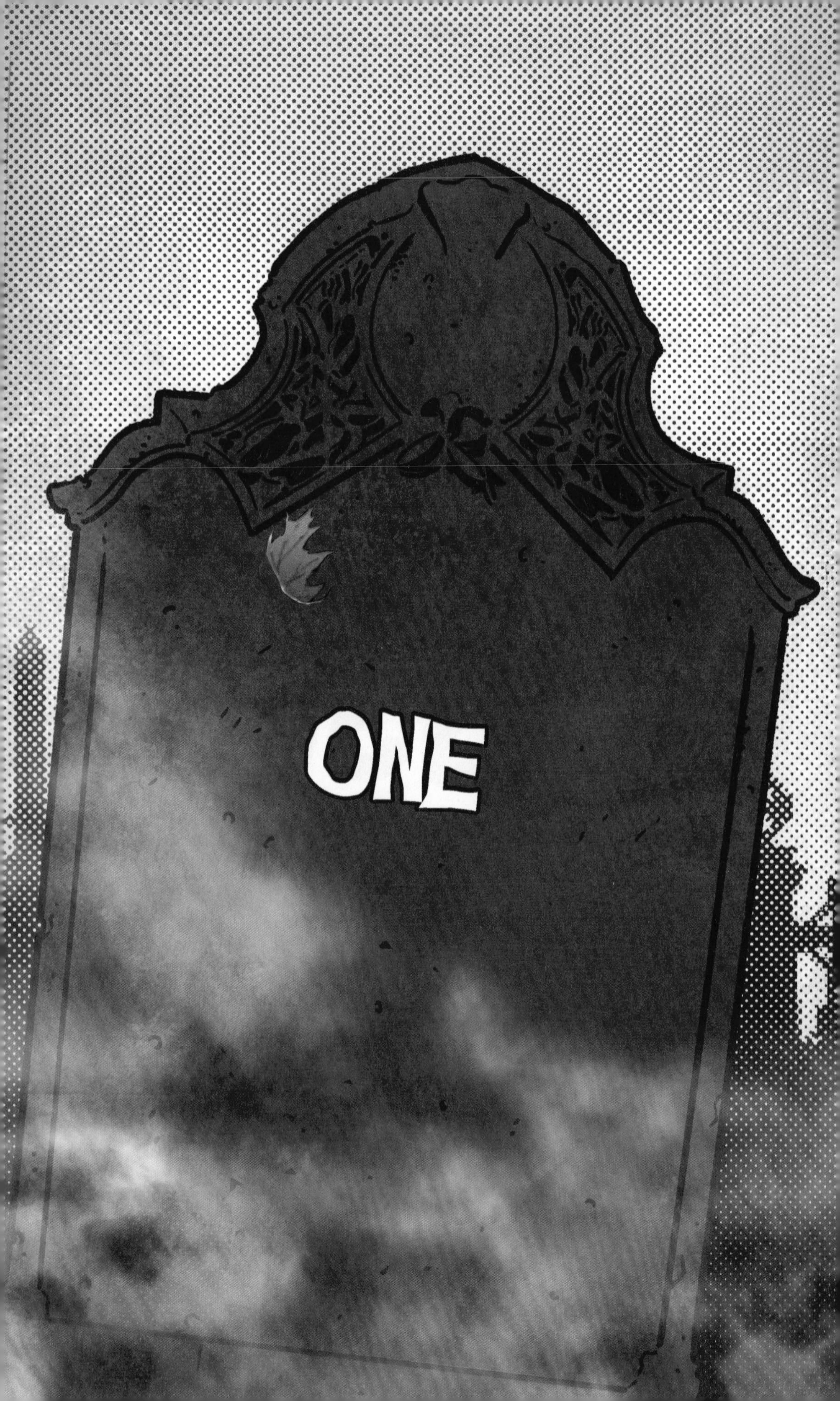
ONE

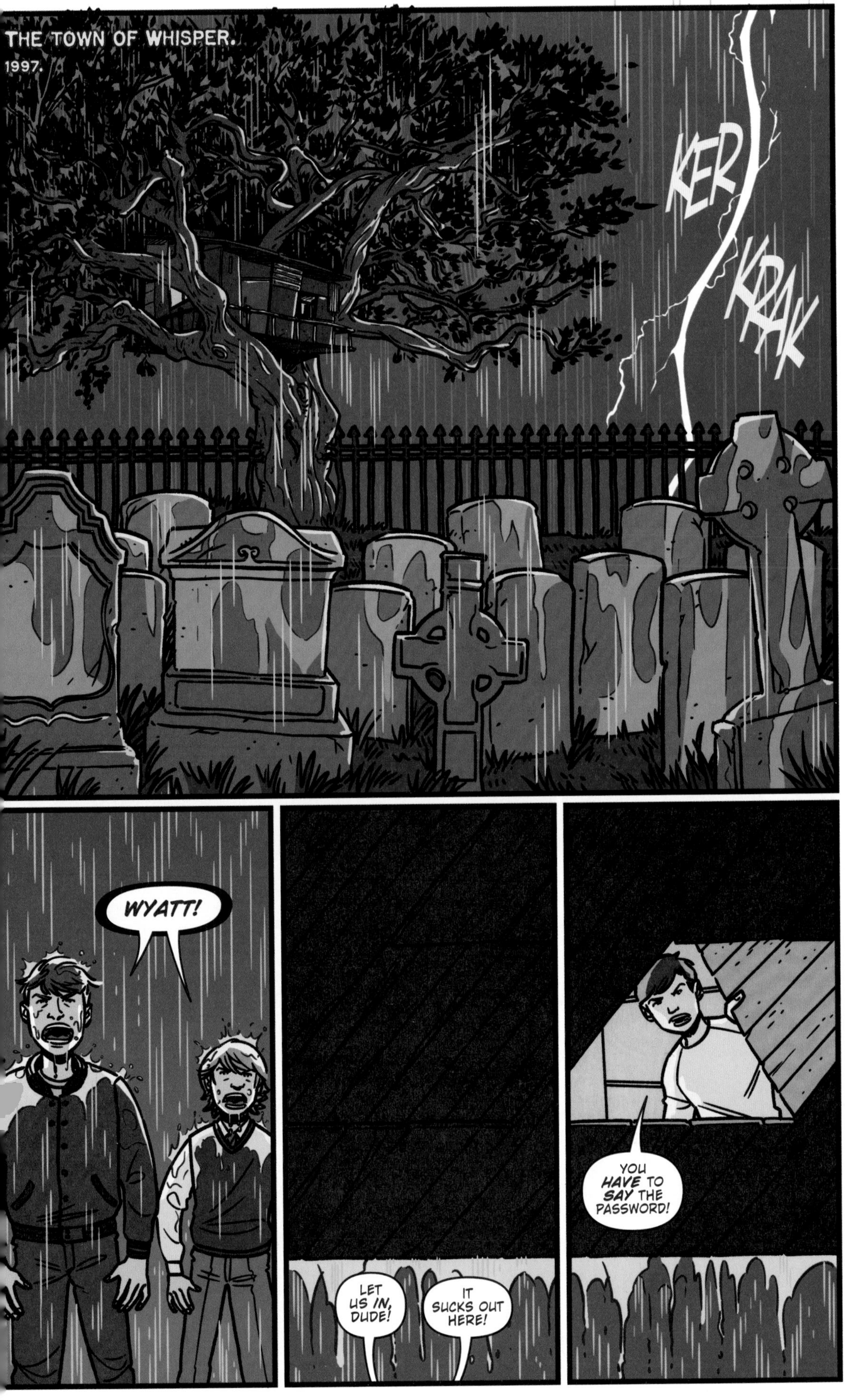
THE TOWN OF WHISPER.
1997.
KER
KRAK
WYATT!
LET US IN, DUDE!
IT SUCKS OUT HERE!
YOU HAVE TO SAY THE PASSWORD!

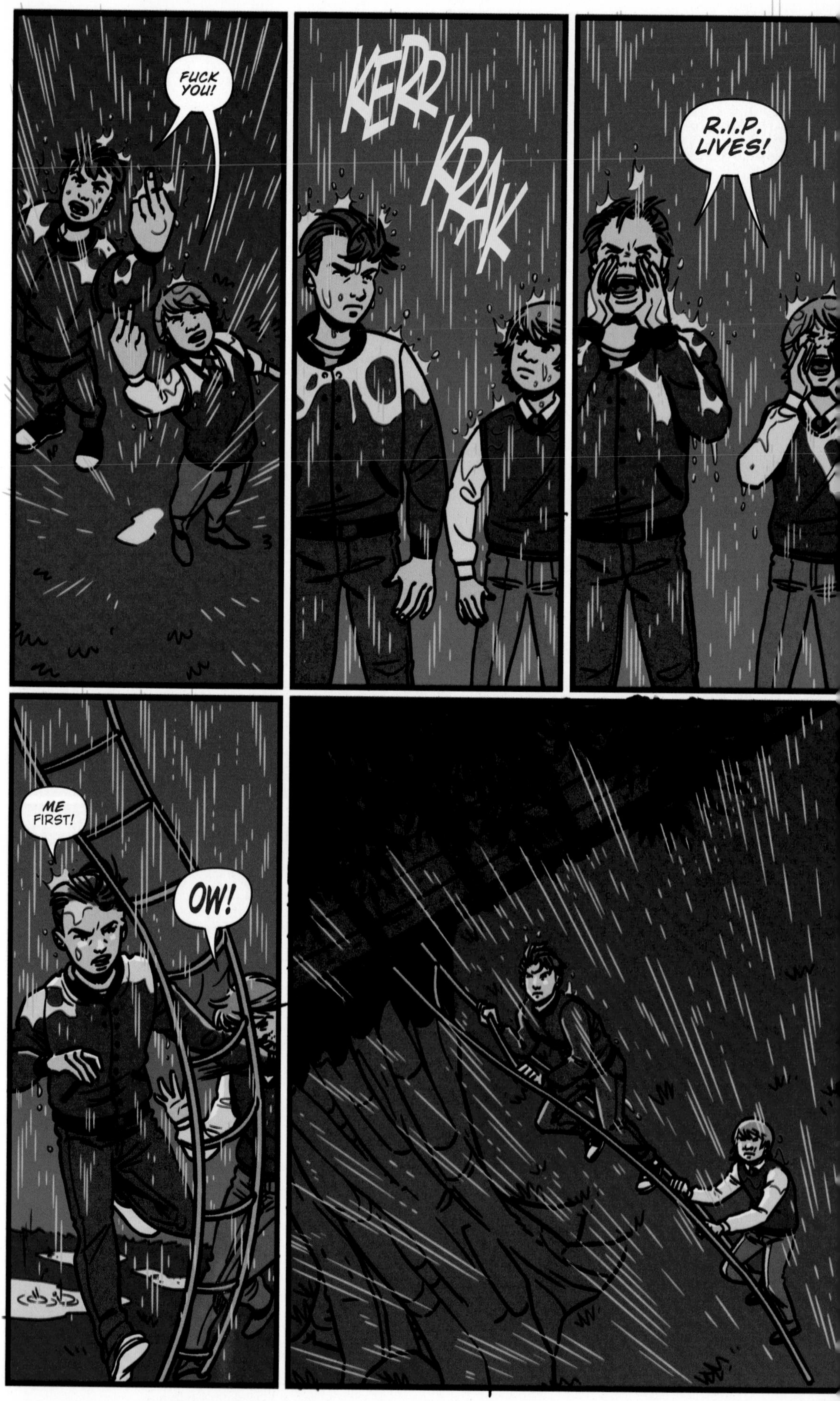
FUCK YOU!
KERR KRAK
R.I.P. LIVES!
ME FIRST!
OW!

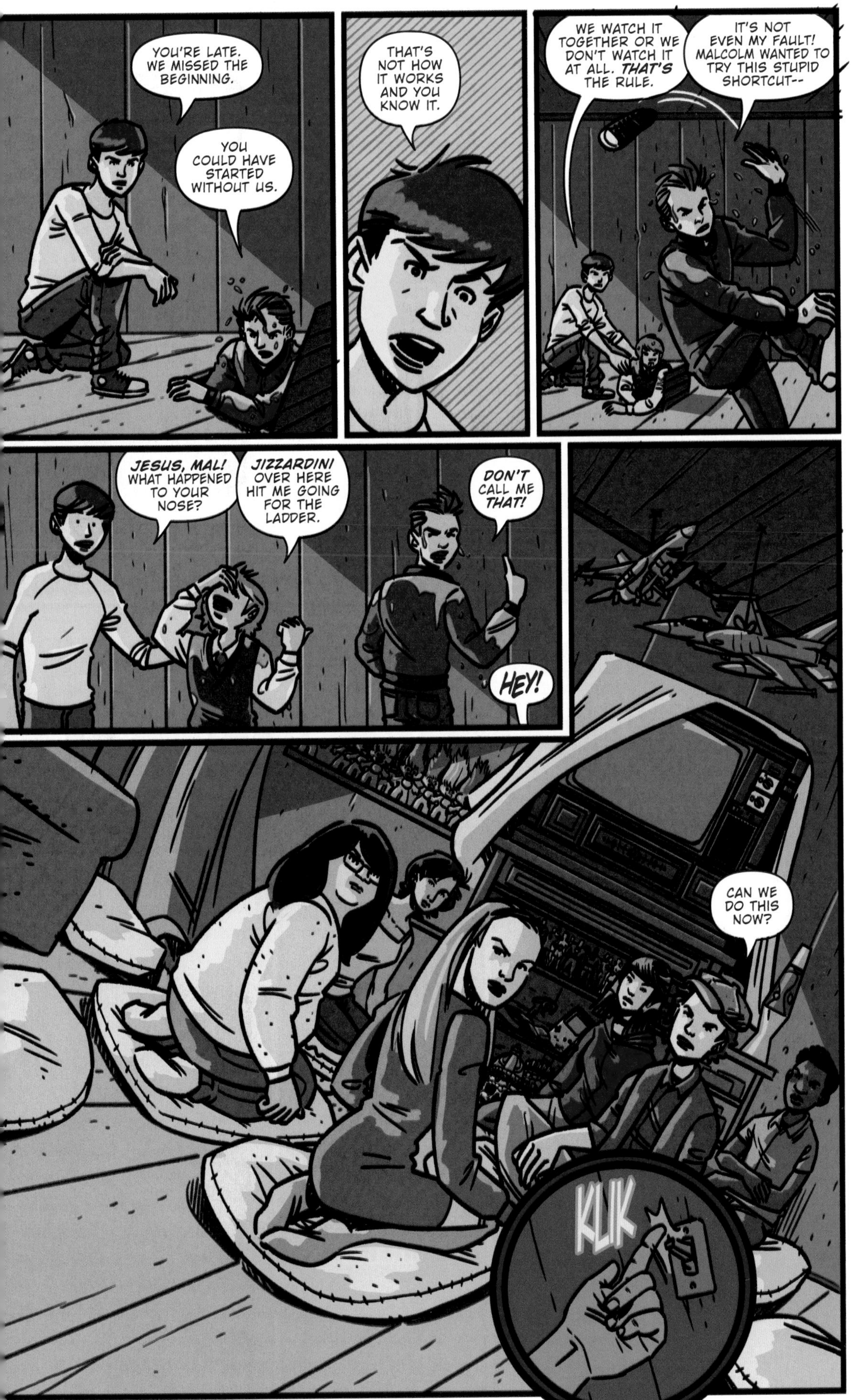

YOU'RE LATE. WE MISSED THE BEGINNING.
YOU COULD HAVE STARTED WITHOUT US.
THAT'S NOT HOW IT WORKS AND YOU KNOW IT.
WE WATCH IT TOGETHER OR WE DON'T WATCH IT AT ALL. *THAT'S* THE RULE.
IT'S NOT EVEN MY FAULT! MALCOLM WANTED TO TRY THIS STUPID SHORTCUT--
JESUS, MAL! WHAT HAPPENED TO YOUR NOSE?
JIZZARDINI OVER HERE HIT ME GOING FOR THE LADDER.
DON'T CALL ME *THAT!*
HEY!
CAN WE DO THIS NOW?
KLIK

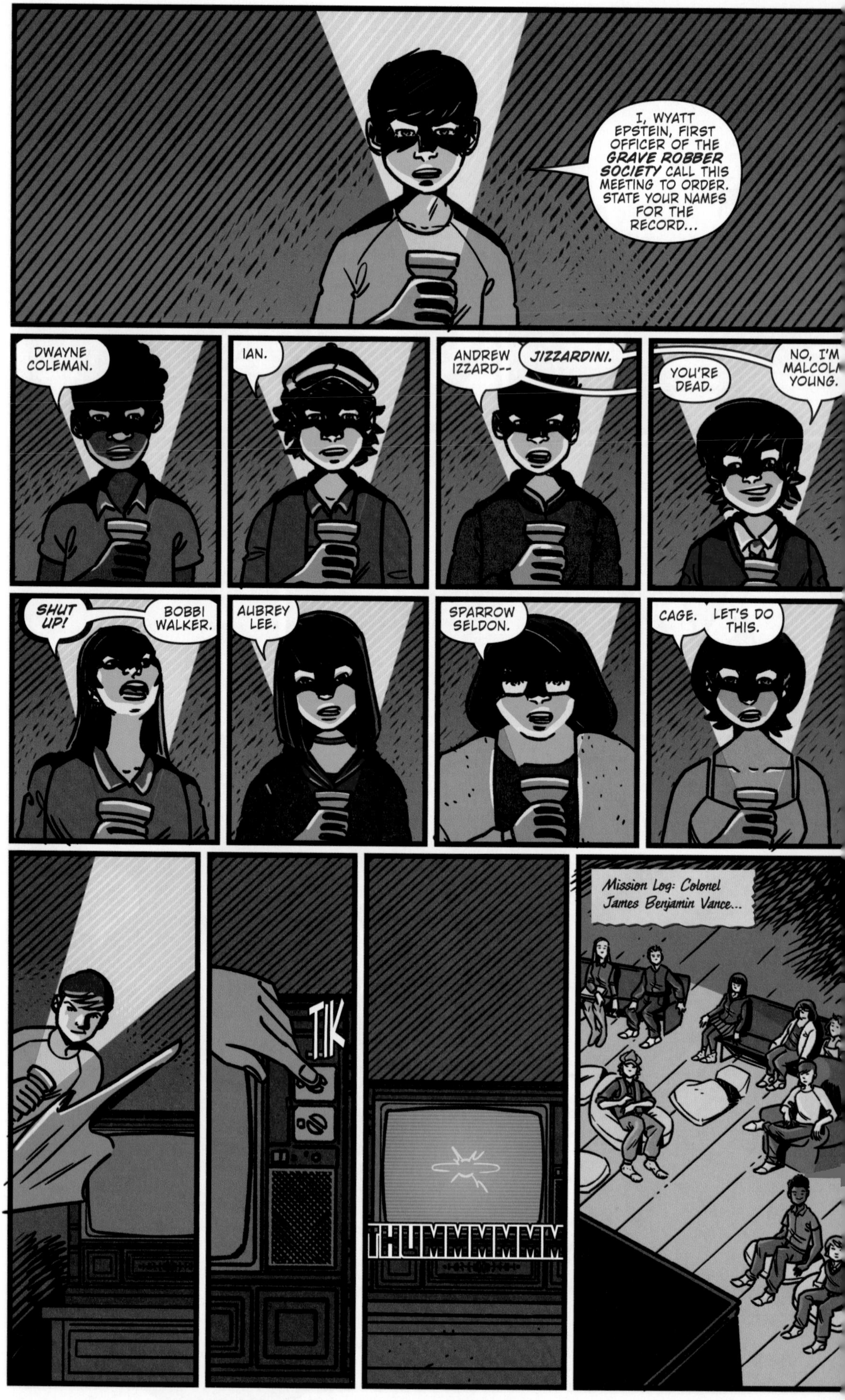
I, WYATT EPSTEIN, FIRST OFFICER OF THE GRAVE ROBBER SOCIETY CALL THIS MEETING TO ORDER. STATE YOUR NAMES FOR THE RECORD...
DWAYNE COLEMAN.
IAN.
ANDREW IZZARD--
JIZZARDINI.
YOU'RE DEAD.
NO, I'M MALCOL YOUNG.
SHUT UP!
BOBBI WALKER.
AUBREY LEE.
SPARROW SELDON.
CAGE.
LET'S DO THIS.
TIK
THUMMMMMMM
Mission Log: Colonel James Benjamin Vance...

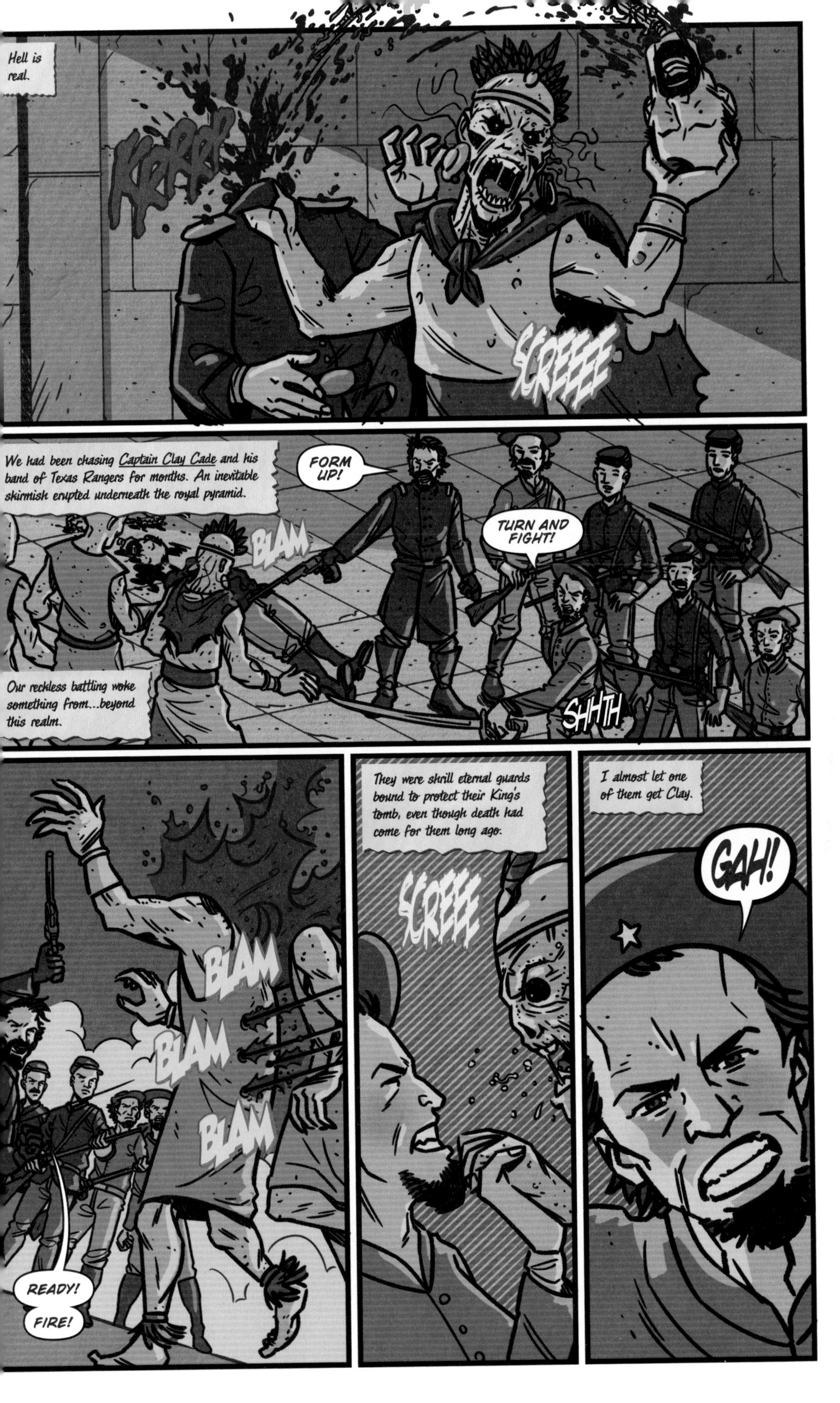

Hell is real.
KRRR
SCREEEE
We had been chasing Captain Clay Cade and his band of Texas Rangers for months. An inevitable skirmish erupted underneath the royal pyramid.
FORM UP!
BLAM
TURN AND FIGHT!
Our reckless battling woke something from...beyond this realm.
SHHTH
BLAM
BLAM
BLAM
READY!
FIRE!
They were shrill eternal guards bound to protect their King's tomb, even though death had come for them long ago.
SCREEE
I almost let one of them get Clay.
GAH!

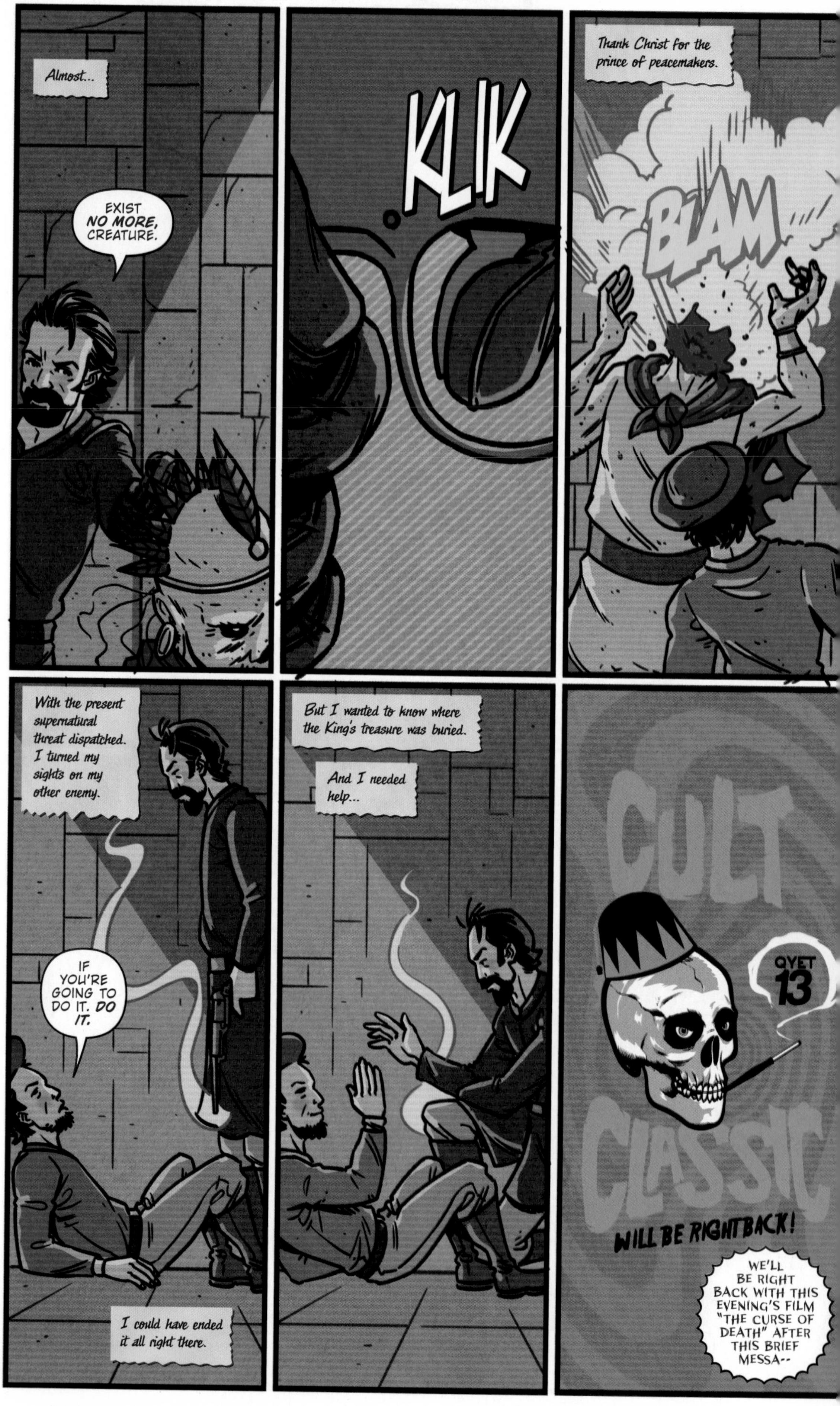

Almost...
EXIST NO MORE, CREATURE.
KLIK
Thank Christ for the prince of peacemakers.
BLAM
With the present supernatural threat dispatched. I turned my sights on my other enemy.
IF YOU'RE GOING TO DO IT. DO IT.
I could have ended it all right there.
But I wanted to know where the King's treasure was buried.
And I needed help...
CULT
QYET 13
CLASSIC
WILL BE RIGHT BACK!
WE'LL BE RIGHT BACK WITH THIS EVENING'S FILM "THE CURSE OF DEATH" AFTER THIS BRIEF MESSA--

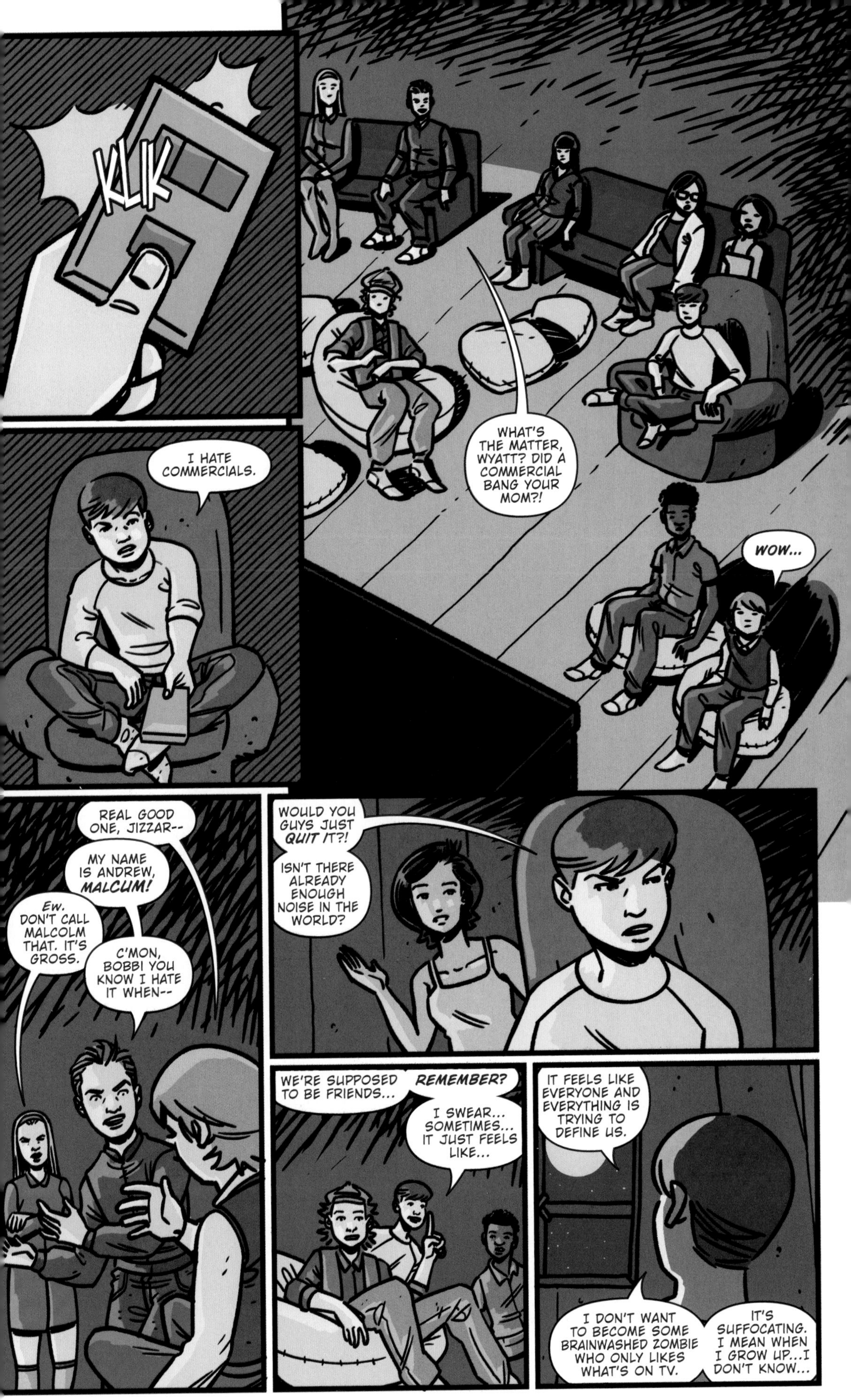
KLIK
I HATE COMMERCIALS.
WHAT'S THE MATTER, WYATT? DID A COMMERCIAL BANG YOUR MOM?!
WOW...
REAL GOOD ONE, JIZZAR--
MY NAME IS ANDREW, MALCUM!
Ew. DON'T CALL MALCOLM THAT. IT'S GROSS.
C'MON, BOBBI YOU KNOW I HATE IT WHEN--
WOULD YOU GUYS JUST QUIT IT?!
ISN'T THERE ALREADY ENOUGH NOISE IN THE WORLD?
WE'RE SUPPOSED TO BE FRIENDS...
REMEMBER?
I SWEAR... SOMETIMES... IT JUST FEELS LIKE...
IT FEELS LIKE EVERYONE AND EVERYTHING IS TRYING TO DEFINE US.
I DON'T WANT TO BECOME SOME BRAINWASHED ZOMBIE WHO ONLY LIKES WHAT'S ON TV.
IT'S SUFFOCATING. I MEAN WHEN I GROW UP...I DON'T KNOW...

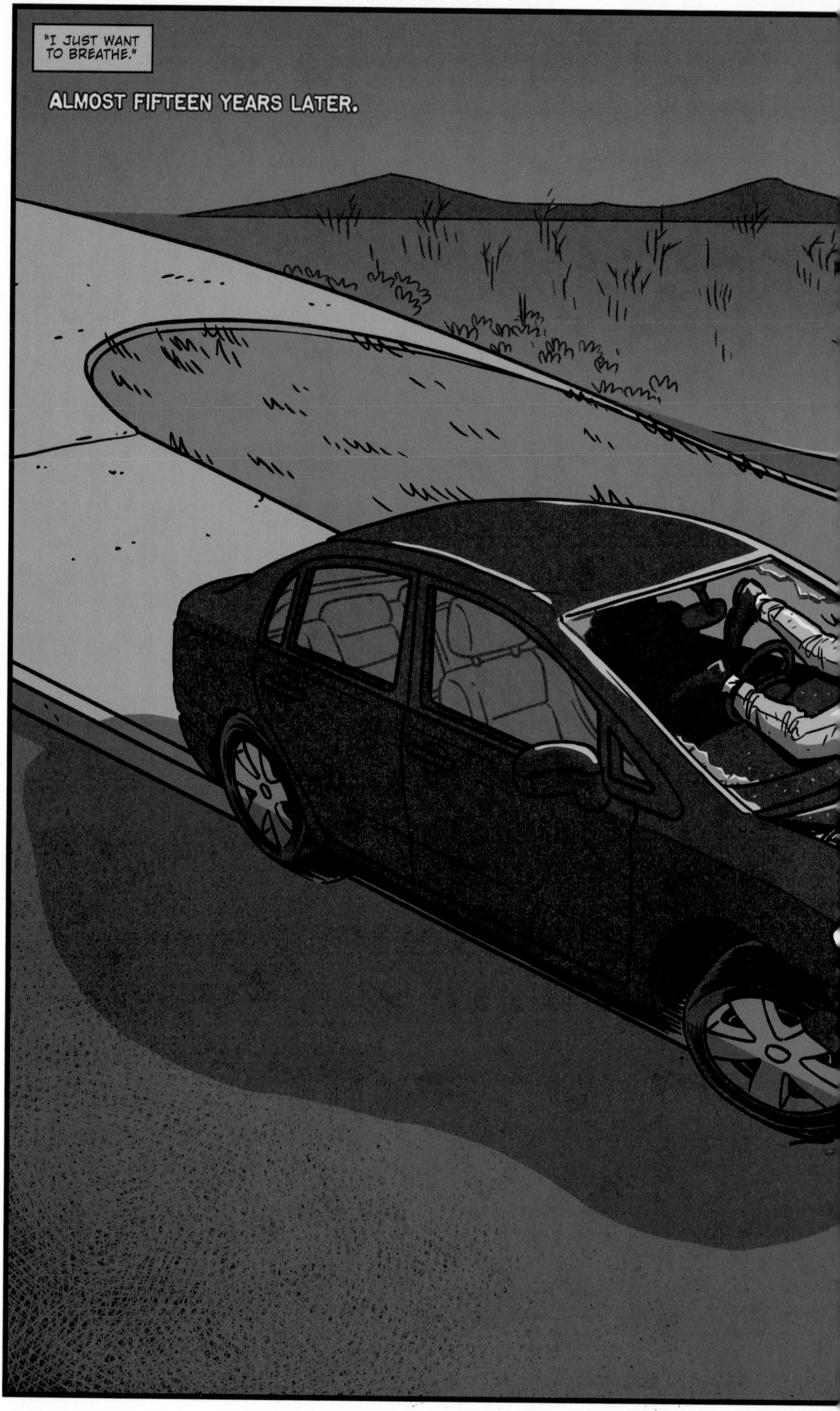
"I JUST WANT TO BREATHE."
ALMOST FIFTEEN YEARS LATER.

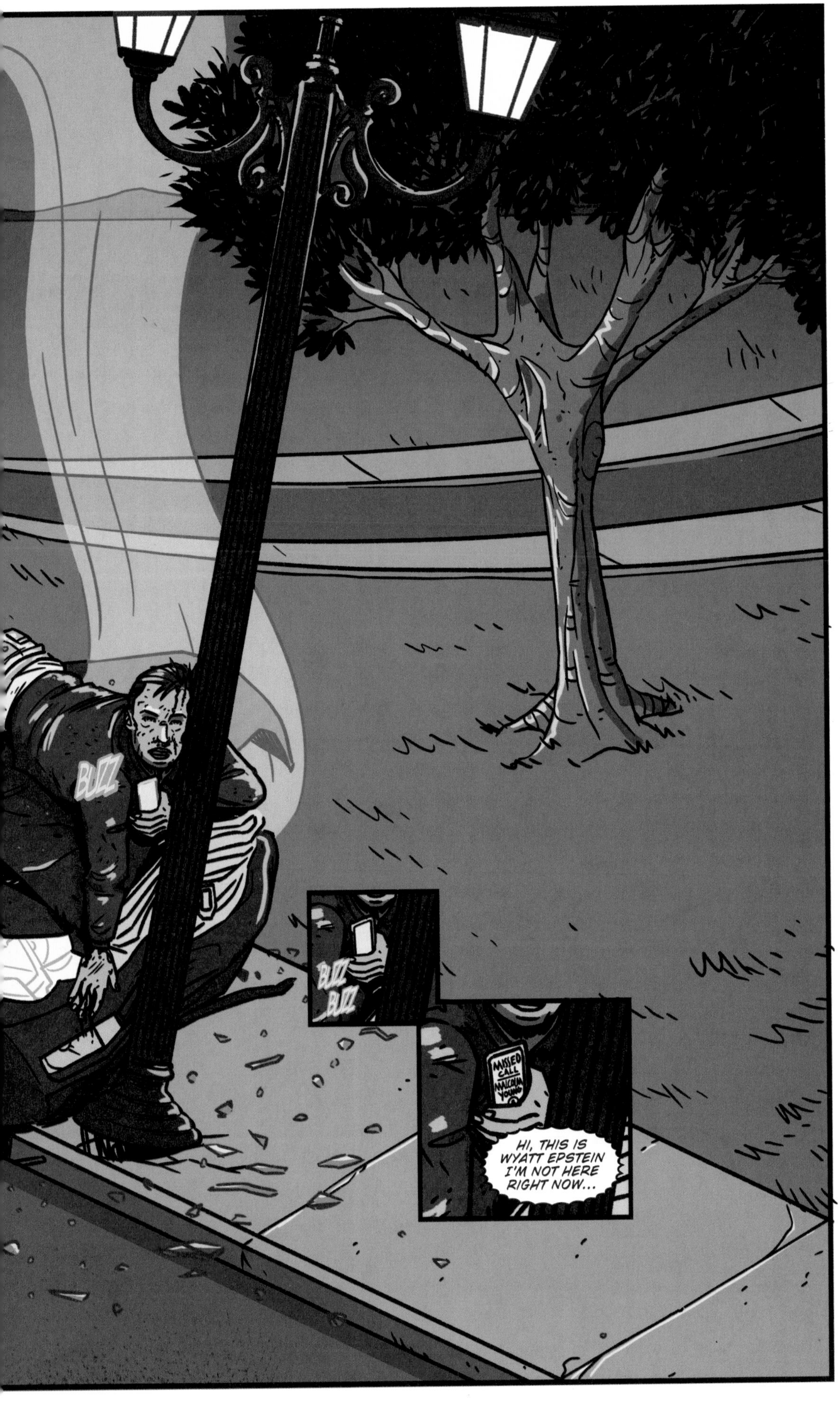
BUZZ
BUZZ BUZZ
MISSED CALL MALCOLM YOUNG
HI, THIS IS WYATT EPSTEIN I'M NOT HERE RIGHT NOW...

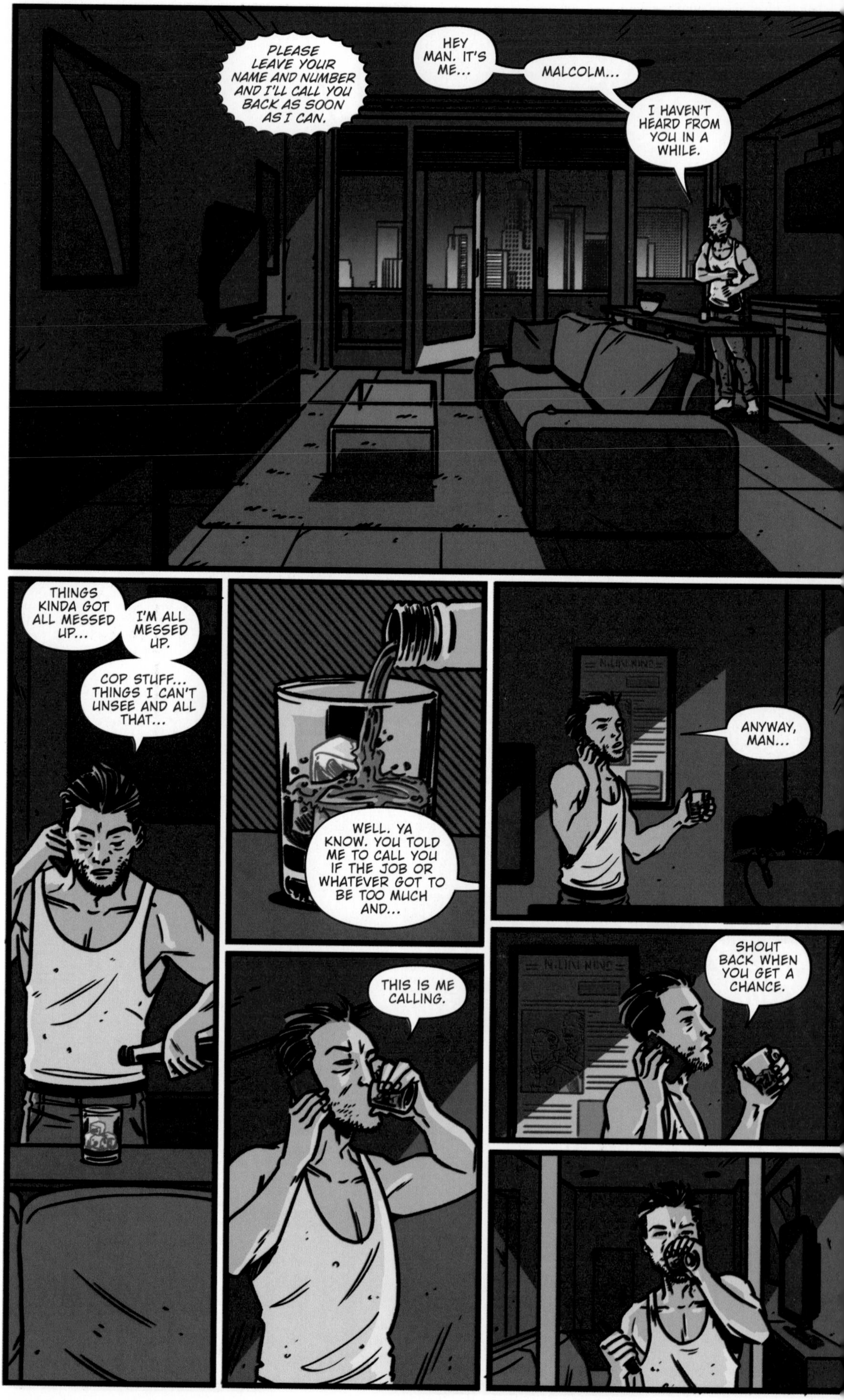
PLEASE LEAVE YOUR NAME AND NUMBER AND I'LL CALL YOU BACK AS SOON AS I CAN.
HEY MAN. IT'S ME...
MALCOLM...
I HAVEN'T HEARD FROM YOU IN A WHILE.
THINGS KINDA GOT ALL MESSED UP...
I'M ALL MESSED UP.
COP STUFF... THINGS I CAN'T UNSEE AND ALL THAT...
WELL. YA KNOW. YOU TOLD ME TO CALL YOU IF THE JOB OR WHATEVER GOT TO BE TOO MUCH AND...
ANYWAY, MAN...
THIS IS ME CALLING.
SHOUT BACK WHEN YOU GET A CHANCE.

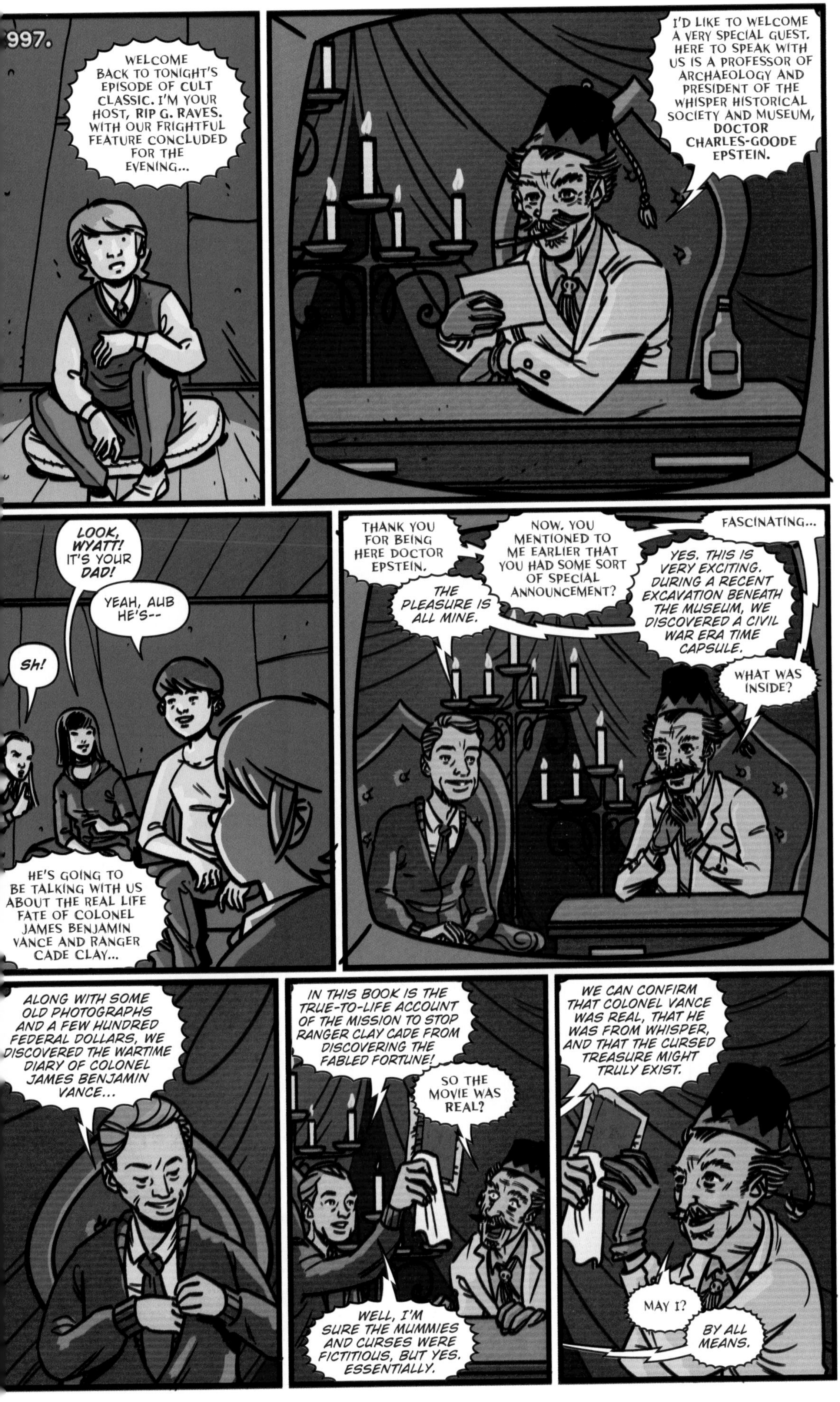
997.
WELCOME BACK TO TONIGHT'S EPISODE OF CULT CLASSIC. I'M YOUR HOST, RIP G. RAVES. WITH OUR FRIGHTFUL FEATURE CONCLUDED FOR THE EVENING...
I'D LIKE TO WELCOME A VERY SPECIAL GUEST. HERE TO SPEAK WITH US IS A PROFESSOR OF ARCHAEOLOGY AND PRESIDENT OF THE WHISPER HISTORICAL SOCIETY AND MUSEUM, DOCTOR CHARLES-GOODE EPSTEIN.
LOOK, WYATT! IT'S YOUR DAD!
YEAH, AUB HE'S--
SH!
HE'S GOING TO BE TALKING WITH US ABOUT THE REAL LIFE FATE OF COLONEL JAMES BENJAMIN VANCE AND RANGER CADE CLAY...
THANK YOU FOR BEING HERE DOCTOR EPSTEIN.
THE PLEASURE IS ALL MINE.
NOW, YOU MENTIONED TO ME EARLIER THAT YOU HAD SOME SORT OF SPECIAL ANNOUNCEMENT?
YES. THIS IS VERY EXCITING. DURING A RECENT EXCAVATION BENEATH THE MUSEUM, WE DISCOVERED A CIVIL WAR ERA TIME CAPSULE.
FASCINATING...
WHAT WAS INSIDE?
ALONG WITH SOME OLD PHOTOGRAPHS AND A FEW HUNDRED FEDERAL DOLLARS, WE DISCOVERED THE WARTIME DIARY OF COLONEL JAMES BENJAMIN VANCE...
IN THIS BOOK IS THE TRUE-TO-LIFE ACCOUNT OF THE MISSION TO STOP RANGER CLAY CADE FROM DISCOVERING THE FABLED FORTUNE!
SO THE MOVIE WAS REAL?
WELL, I'M SURE THE MUMMIES AND CURSES WERE FICTITIOUS, BUT YES. ESSENTIALLY.
WE CAN CONFIRM THAT COLONEL VANCE WAS REAL, THAT HE WAS FROM WHISPER, AND THAT THE CURSED TREASURE MIGHT TRULY EXIST.
MAY I?
BY ALL MEANS.

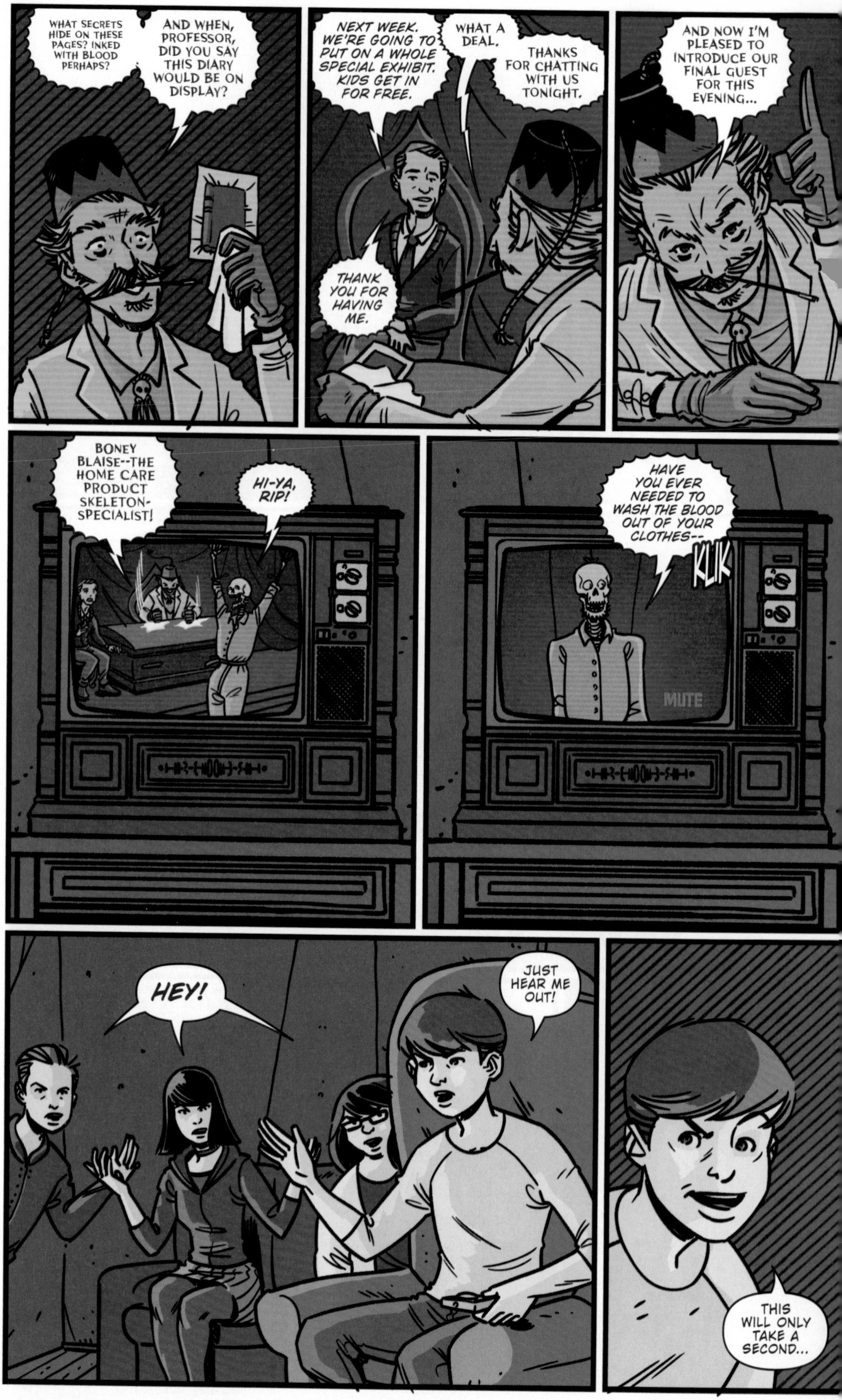

WHAT SECRETS HIDE ON THESE PAGES? INKED WITH BLOOD PERHAPS?
AND WHEN, PROFESSOR, DID YOU SAY THIS DIARY WOULD BE ON DISPLAY?
NEXT WEEK. WE'RE GOING TO PUT ON A WHOLE SPECIAL EXHIBIT. KIDS GET IN FOR FREE.
WHAT A DEAL.
THANKS FOR CHATTING WITH US TONIGHT.
THANK YOU FOR HAVING ME.
AND NOW I'M PLEASED TO INTRODUCE OUR FINAL GUEST FOR THIS EVENING...
BONEY BLAISE--THE HOME CARE PRODUCT SKELETON-SPECIALIST!
HI-YA, RIP!
HAVE YOU EVER NEEDED TO WASH THE BLOOD OUT OF YOUR CLOTHES--
KLIK
MUTE
HEY!
JUST HEAR ME OUT!
THIS WILL ONLY TAKE A SECOND...

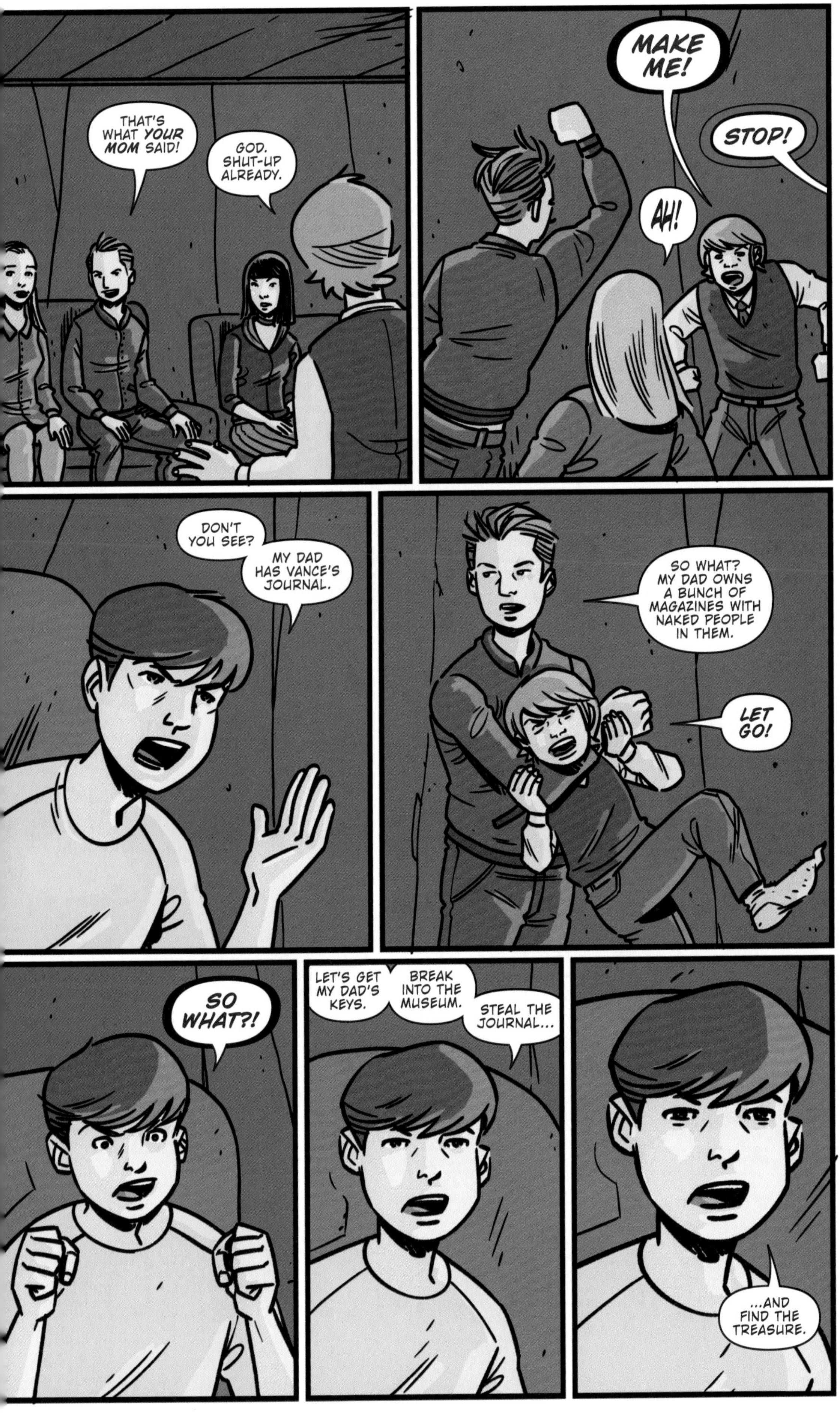
THAT'S WHAT YOUR MOM SAID!
GOD. SHUT-UP ALREADY.
MAKE ME!
AH!
STOP!
DON'T YOU SEE?
MY DAD HAS VANCE'S JOURNAL.
SO WHAT? MY DAD OWNS A BUNCH OF MAGAZINES WITH NAKED PEOPLE IN THEM.
LET GO!
SO WHAT?!
LET'S GET MY DAD'S KEYS.
BREAK INTO THE MUSEUM.
STEAL THE JOURNAL...
...AND FIND THE TREASURE.

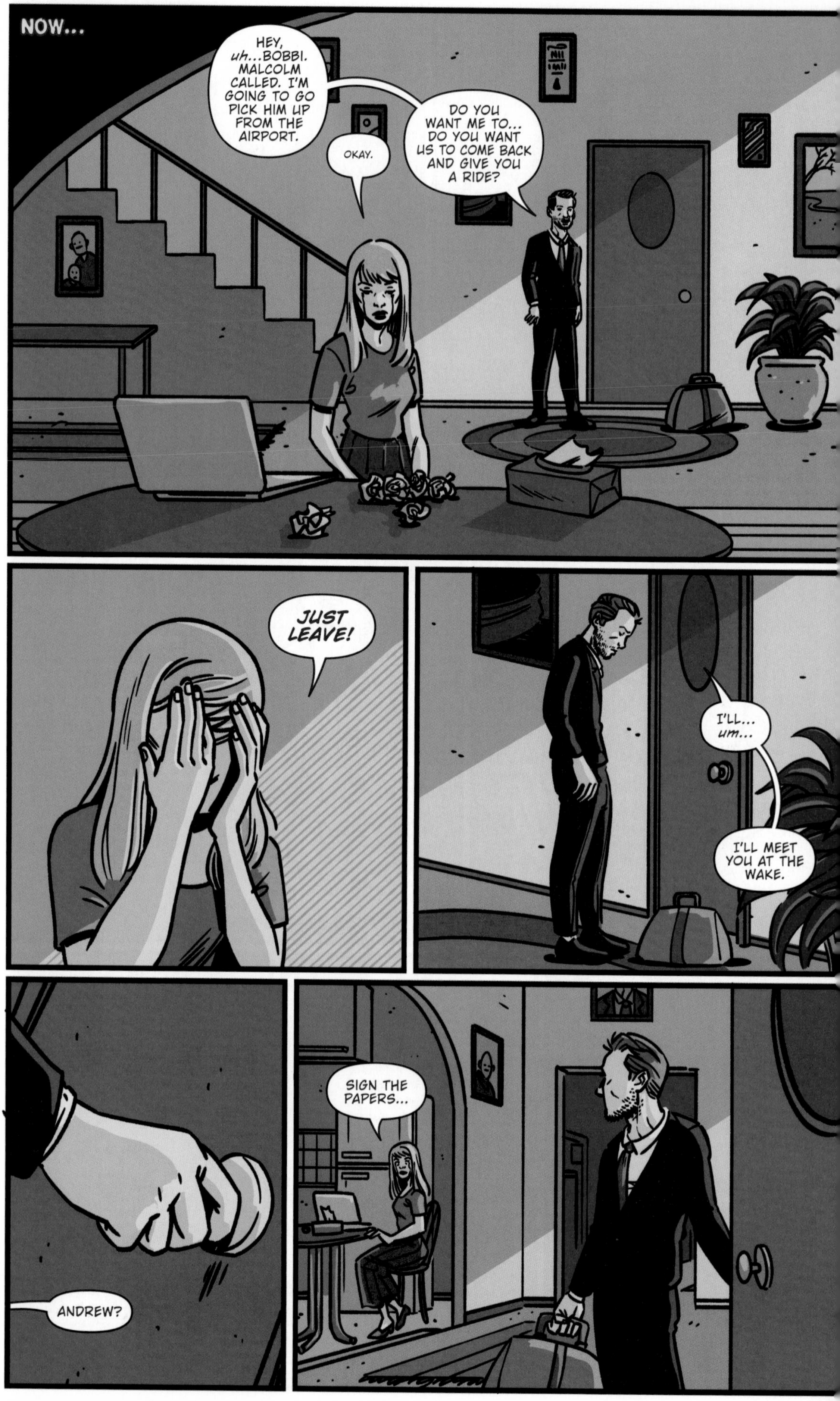
NOW...
HEY, *uh*...BOBBI. MALCOLM CALLED. I'M GOING TO GO PICK HIM UP FROM THE AIRPORT.
OKAY.
DO YOU WANT ME TO... DO YOU WANT US TO COME BACK AND GIVE YOU A RIDE?
JUST LEAVE!
I'LL... *um*...
I'LL MEET YOU AT THE WAKE.
ANDREW?
SIGN THE PAPERS...

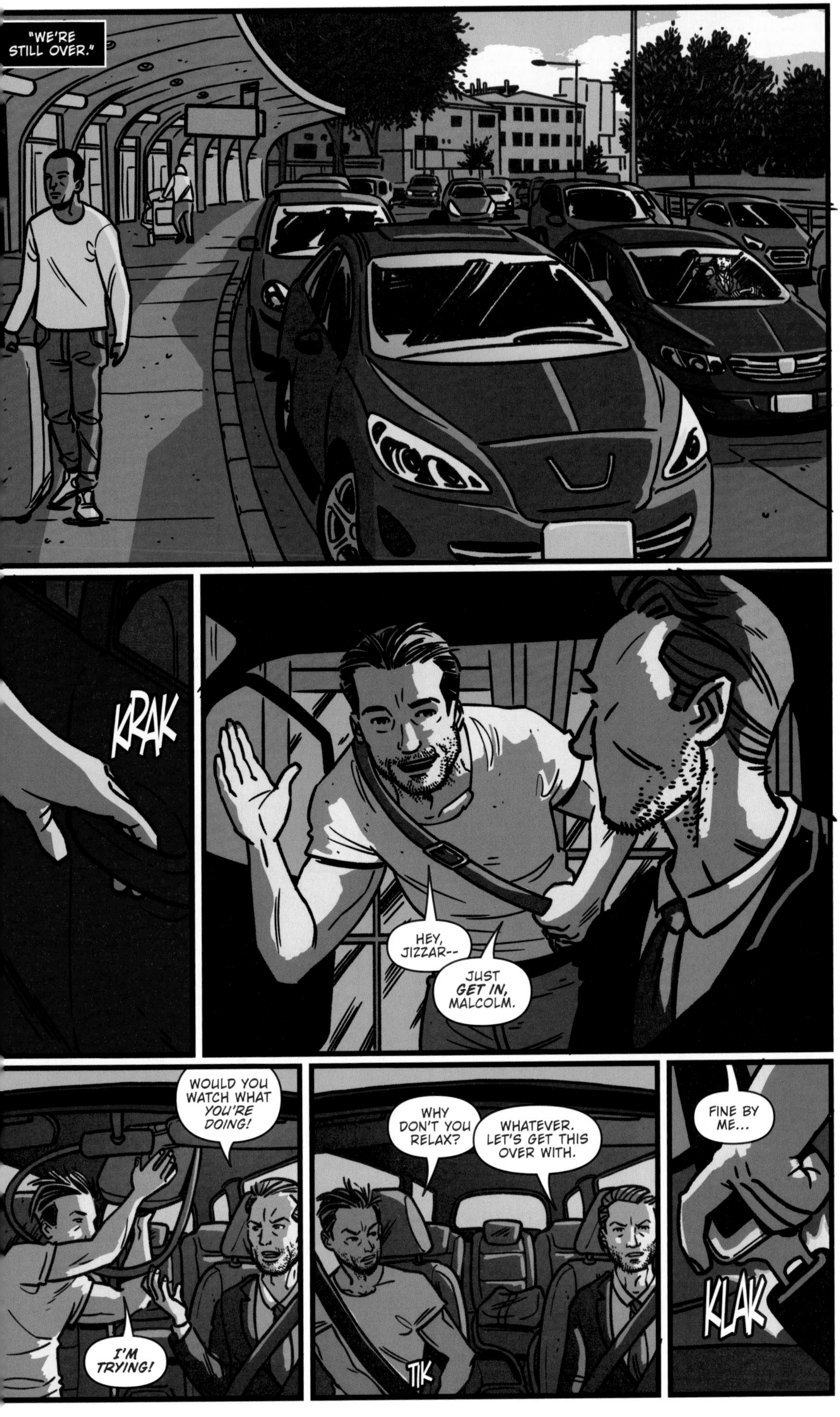
"WE'RE STILL OVER."
KRAK
HEY, JIZZAR--
JUST GET IN, MALCOLM.
WOULD YOU WATCH WHAT YOU'RE DOING!
I'M TRYING!
WHY DON'T YOU RELAX?
WHATEVER. LET'S GET THIS OVER WITH.
TIK
FINE BY ME...
KLAK

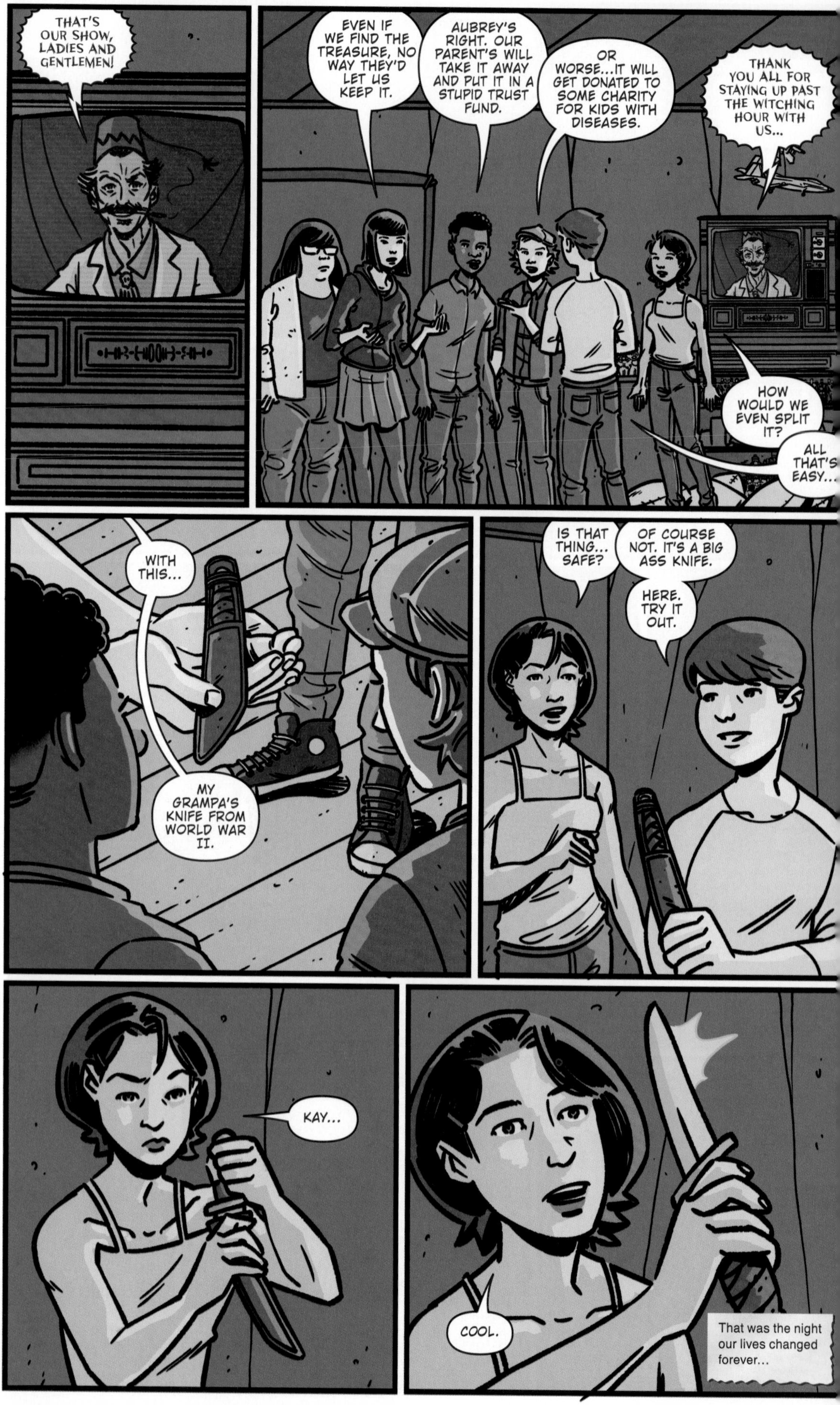
THAT'S OUR SHOW, LADIES AND GENTLEMEN!
EVEN IF WE FIND THE TREASURE, NO WAY THEY'D LET US KEEP IT.
AUBREY'S RIGHT. OUR PARENT'S WILL TAKE IT AWAY AND PUT IT IN A STUPID TRUST FUND.
OR WORSE...IT WILL GET DONATED TO SOME CHARITY FOR KIDS WITH DISEASES.
THANK YOU ALL FOR STAYING UP PAST THE WITCHING HOUR WITH US...
HOW WOULD WE EVEN SPLIT IT?
ALL THAT'S EASY...
WITH THIS...
MY GRAMPA'S KNIFE FROM WORLD WAR II.
IS THAT THING... SAFE?
OF COURSE NOT. IT'S A BIG ASS KNIFE.
HERE. TRY IT OUT.
KAY...
COOL.
That was the night our lives changed forever...

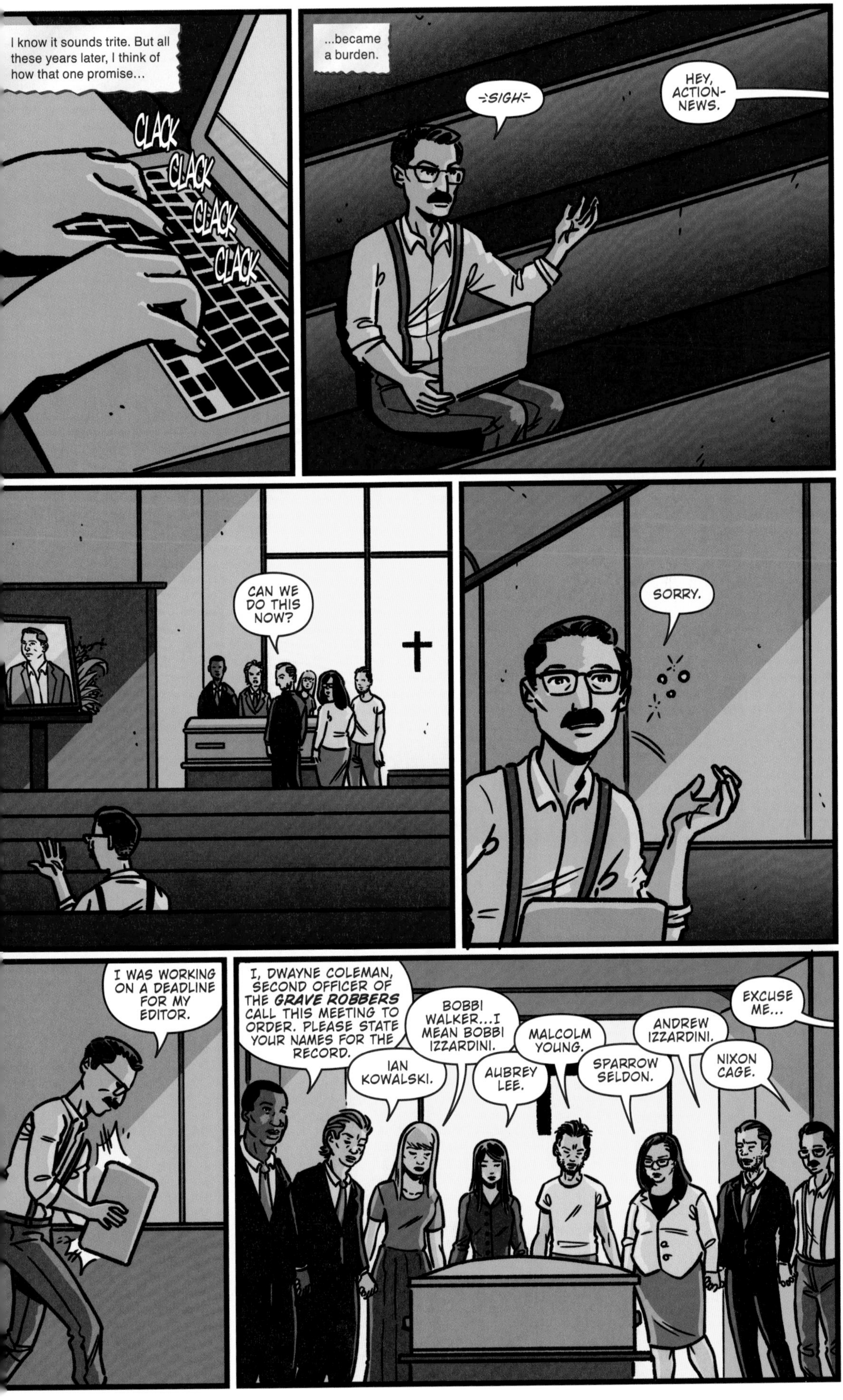

I know it sounds trite. But all these years later, I think of how that one promise…
CLACK
CLACK
CLACK
CLACK
...became a burden.
-SIGH-
HEY, ACTION-NEWS.
CAN WE DO THIS NOW?
SORRY.
I WAS WORKING ON A DEADLINE FOR MY EDITOR.
I, DWAYNE COLEMAN, SECOND OFFICER OF THE GRAVE ROBBERS CALL THIS MEETING TO ORDER. PLEASE STATE YOUR NAMES FOR THE RECORD.
IAN KOWALSKI.
BOBBI WALKER...I MEAN BOBBI IZZARDINI.
AUBREY LEE.
MALCOLM YOUNG.
SPARROW SELDON.
ANDREW IZZARDINI.
NIXON CAGE.
EXCUSE ME...

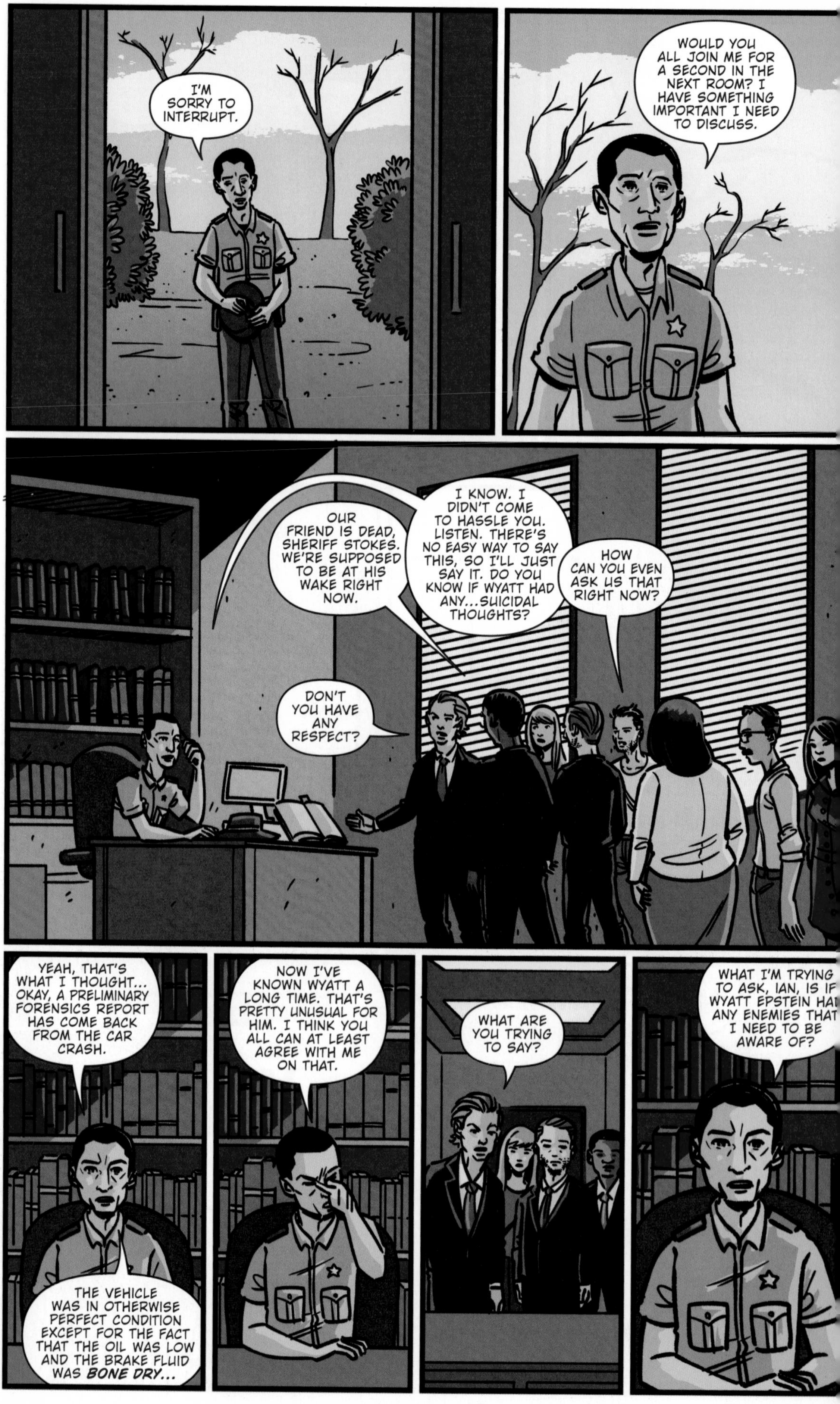
I'M SORRY TO INTERRUPT.
WOULD YOU ALL JOIN ME FOR A SECOND IN THE NEXT ROOM? I HAVE SOMETHING IMPORTANT I NEED TO DISCUSS.
OUR FRIEND IS DEAD, SHERIFF STOKES. WE'RE SUPPOSED TO BE AT HIS WAKE RIGHT NOW.
I KNOW. I DIDN'T COME TO HASSLE YOU. LISTEN. THERE'S NO EASY WAY TO SAY THIS, SO I'LL JUST SAY IT. DO YOU KNOW IF WYATT HAD ANY...SUICIDAL THOUGHTS?
HOW CAN YOU EVEN ASK US THAT RIGHT NOW?
DON'T YOU HAVE ANY RESPECT?
YEAH, THAT'S WHAT I THOUGHT... OKAY, A PRELIMINARY FORENSICS REPORT HAS COME BACK FROM THE CAR CRASH.
THE VEHICLE WAS IN OTHERWISE PERFECT CONDITION EXCEPT FOR THE FACT THAT THE OIL WAS LOW AND THE BRAKE FLUID WAS ***BONE DRY...***
NOW I'VE KNOWN WYATT A LONG TIME. THAT'S PRETTY UNUSUAL FOR HIM. I THINK YOU ALL CAN AT LEAST AGREE WITH ME ON THAT.
WHAT ARE YOU TRYING TO SAY?
WHAT I'M TRYING TO ASK, IAN, IS IF WYATT EPSTEIN HAD ANY ENEMIES THAT I NEED TO BE AWARE OF?

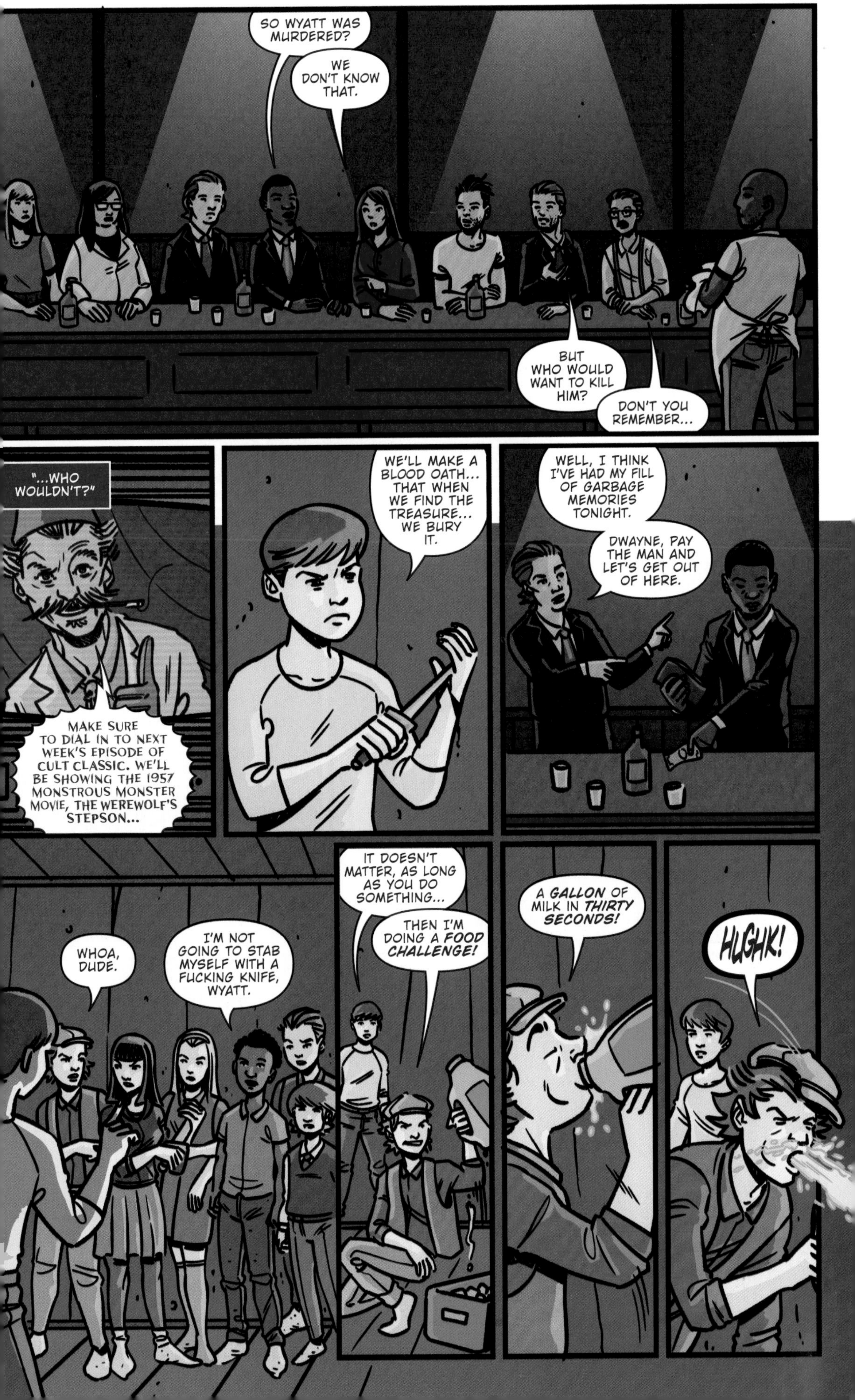
SO WYATT WAS MURDERED?
WE DON'T KNOW THAT.
BUT WHO WOULD WANT TO KILL HIM?
DON'T YOU REMEMBER...
"...WHO WOULDN'T?"
MAKE SURE TO DIAL IN TO NEXT WEEK'S EPISODE OF CULT CLASSIC. WE'LL BE SHOWING THE 1957 MONSTROUS MONSTER MOVIE, THE WEREWOLF'S STEPSON...
WE'LL MAKE A BLOOD OATH... THAT WHEN WE FIND THE TREASURE... WE BURY IT.
WELL, I THINK I'VE HAD MY FILL OF GARBAGE MEMORIES TONIGHT.
DWAYNE, PAY THE MAN AND LET'S GET OUT OF HERE.
WHOA, DUDE.
I'M NOT GOING TO STAB MYSELF WITH A FUCKING KNIFE, WYATT.
IT DOESN'T MATTER, AS LONG AS YOU DO SOMETHING...
THEN I'M DOING A *FOOD CHALLENGE!*
A *GALLON* OF MILK IN *THIRTY SECONDS!*
HUGHK!

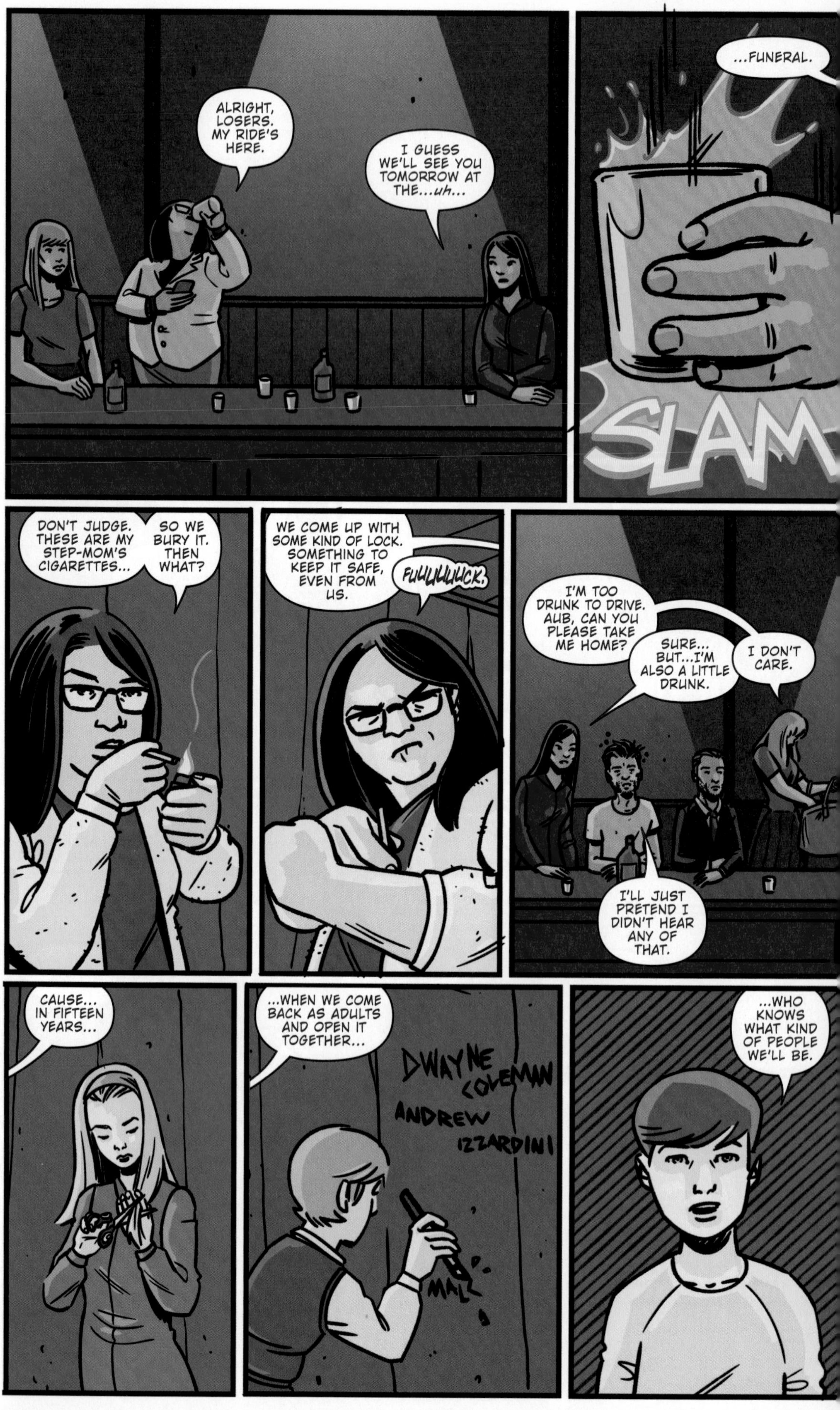
ALRIGHT, LOSERS. MY RIDE'S HERE.
I GUESS WE'LL SEE YOU TOMORROW AT THE...uh...
...FUNERAL.
SLAM
DON'T JUDGE. THESE ARE MY STEP-MOM'S CIGARETTES...
SO WE BURY IT. THEN WHAT?
WE COME UP WITH SOME KIND OF LOCK. SOMETHING TO KEEP IT SAFE, EVEN FROM US.
FUUUUUUCK.
I'M TOO DRUNK TO DRIVE. AUB, CAN YOU PLEASE TAKE ME HOME?
SURE... BUT...I'M ALSO A LITTLE DRUNK.
I DON'T CARE.
I'LL JUST PRETEND I DIDN'T HEAR ANY OF THAT.
CAUSE... IN FIFTEEN YEARS...
...WHEN WE COME BACK AS ADULTS AND OPEN IT TOGETHER...
DWAYNE COLEMAN
ANDREW IZZARDINI
MAL
...WHO KNOWS WHAT KIND OF PEOPLE WE'LL BE.

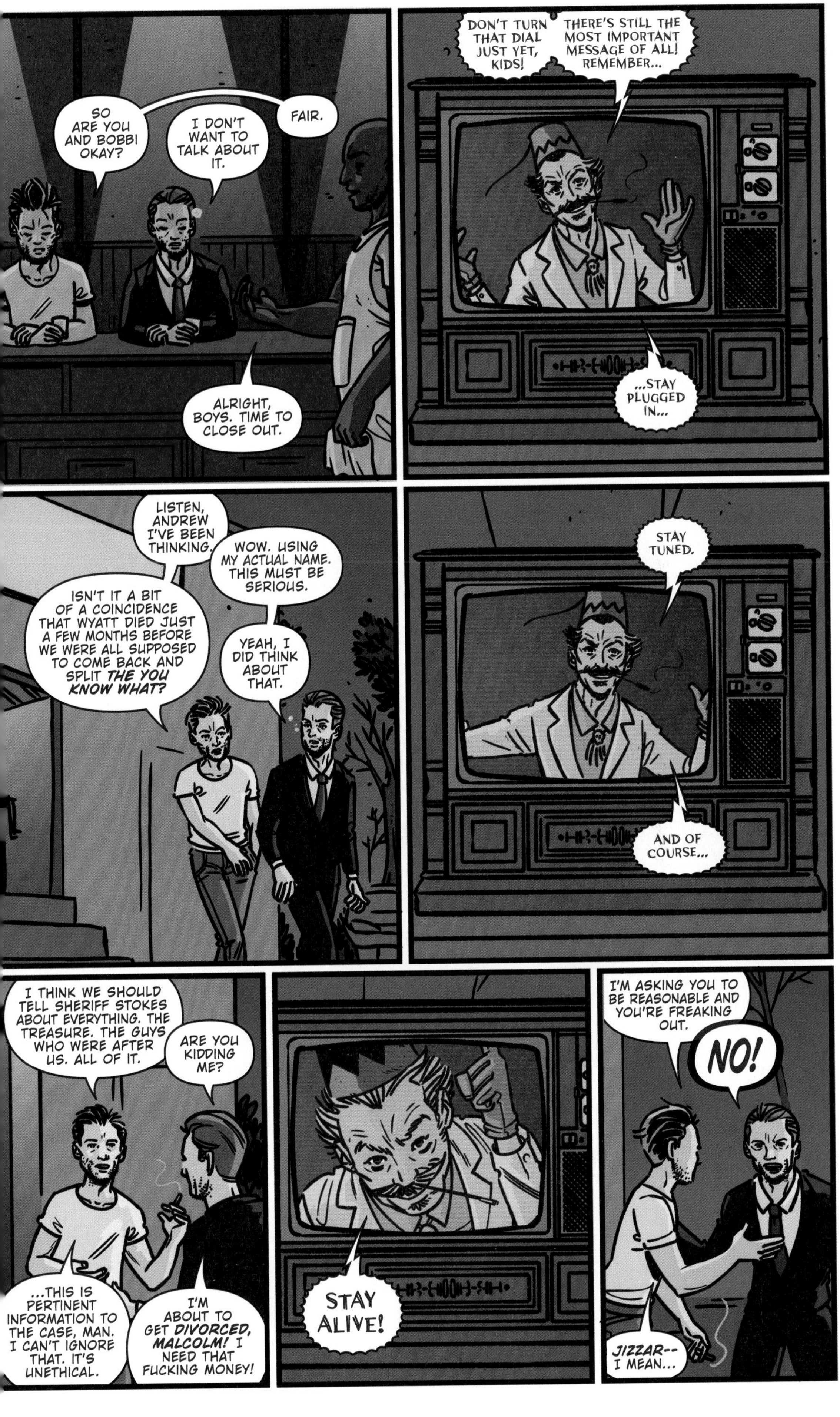
SO ARE YOU AND BOBBI OKAY?
I DON'T WANT TO TALK ABOUT IT.
FAIR.
ALRIGHT, BOYS. TIME TO CLOSE OUT.
DON'T TURN THAT DIAL JUST YET, KIDS!
THERE'S STILL THE MOST IMPORTANT MESSAGE OF ALL! REMEMBER...
...STAY PLUGGED IN...
LISTEN, ANDREW I'VE BEEN THINKING.
WOW. USING MY ACTUAL NAME. THIS MUST BE SERIOUS.
ISN'T IT A BIT OF A COINCIDENCE THAT WYATT DIED JUST A FEW MONTHS BEFORE WE WERE ALL SUPPOSED TO COME BACK AND SPLIT *THE YOU KNOW WHAT?*
YEAH, I DID THINK ABOUT THAT.
STAY TUNED.
AND OF COURSE...
I THINK WE SHOULD TELL SHERIFF STOKES ABOUT EVERYTHING. THE TREASURE. THE GUYS WHO WERE AFTER US. ALL OF IT.
ARE YOU KIDDING ME?
...THIS IS PERTINENT INFORMATION TO THE CASE, MAN. I CAN'T IGNORE THAT. IT'S UNETHICAL.
I'M ABOUT TO GET *DIVORCED, MALCOLM!* I NEED THAT FUCKING MONEY!
STAY ALIVE!
I'M ASKING YOU TO BE REASONABLE AND YOU'RE FREAKING OUT.
NO!
JIZZAR-- I MEAN...

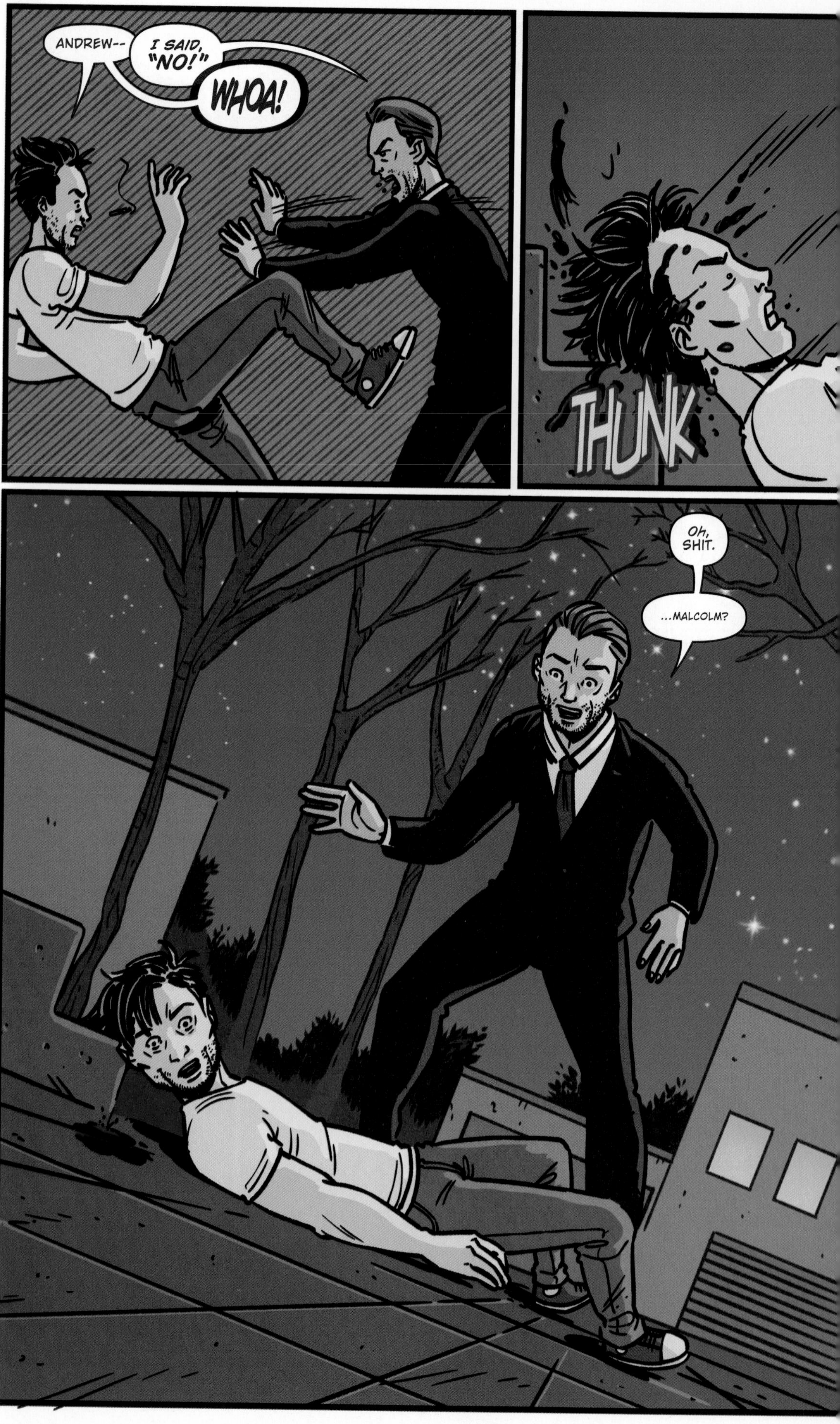
ANDREW--
I SAID, "NO!"
WHOA!
THUNK
OH, SHIT.
...MALCOLM?

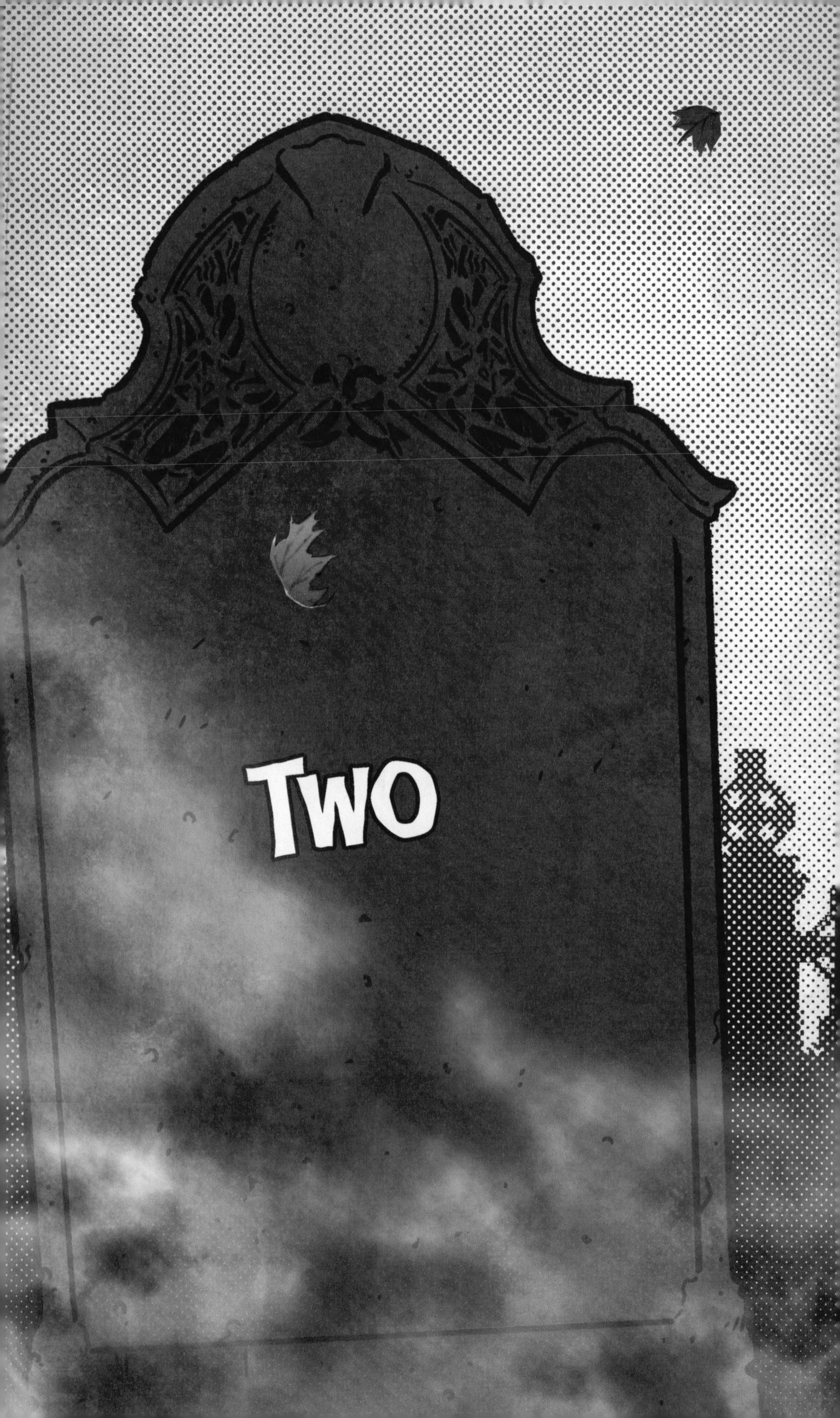
TWO

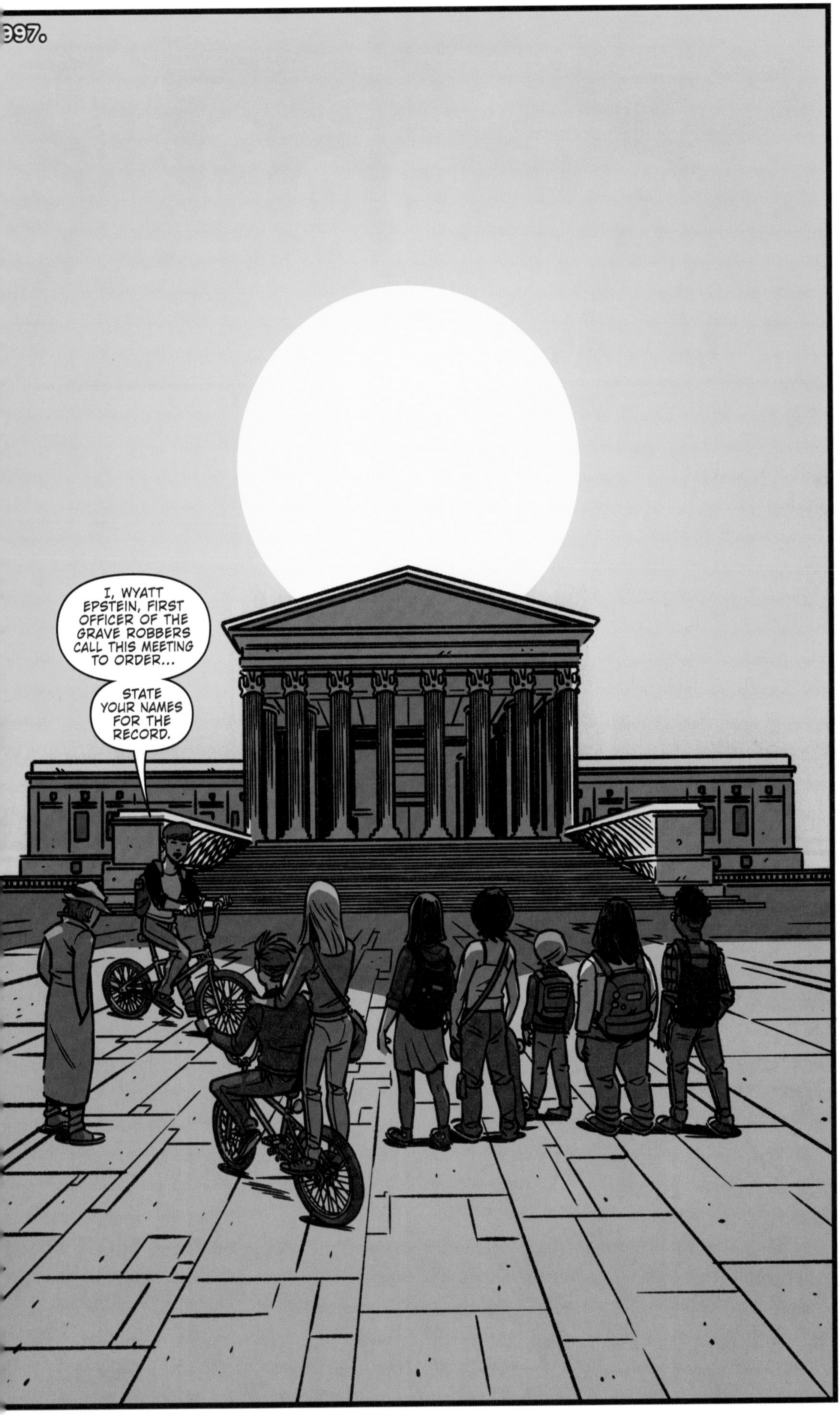
1997.
I, WYATT EPSTEIN, FIRST OFFICER OF THE GRAVE ROBBERS CALL THIS MEETING TO ORDER...
STATE YOUR NAMES FOR THE RECORD.

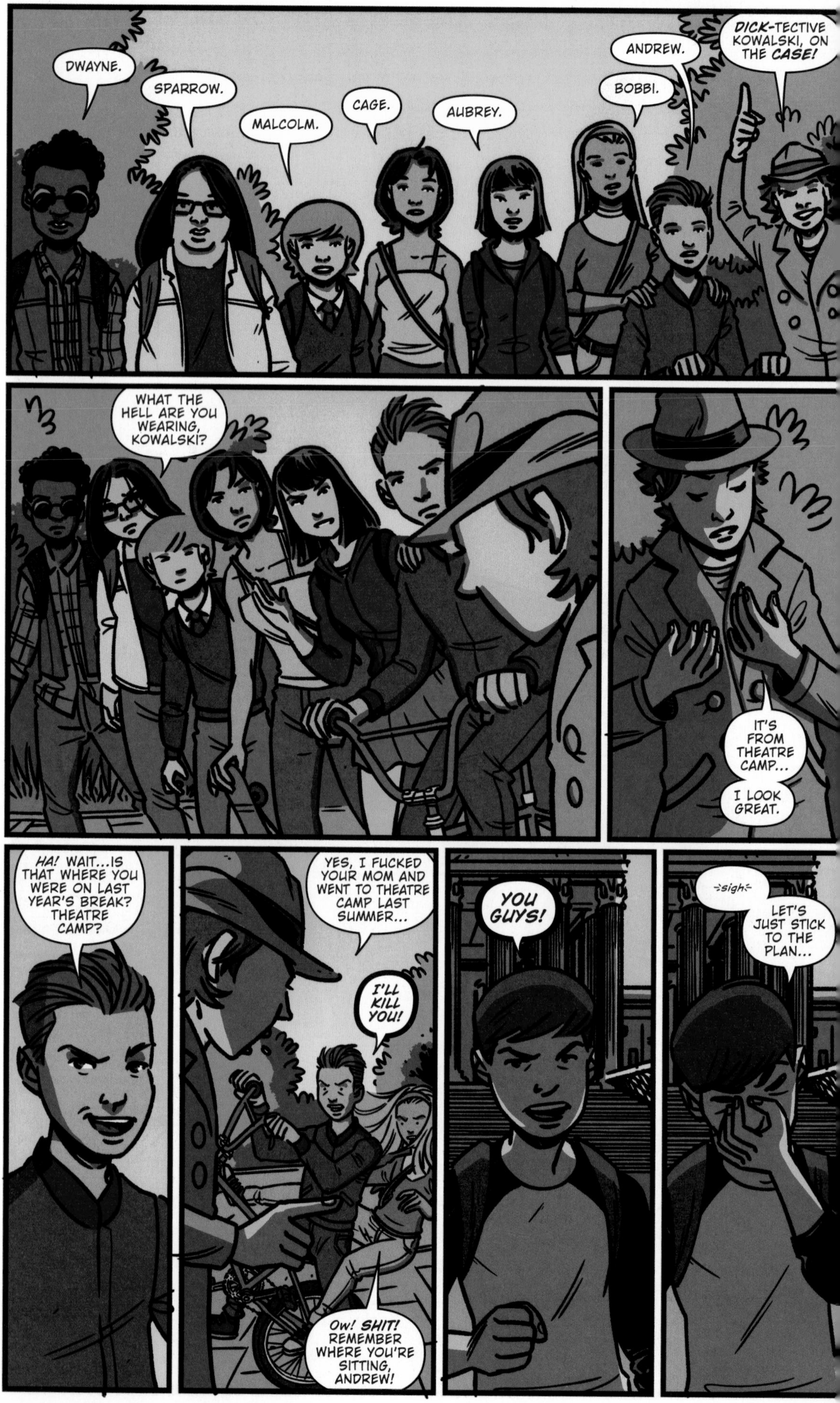
DWAYNE.
SPARROW.
MALCOLM.
CAGE.
AUBREY.
BOBBI.
ANDREW.
DICK-TECTIVE KOWALSKI, ON THE CASE!
WHAT THE HELL ARE YOU WEARING, KOWALSKI?
IT'S FROM THEATRE CAMP...
I LOOK GREAT.
HA! WAIT...IS THAT WHERE YOU WERE ON LAST YEAR'S BREAK? THEATRE CAMP?
YES, I FUCKED YOUR MOM AND WENT TO THEATRE CAMP LAST SUMMER...
I'LL KILL YOU!
Ow! SHIT! REMEMBER WHERE YOU'RE SITTING, ANDREW!
YOU GUYS!
-sigh-
LET'S JUST STICK TO THE PLAN...

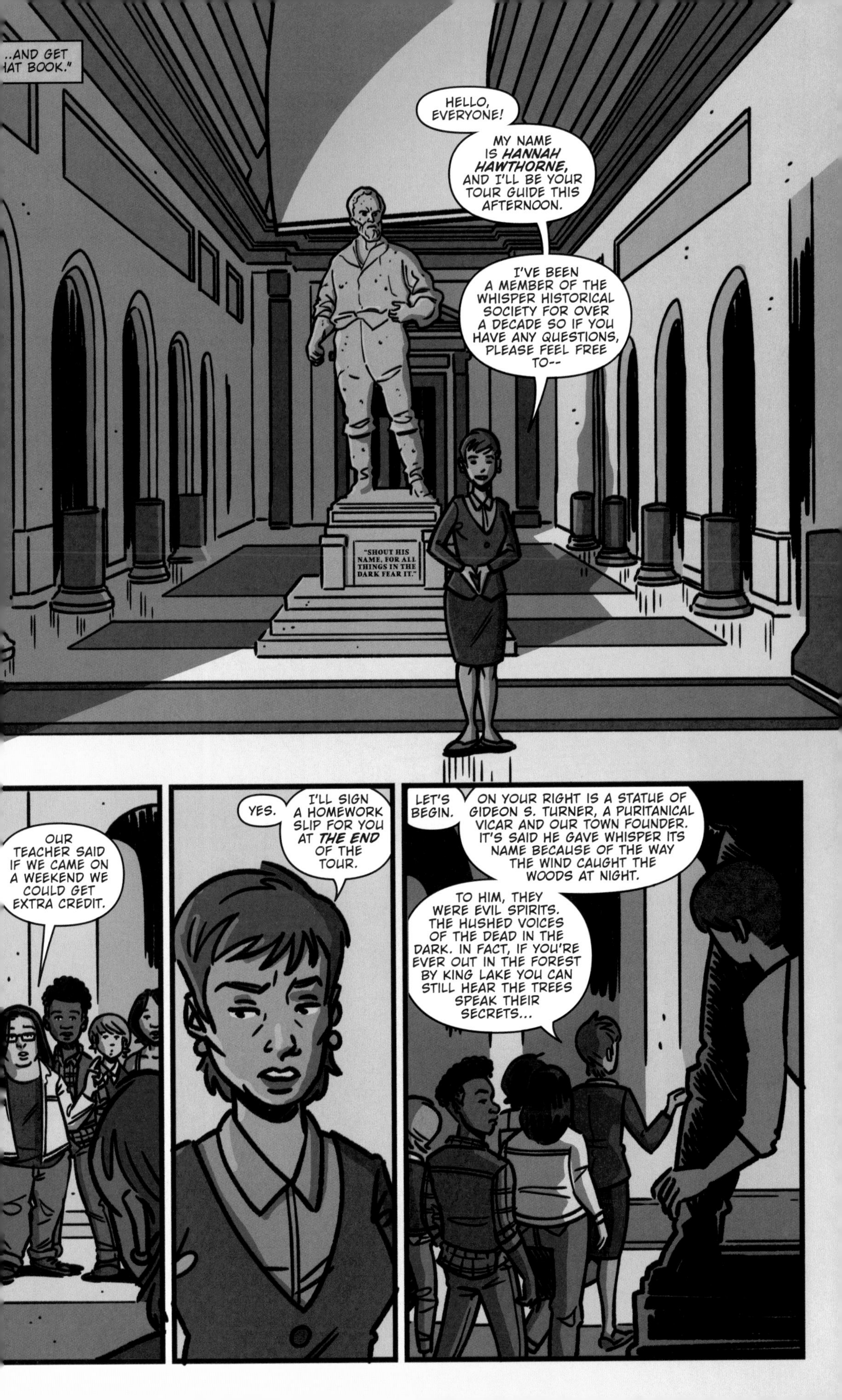

..AND GET
AT BOOK."
HELLO, EVERYONE!
MY NAME IS HANNAH HAWTHORNE, AND I'LL BE YOUR TOUR GUIDE THIS AFTERNOON.
I'VE BEEN A MEMBER OF THE WHISPER HISTORICAL SOCIETY FOR OVER A DECADE SO IF YOU HAVE ANY QUESTIONS, PLEASE FEEL FREE TO--
"SHOUT HIS NAME, FOR ALL THINGS IN THE DARK FEAR IT."
OUR TEACHER SAID IF WE CAME ON A WEEKEND WE COULD GET EXTRA CREDIT.
YES.
I'LL SIGN A HOMEWORK SLIP FOR YOU AT THE END OF THE TOUR.
LET'S BEGIN.
ON YOUR RIGHT IS A STATUE OF GIDEON S. TURNER, A PURITANICAL VICAR AND OUR TOWN FOUNDER. IT'S SAID HE GAVE WHISPER ITS NAME BECAUSE OF THE WAY THE WIND CAUGHT THE WOODS AT NIGHT.
TO HIM, THEY WERE EVIL SPIRITS. THE HUSHED VOICES OF THE DEAD IN THE DARK. IN FACT, IF YOU'RE EVER OUT IN THE FOREST BY KING LAKE YOU CAN STILL HEAR THE TREES SPEAK THEIR SECRETS...

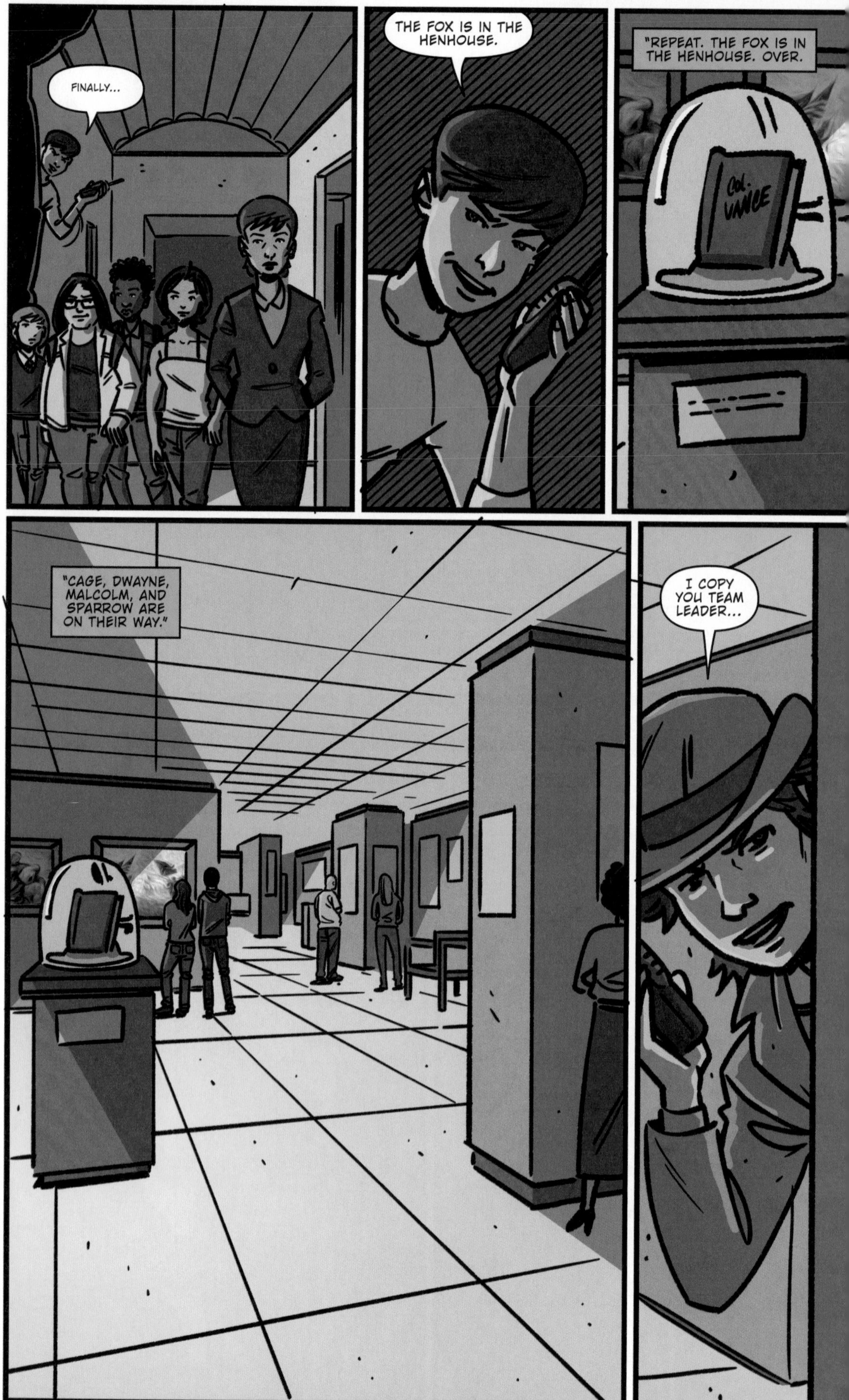
FINALLY...
THE FOX IS IN THE HENHOUSE.
"REPEAT. THE FOX IS IN THE HENHOUSE. OVER.
COL. VANCE
"CAGE, DWAYNE, MALCOLM, AND SPARROW ARE ON THEIR WAY."
I COPY YOU TEAM LEADER...

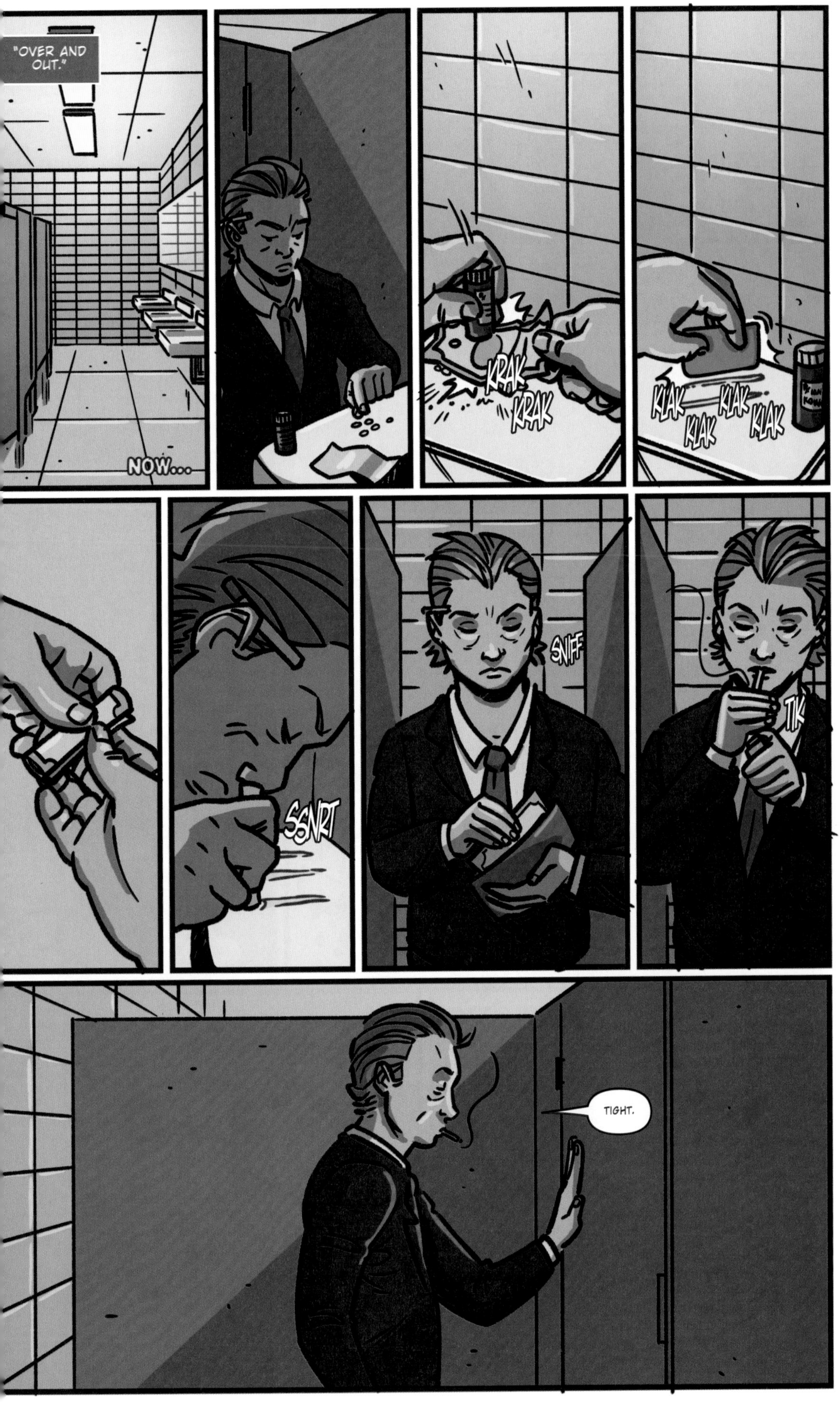
"OVER AND OUT."
NOW...
KRAK
KRAK
KLAK
KLAK
KLAK
KLAK
SSNRT
SNIFF
TIK
TIGHT.

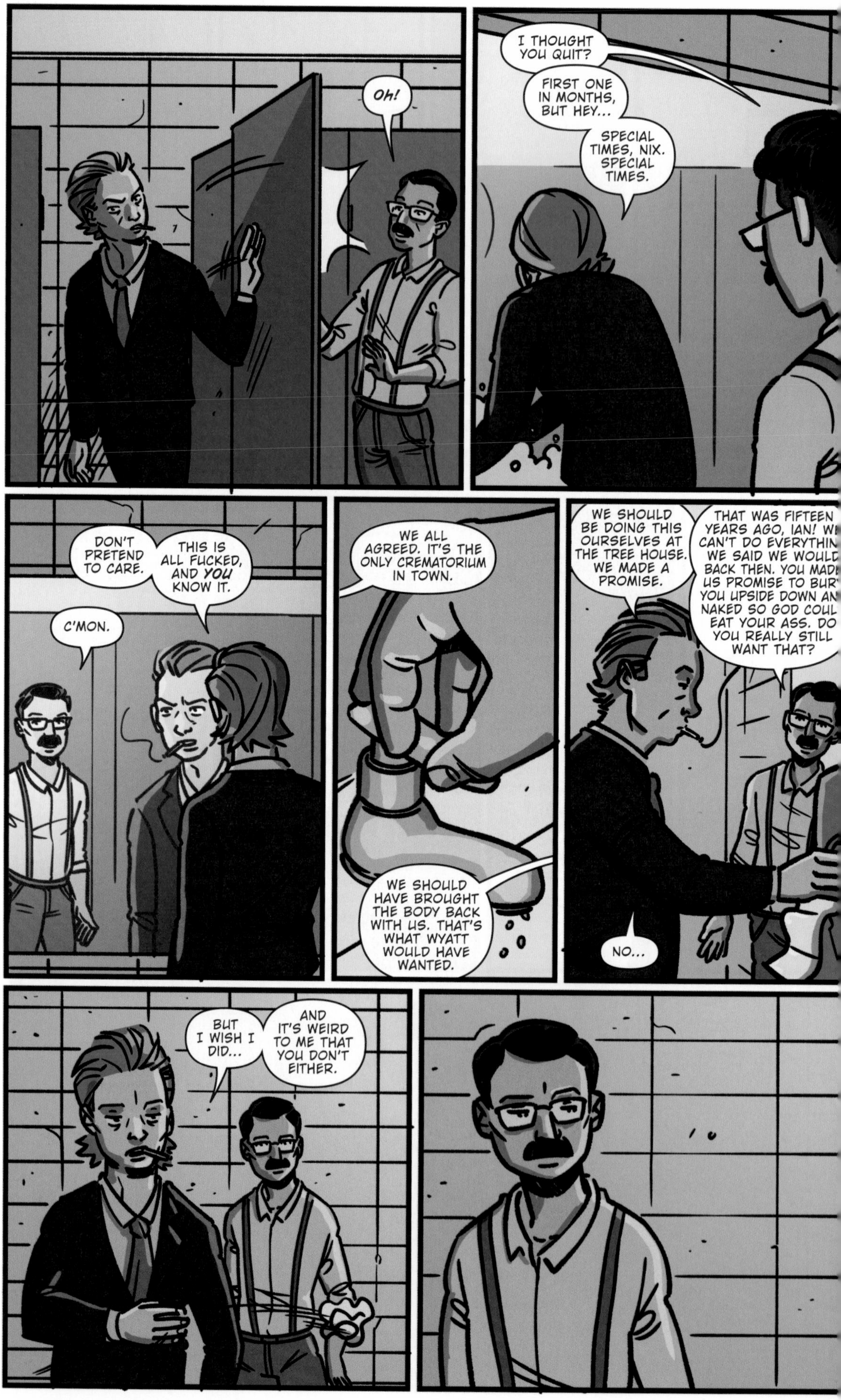

Oh!
I THOUGHT YOU QUIT?
FIRST ONE IN MONTHS, BUT HEY...
SPECIAL TIMES, NIX. SPECIAL TIMES.
DON'T PRETEND TO CARE.
THIS IS ALL FUCKED, AND *YOU* KNOW IT.
C'MON.
WE ALL AGREED. IT'S THE ONLY CREMATORIUM IN TOWN.
WE SHOULD HAVE BROUGHT THE BODY BACK WITH US. THAT'S WHAT WYATT WOULD HAVE WANTED.
WE SHOULD BE DOING THIS OURSELVES AT THE TREE HOUSE. WE MADE A PROMISE.
NO...
BUT I WISH I DID...
AND IT'S WEIRD TO ME THAT YOU DON'T EITHER.

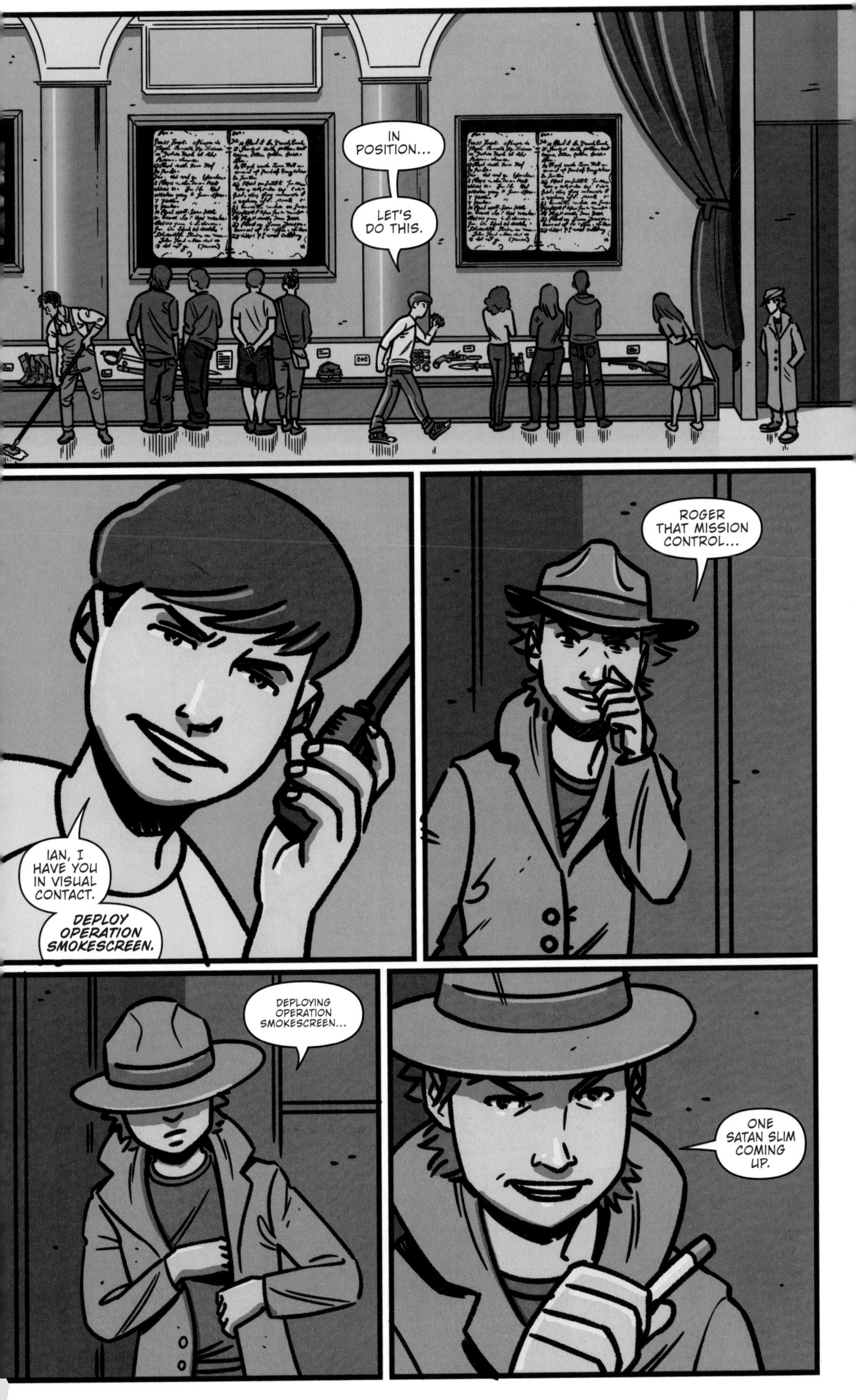
IN POSITION...
LET'S DO THIS.
IAN, I HAVE YOU IN VISUAL CONTACT.
DEPLOY OPERATION SMOKESCREEN.
ROGER THAT MISSION CONTROL...
DEPLOYING OPERATION SMOKESCREEN...
ONE SATAN SLIM COMING UP.

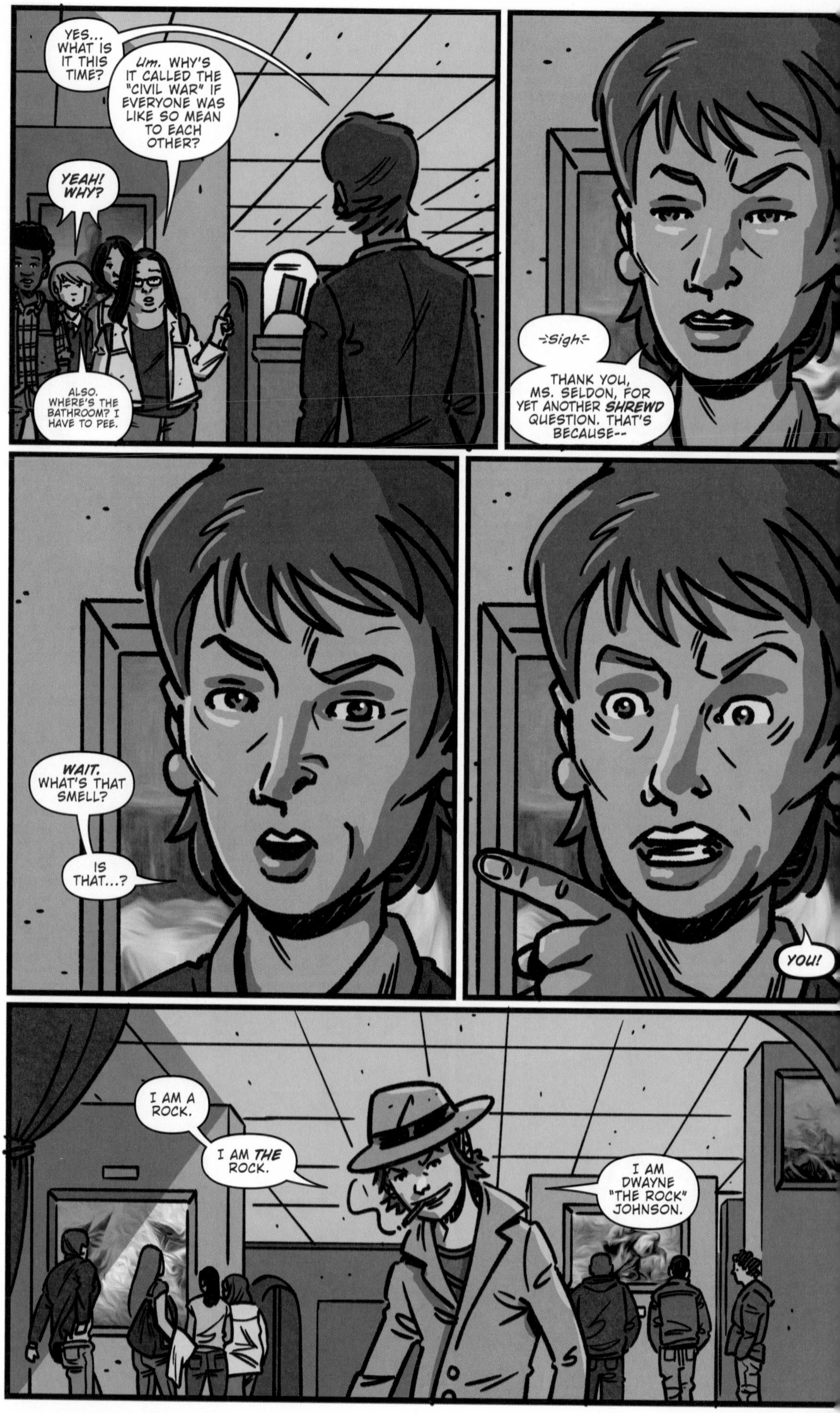

YES... WHAT IS IT THIS TIME?
Um. WHY'S IT CALLED THE "CIVIL WAR" IF EVERYONE WAS LIKE SO MEAN TO EACH OTHER?
YEAH! WHY?
ALSO. WHERE'S THE BATHROOM? I HAVE TO PEE.
Sigh
THANK YOU, MS. SELDON, FOR YET ANOTHER SHREWD QUESTION. THAT'S BECAUSE--
WAIT. WHAT'S THAT SMELL?
IS THAT...?
YOU!
I AM A ROCK.
I AM THE ROCK.
I AM DWAYNE "THE ROCK" JOHNSON.

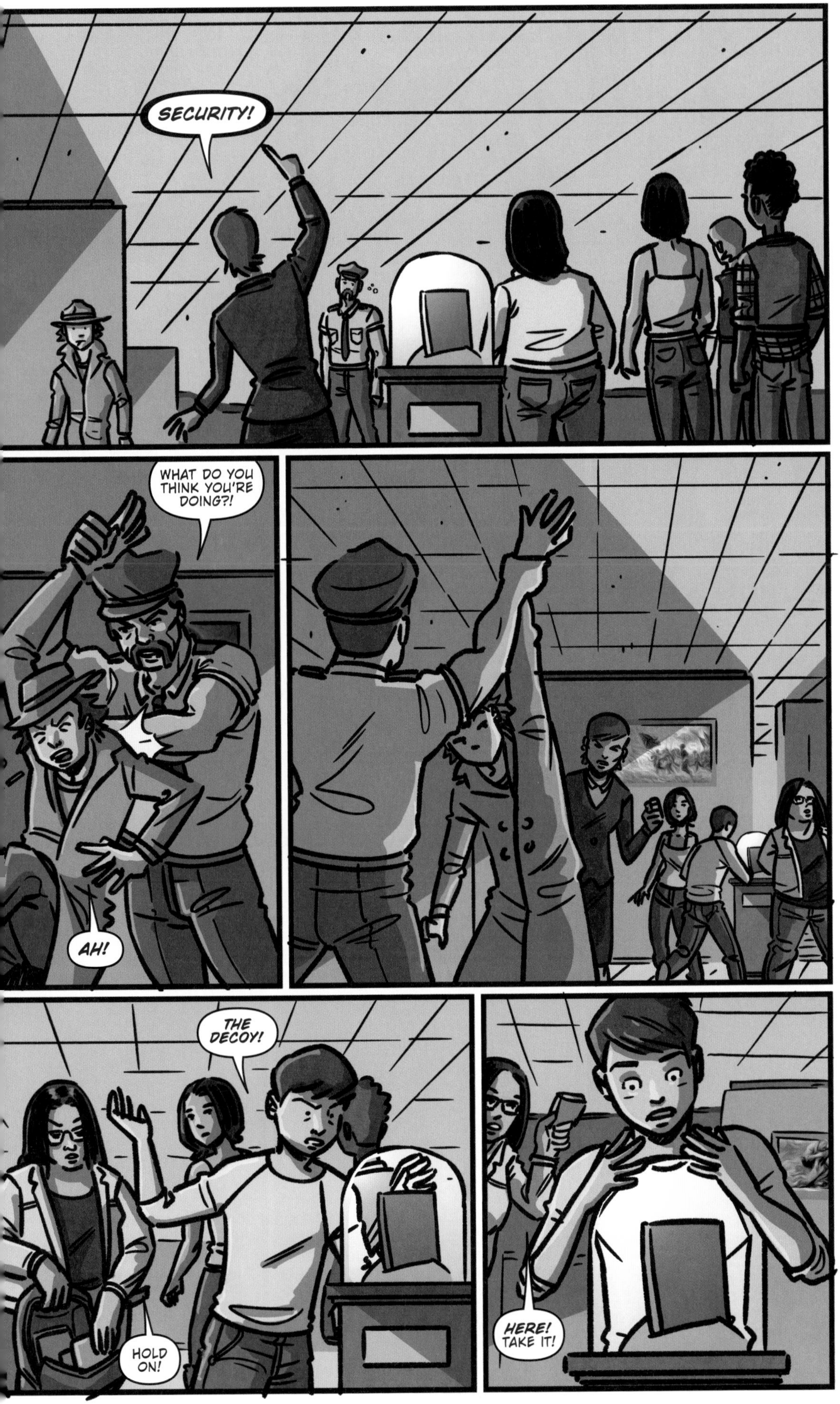
SECURITY!
WHAT DO YOU THINK YOU'RE DOING?!
AH!
THE DECOY!
HOLD ON!
HERE! TAKE IT!

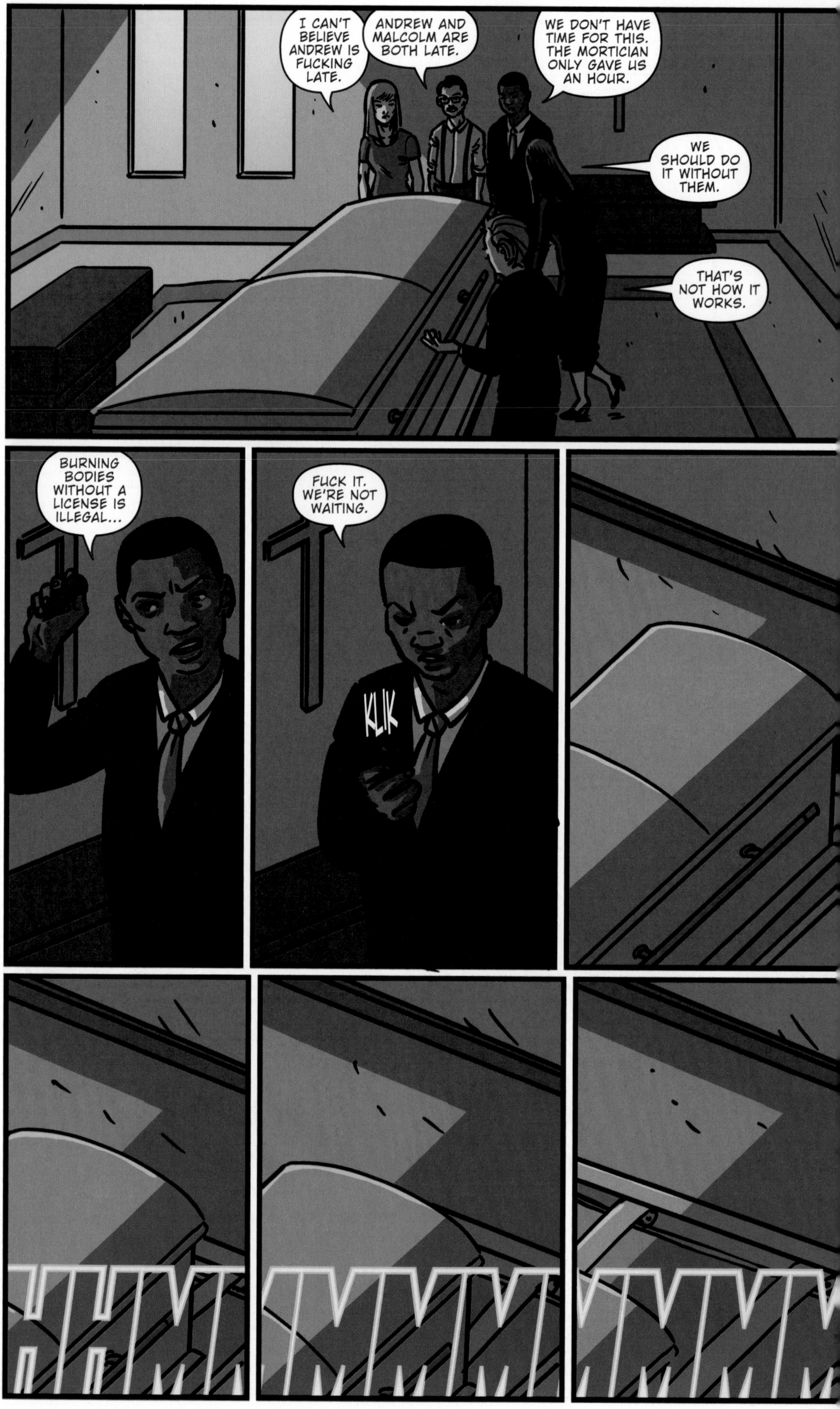
I CAN'T BELIEVE ANDREW IS FUCKING LATE.
ANDREW AND MALCOLM ARE BOTH LATE.
WE DON'T HAVE TIME FOR THIS. THE MORTICIAN ONLY GAVE US AN HOUR.
WE SHOULD DO IT WITHOUT THEM.
THAT'S NOT HOW IT WORKS.
BURNING BODIES WITHOUT A LICENSE IS ILLEGAL...
FUCK IT. WE'RE NOT WAITING.
KLIK

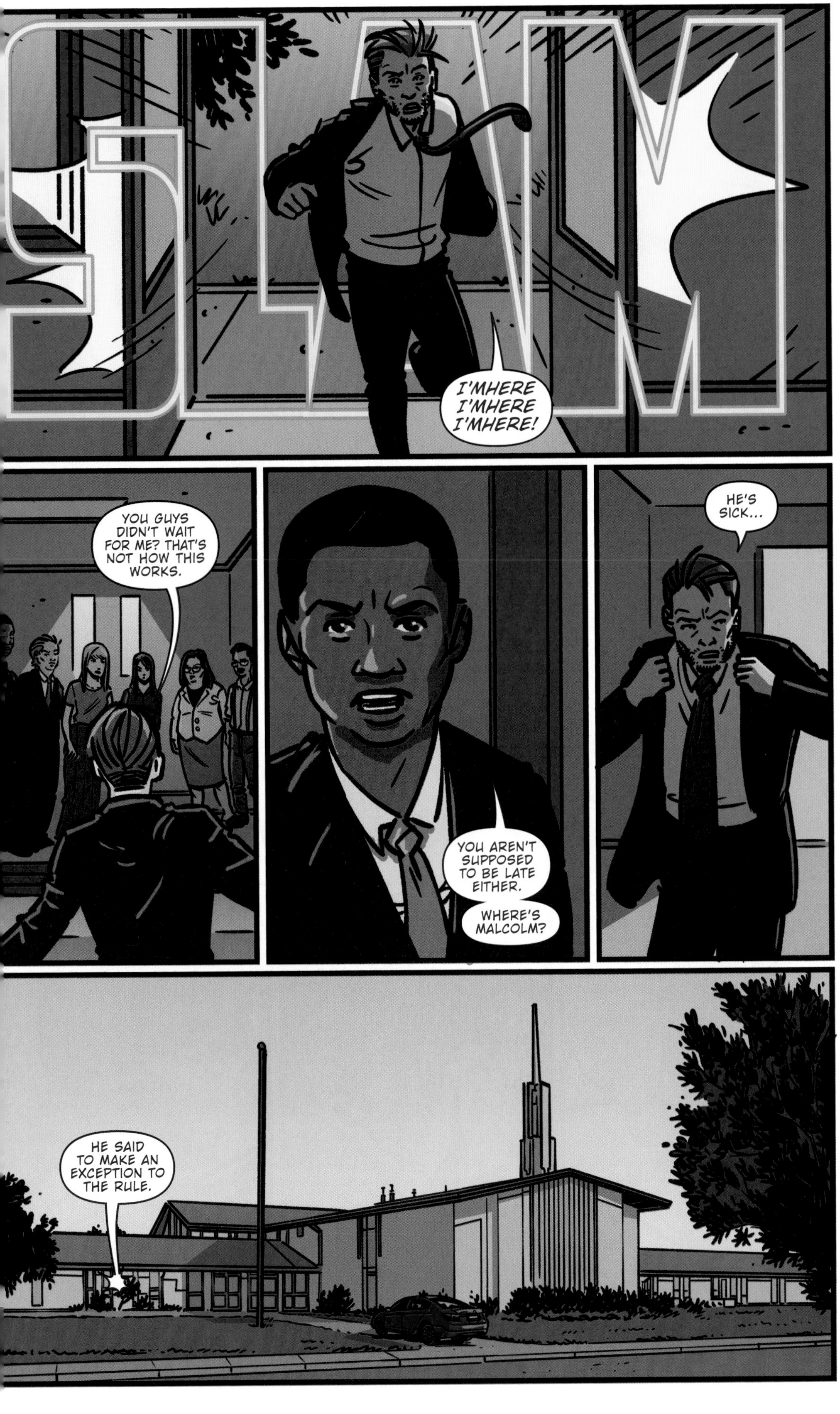
SLAM
I'MHERE I'MHERE I'MHERE!
YOU GUYS DIDN'T WAIT FOR ME? THAT'S NOT HOW THIS WORKS.
YOU AREN'T SUPPOSED TO BE LATE EITHER.
WHERE'S MALCOLM?
HE'S SICK...
HE SAID TO MAKE AN EXCEPTION TO THE RULE.

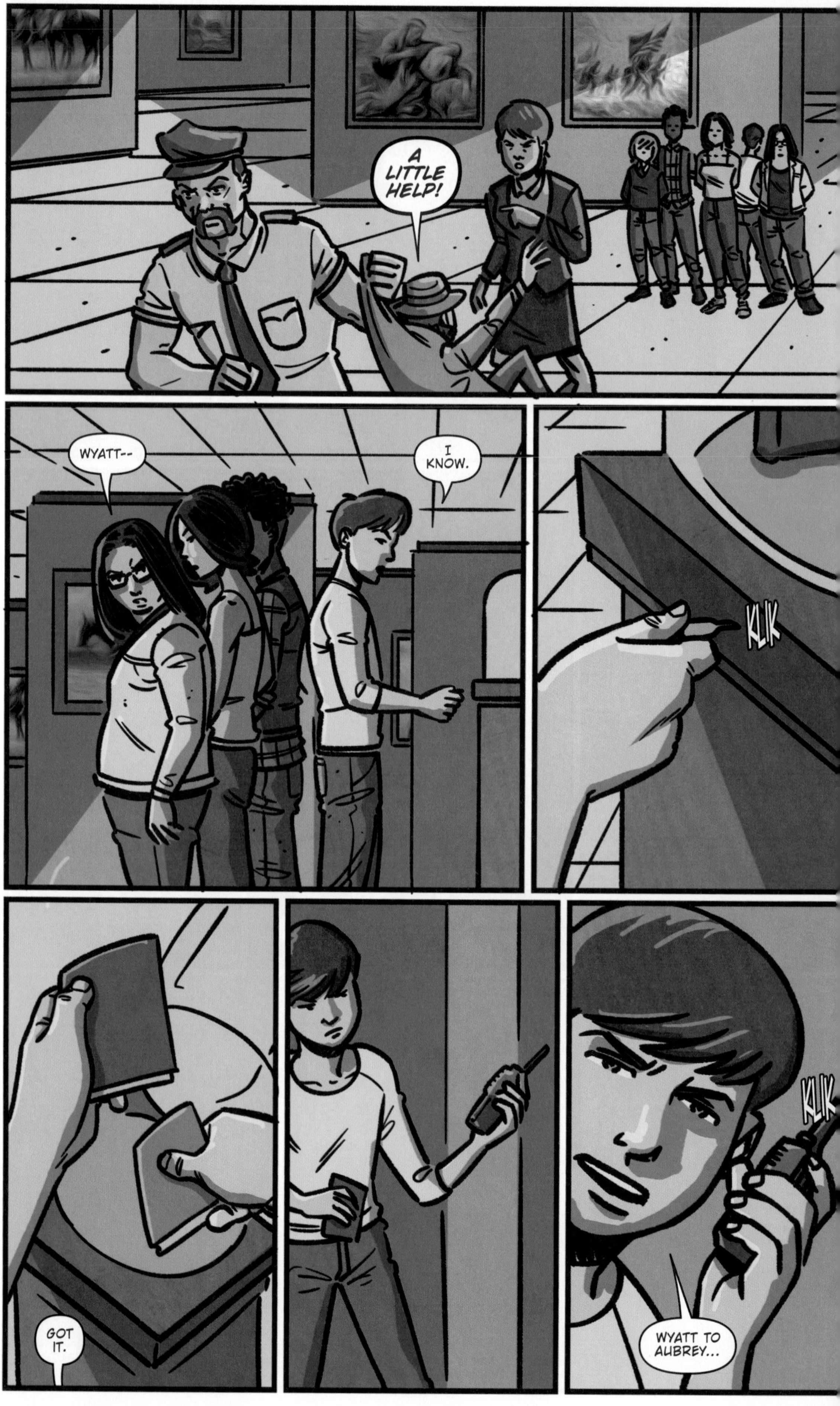
A LITTLE HELP!
WYATT--
I KNOW.
KLIK
GOT IT.
KLIK
WYATT TO AUBREY...

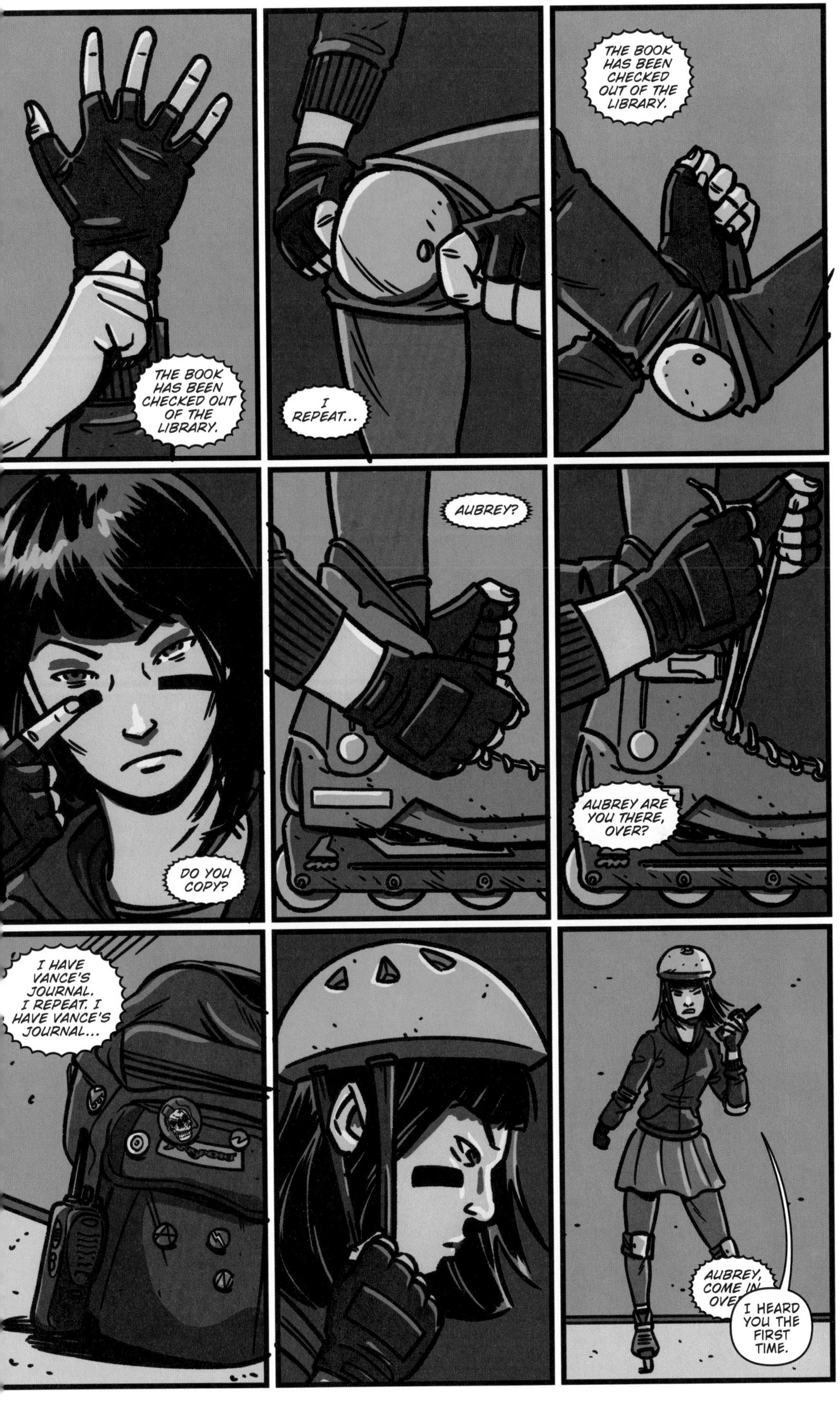

THE BOOK HAS BEEN CHECKED OUT OF THE LIBRARY.
I REPEAT...
THE BOOK HAS BEEN CHECKED OUT OF THE LIBRARY.
DO YOU COPY?
AUBREY?
AUBREY ARE YOU THERE, OVER?
I HAVE VANCE'S JOURNAL. I REPEAT. I HAVE VANCE'S JOURNAL...
AUBREY, COME IN, OVE
I HEARD YOU THE FIRST TIME.

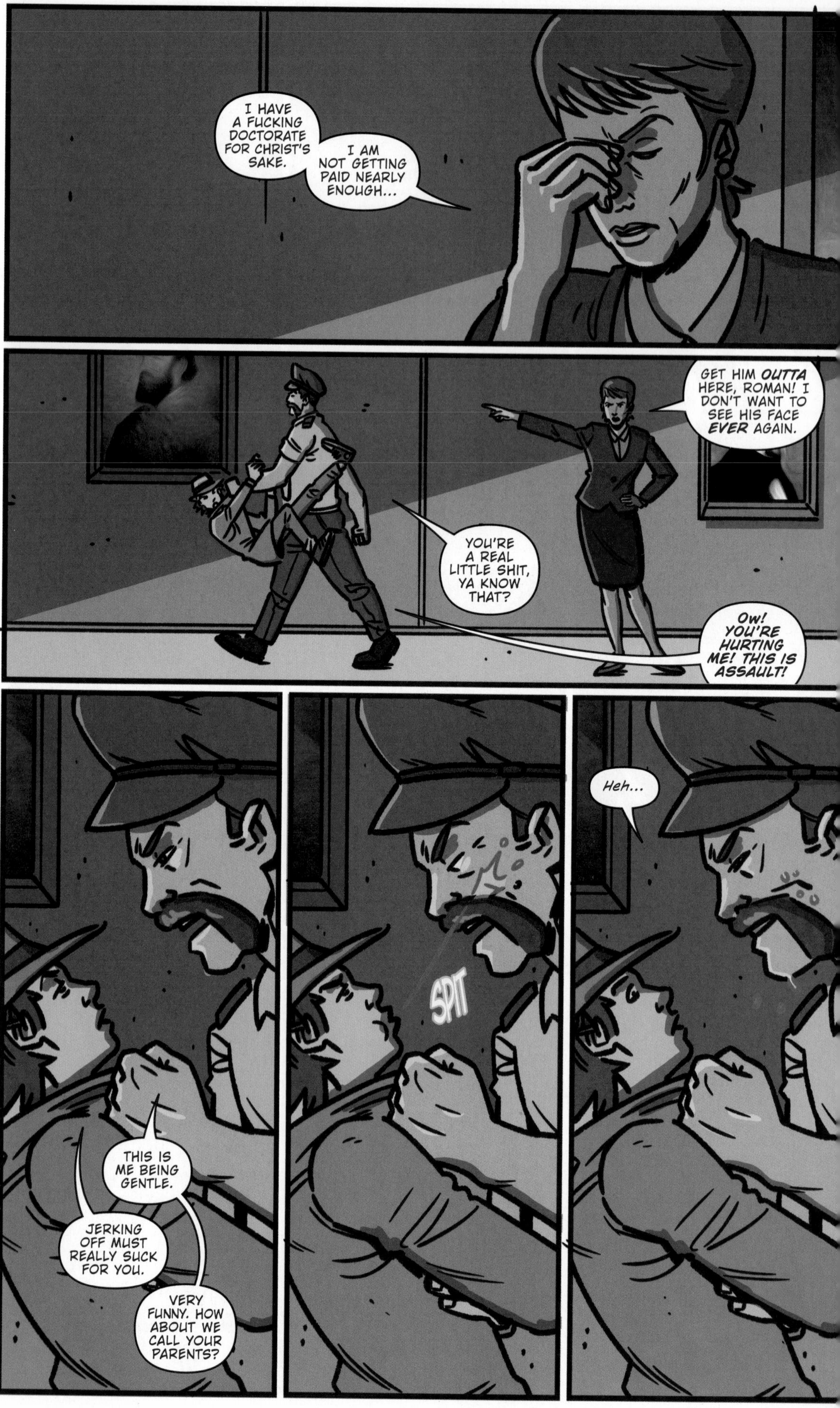
I HAVE A FUCKING DOCTORATE FOR CHRIST'S SAKE.
I AM NOT GETTING PAID NEARLY ENOUGH...
GET HIM OUTTA HERE, ROMAN! I DON'T WANT TO SEE HIS FACE EVER AGAIN.
YOU'RE A REAL LITTLE SHIT, YA KNOW THAT?
OW! YOU'RE HURTING ME! THIS IS ASSAULT!
THIS IS ME BEING GENTLE.
JERKING OFF MUST REALLY SUCK FOR YOU.
VERY FUNNY. HOW ABOUT WE CALL YOUR PARENTS?
SPIT
Heh...

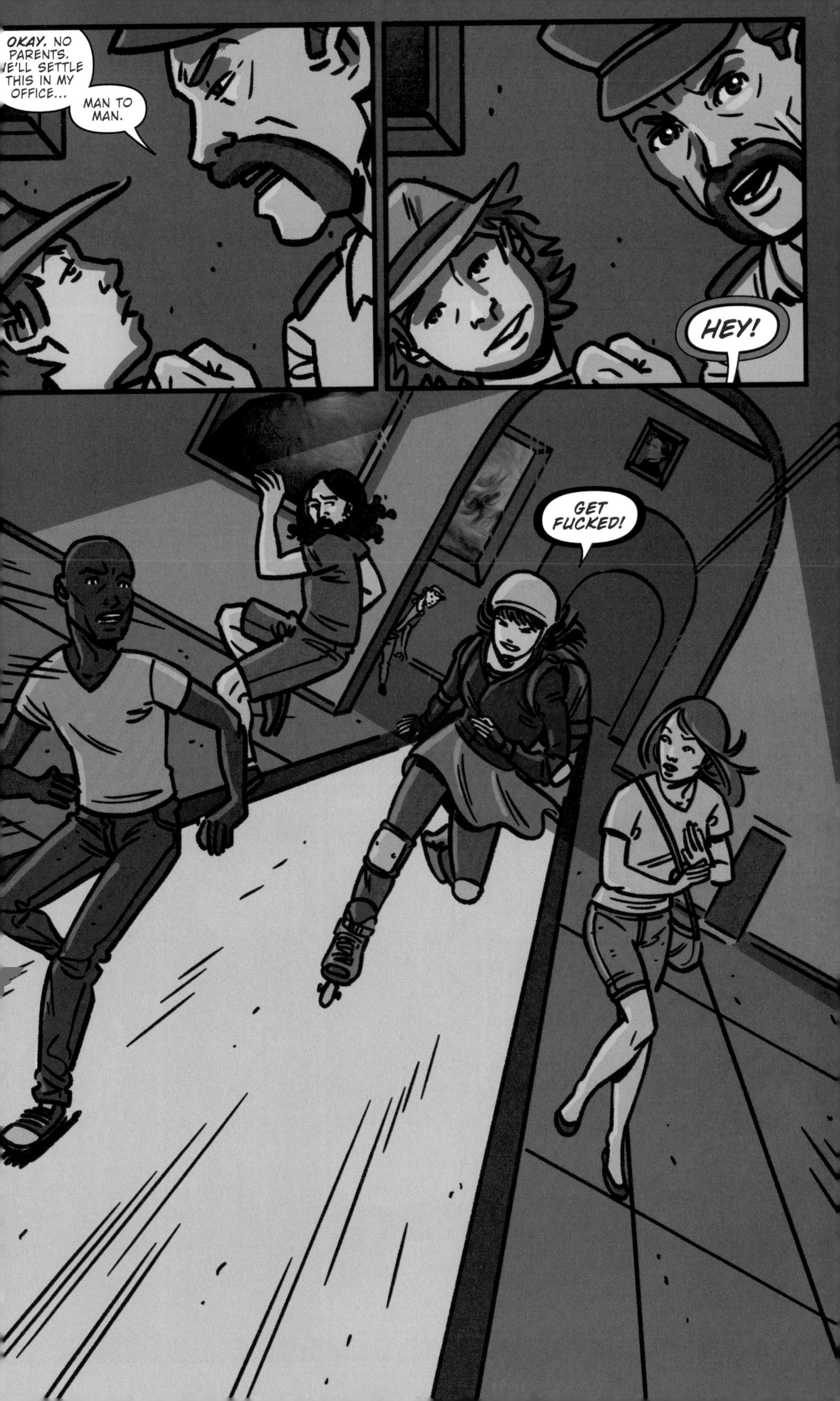
OKAY. NO PARENTS. WE'LL SETTLE THIS IN MY OFFICE...
MAN TO MAN.
HEY!
GET FUCKED!

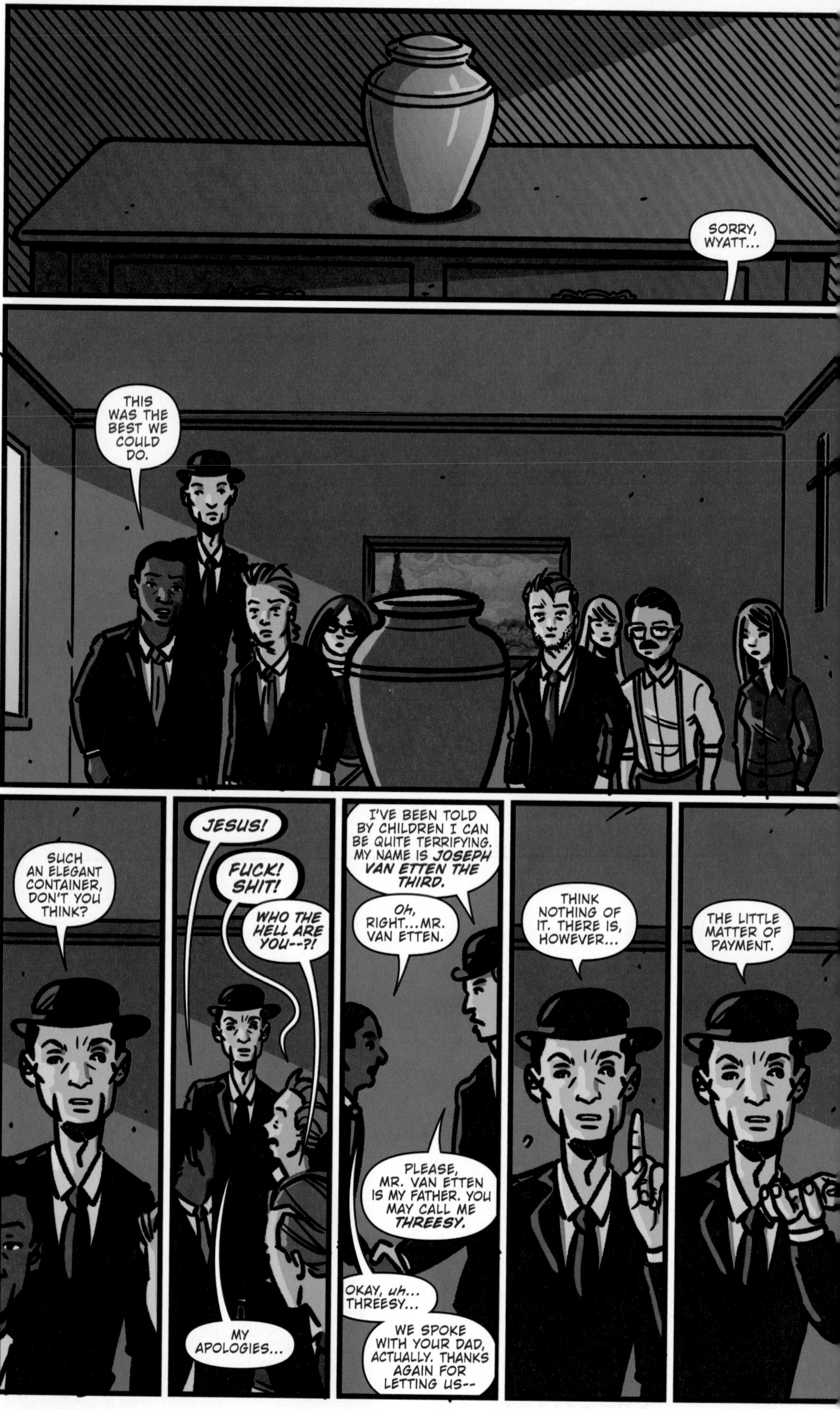
SORRY, WYATT...
THIS WAS THE BEST WE COULD DO.
SUCH AN ELEGANT CONTAINER, DON'T YOU THINK?
JESUS!
FUCK! SHIT!
WHO THE HELL ARE YOU--?!
MY APOLOGIES...
I'VE BEEN TOLD BY CHILDREN I CAN BE QUITE TERRIFYING. MY NAME IS JOSEPH VAN ETTEN THE THIRD.
Oh, RIGHT...MR. VAN ETTEN.
PLEASE, MR. VAN ETTEN IS MY FATHER. YOU MAY CALL ME THREESY.
OKAY, uh... THREESY...
WE SPOKE WITH YOUR DAD, ACTUALLY. THANKS AGAIN FOR LETTING US--
THINK NOTHING OF IT. THERE IS, HOWEVER...
THE LITTLE MATTER OF PAYMENT.

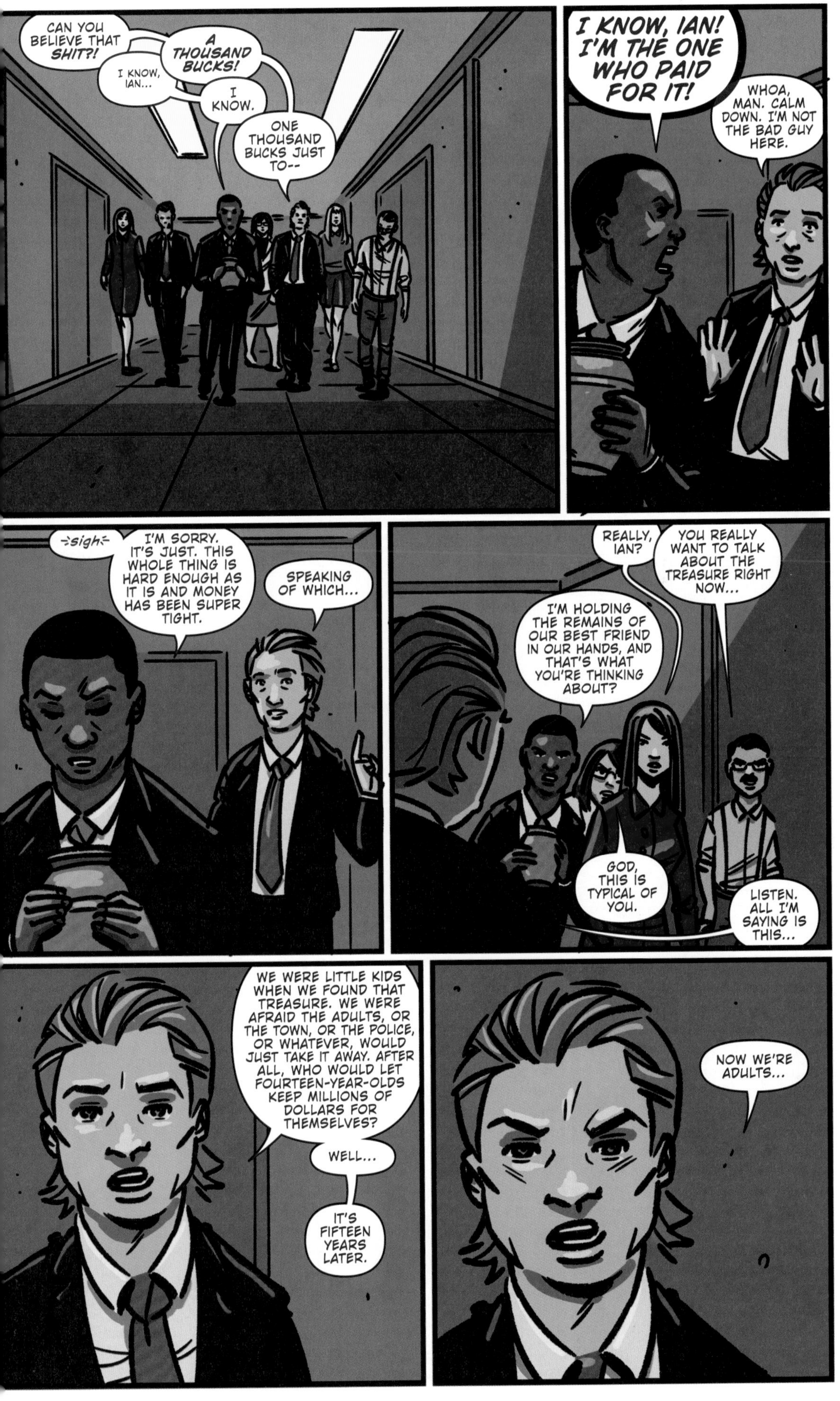

CAN YOU BELIEVE THAT *SHIT?!*
I KNOW, IAN...
A THOUSAND BUCKS!
I KNOW.
ONE THOUSAND BUCKS JUST TO--
I KNOW, IAN! I'M THE ONE WHO PAID FOR IT!
WHOA, MAN. CALM DOWN. I'M NOT THE BAD GUY HERE.
sigh
I'M SORRY. IT'S JUST. THIS WHOLE THING IS HARD ENOUGH AS IT IS AND MONEY HAS BEEN SUPER TIGHT.
SPEAKING OF WHICH...
REALLY, IAN?
YOU REALLY WANT TO TALK ABOUT THE TREASURE RIGHT NOW...
I'M HOLDING THE REMAINS OF OUR BEST FRIEND IN OUR HANDS, AND THAT'S WHAT YOU'RE THINKING ABOUT?
GOD, THIS IS TYPICAL OF YOU.
LISTEN. ALL I'M SAYING IS THIS...
WE WERE LITTLE KIDS WHEN WE FOUND THAT TREASURE. WE WERE AFRAID THE ADULTS, OR THE TOWN, OR THE POLICE, OR WHATEVER, WOULD JUST TAKE IT AWAY. AFTER ALL, WHO WOULD LET FOURTEEN-YEAR-OLDS KEEP MILLIONS OF DOLLARS FOR THEMSELVES?
WELL...
IT'S FIFTEEN YEARS LATER.
NOW WE'RE ADULTS...

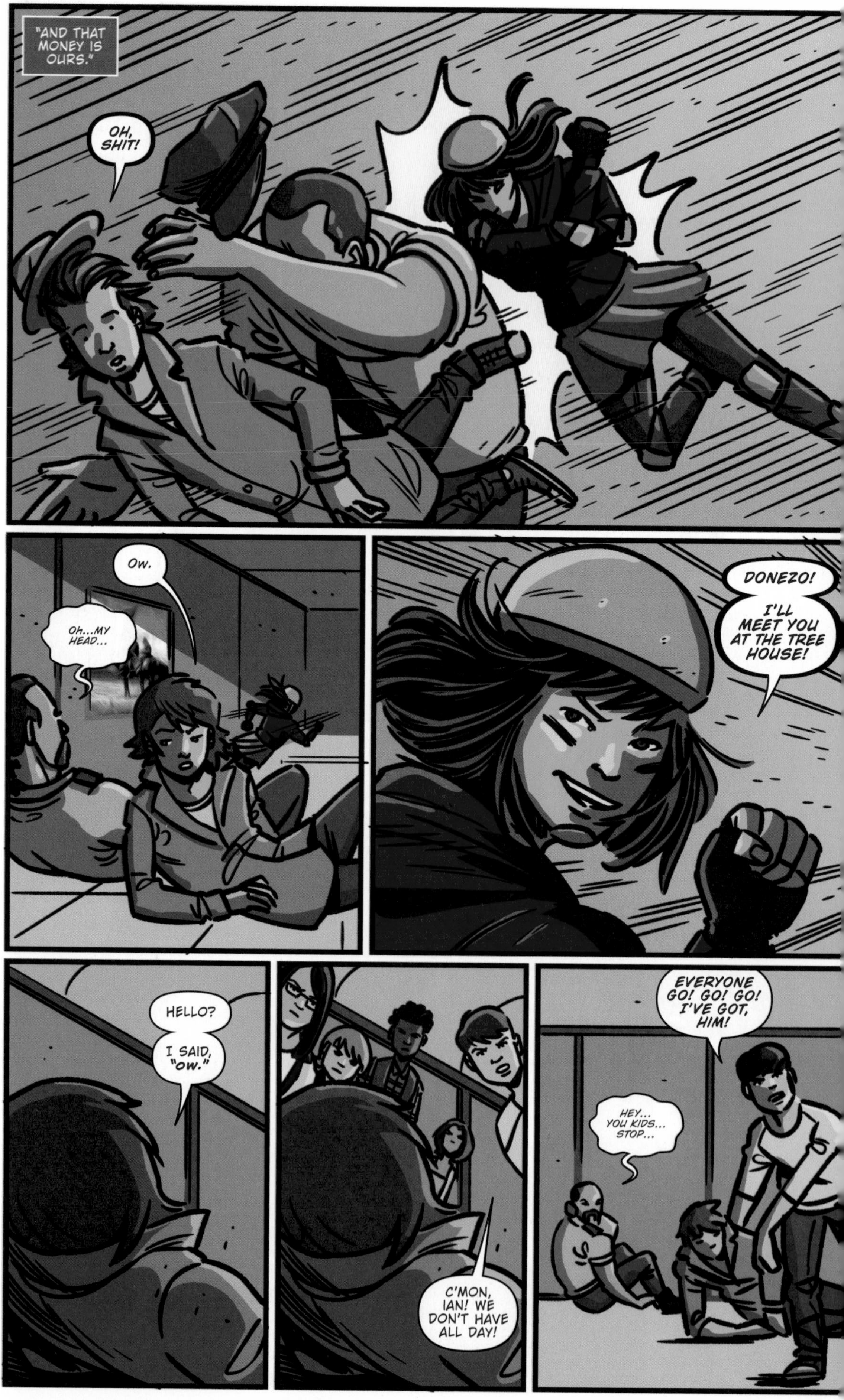
"AND THAT MONEY IS OURS."
OH, SHIT!
OW.
OH...MY HEAD...
DONEZO!
I'LL MEET YOU AT THE TREE HOUSE!
HELLO?
I SAID, "OW."
C'MON, IAN! WE DON'T HAVE ALL DAY!
EVERYONE GO! GO! GO! I'VE GOT, HIM!
HEY... YOU KIDS... STOP...

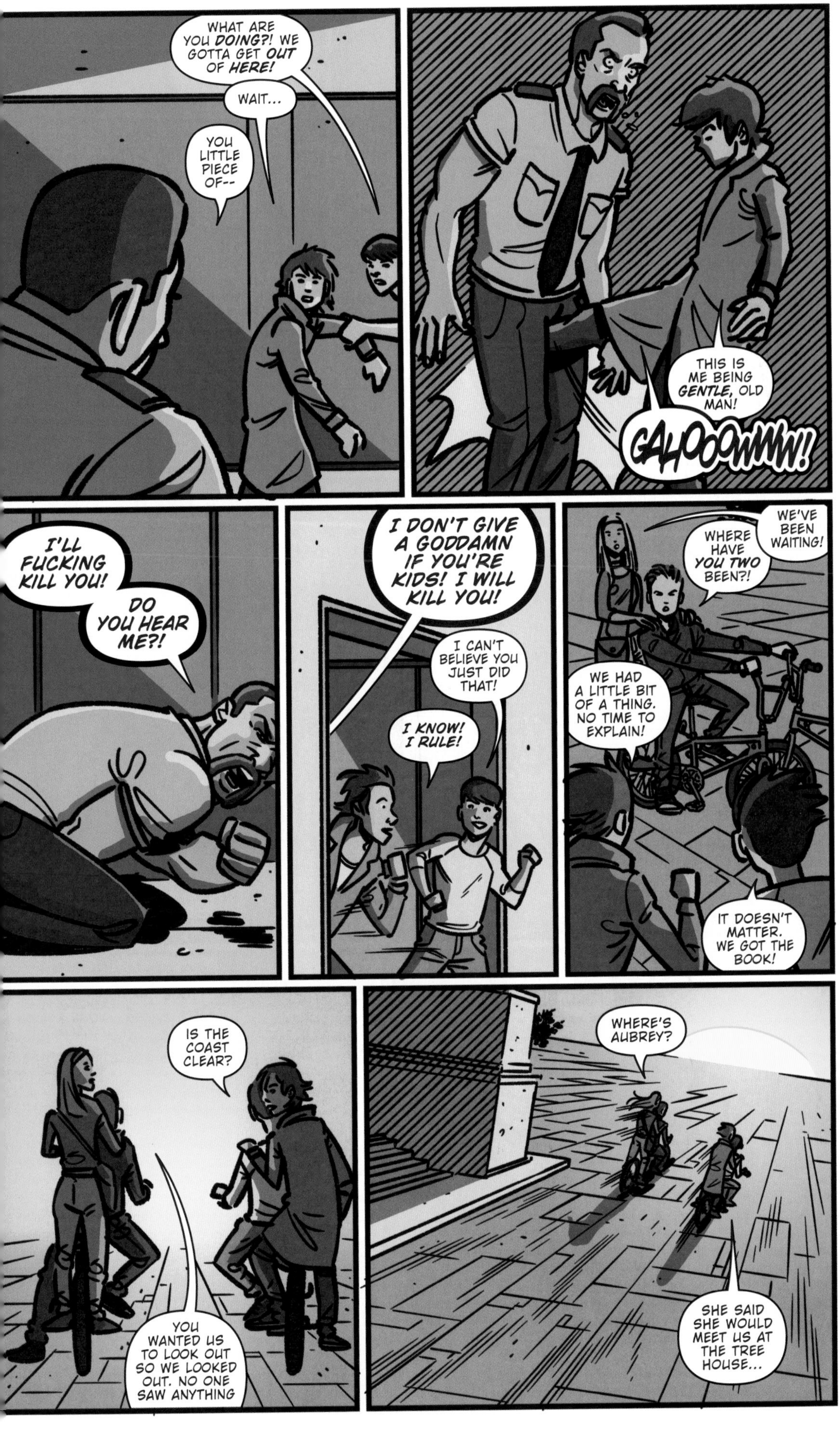
WHAT ARE YOU DOING?! WE GOTTA GET OUT OF HERE!
WAIT...
YOU LITTLE PIECE OF--
THIS IS ME BEING GENTLE, OLD MAN!
GALOOOWWW!
I'LL FUCKING KILL YOU!
DO YOU HEAR ME?!
I DON'T GIVE A GODDAMN IF YOU'RE KIDS! I WILL KILL YOU!
I CAN'T BELIEVE YOU JUST DID THAT!
I KNOW! I RULE!
WHERE HAVE YOU TWO BEEN?!
WE'VE BEEN WAITING!
WE HAD A LITTLE BIT OF A THING. NO TIME TO EXPLAIN!
IT DOESN'T MATTER. WE GOT THE BOOK!
IS THE COAST CLEAR?
YOU WANTED US TO LOOK OUT SO WE LOOKED OUT. NO ONE SAW ANYTHING
WHERE'S AUBREY?
SHE SAID SHE WOULD MEET US AT THE TREE HOUSE...

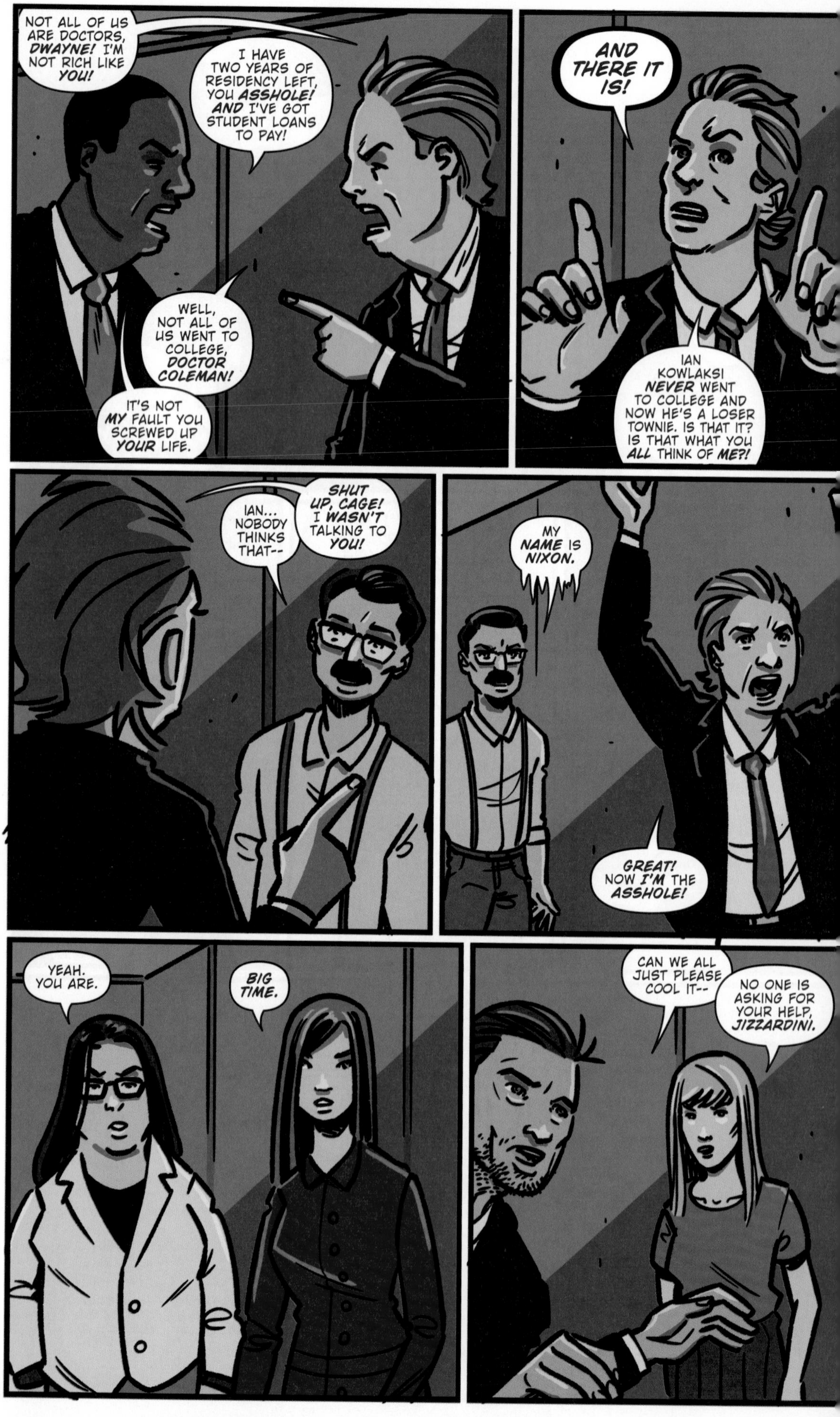

NOT ALL OF US ARE DOCTORS, DWAYNE! I'M NOT RICH LIKE YOU!
I HAVE TWO YEARS OF RESIDENCY LEFT, YOU ASSHOLE! AND I'VE GOT STUDENT LOANS TO PAY!
WELL, NOT ALL OF US WENT TO COLLEGE, DOCTOR COLEMAN!
IT'S NOT MY FAULT YOU SCREWED UP YOUR LIFE.
AND THERE IT IS!
IAN KOWLAKSI NEVER WENT TO COLLEGE AND NOW HE'S A LOSER TOWNIE. IS THAT IT? IS THAT WHAT YOU ALL THINK OF ME?!
IAN... NOBODY THINKS THAT--
SHUT UP, CAGE! I WASN'T TALKING TO YOU!
MY NAME IS NIXON.
GREAT! NOW I'M THE ASSHOLE!
YEAH. YOU ARE.
BIG TIME.
CAN WE ALL JUST PLEASE COOL IT--
NO ONE IS ASKING FOR YOUR HELP, JIZZARDINI.

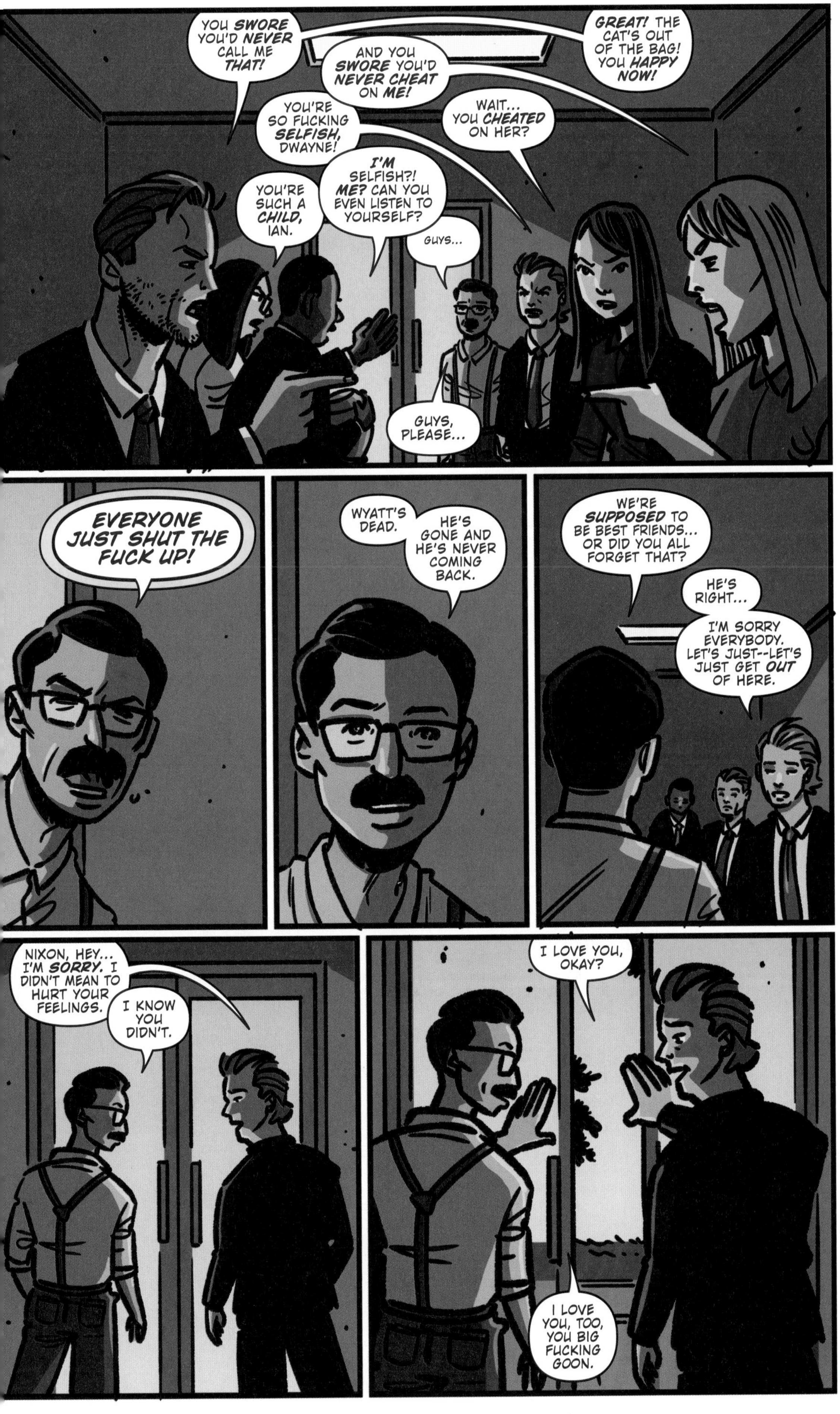
YOU SWORE YOU'D NEVER CALL ME THAT!
GREAT! THE CAT'S OUT OF THE BAG! YOU HAPPY NOW!
AND YOU SWORE YOU'D NEVER CHEAT ON ME!
YOU'RE SO FUCKING SELFISH, DWAYNE!
WAIT... YOU CHEATED ON HER?
YOU'RE SUCH A CHILD, IAN.
I'M SELFISH?! ME? CAN YOU EVEN LISTEN TO YOURSELF?
GUYS...
GUYS, PLEASE...
EVERYONE JUST SHUT THE FUCK UP!
WYATT'S DEAD.
HE'S GONE AND HE'S NEVER COMING BACK.
WE'RE SUPPOSED TO BE BEST FRIENDS... OR DID YOU ALL FORGET THAT?
HE'S RIGHT...
I'M SORRY EVERYBODY. LET'S JUST--LET'S JUST GET OUT OF HERE.
NIXON, HEY... I'M SORRY. I DIDN'T MEAN TO HURT YOUR FEELINGS.
I KNOW YOU DIDN'T.
I LOVE YOU, OKAY?
I LOVE YOU, TOO, YOU BIG FUCKING GOON.

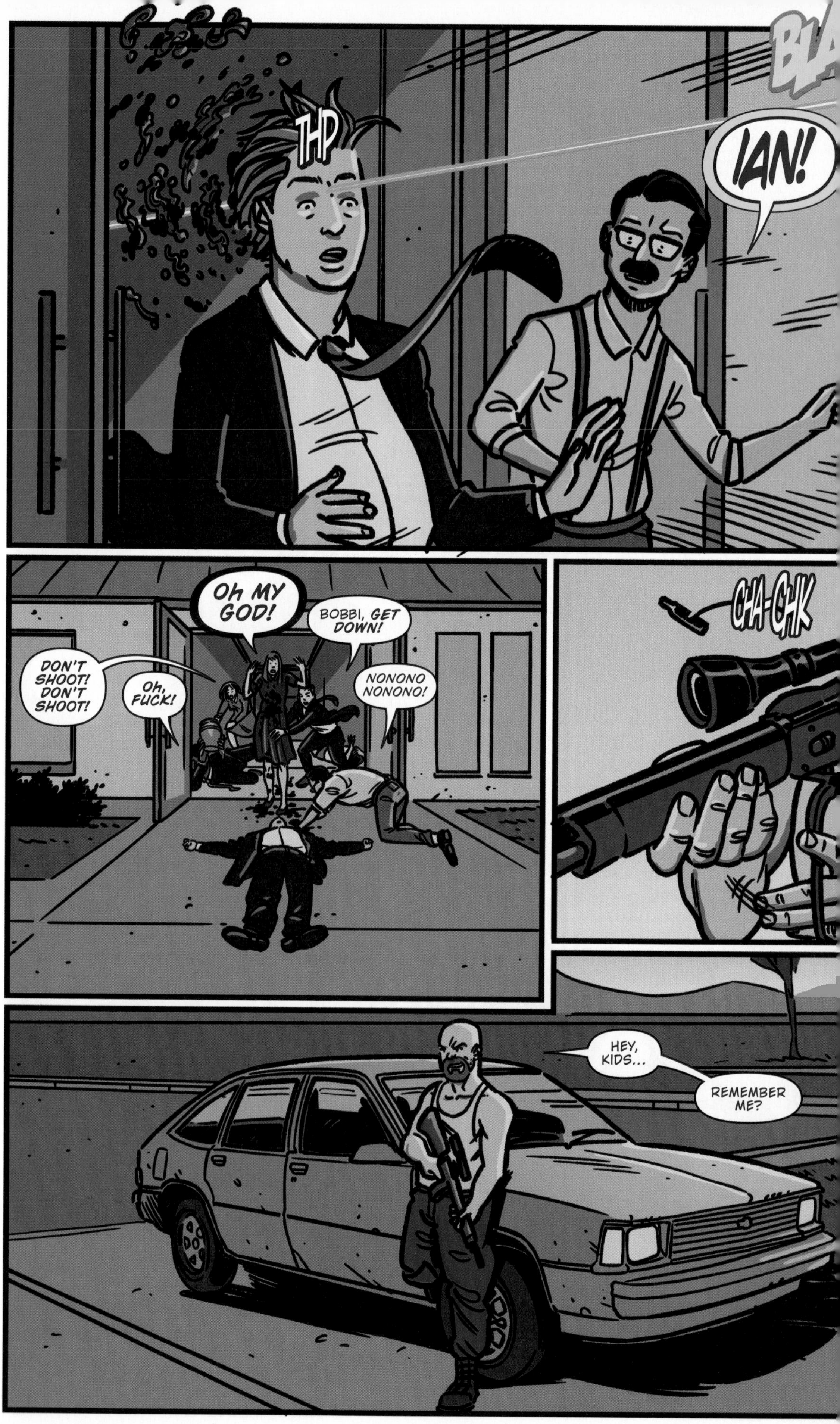
THP
IAN!
Oh MY GOD!
BOBBI, GET DOWN!
DON'T SHOOT! DON'T SHOOT!
Oh, FUCK!
NONONO NONONO!
CHA-CHK
HEY, KIDS...
REMEMBER ME?

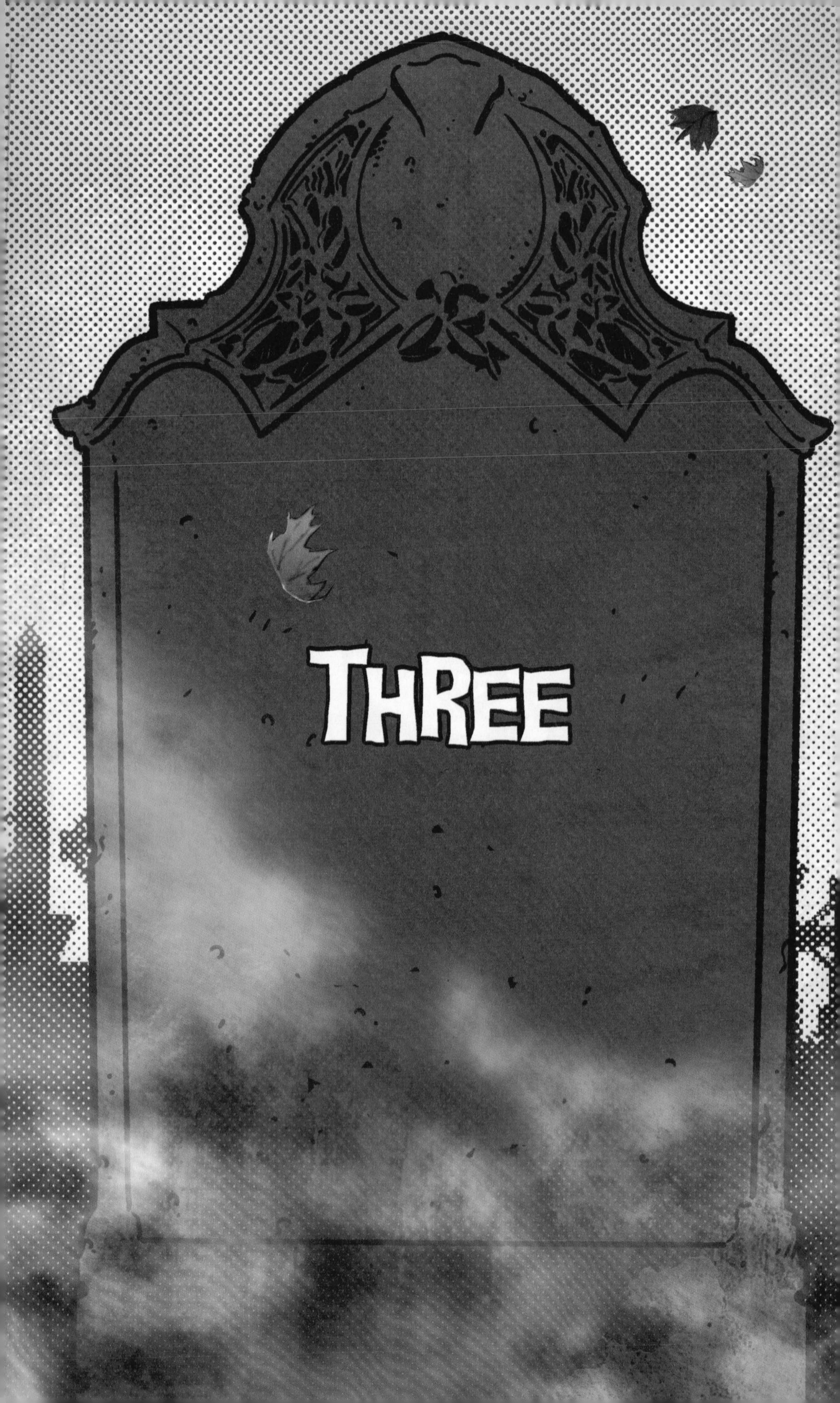
THREE

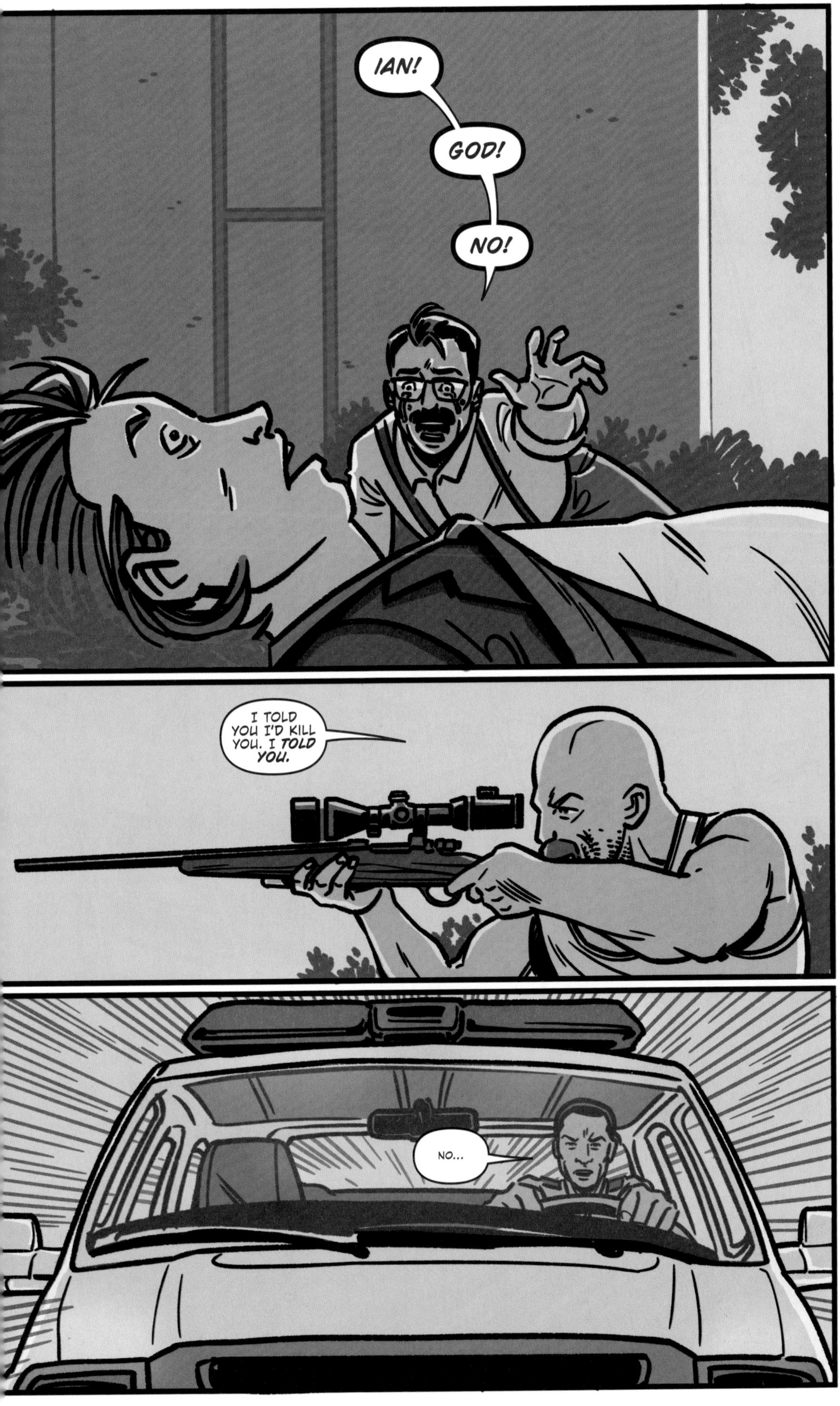
IAN!
GOD!
NO!
I TOLD YOU I'D KILL YOU. I *TOLD* *YOU.*
NO...

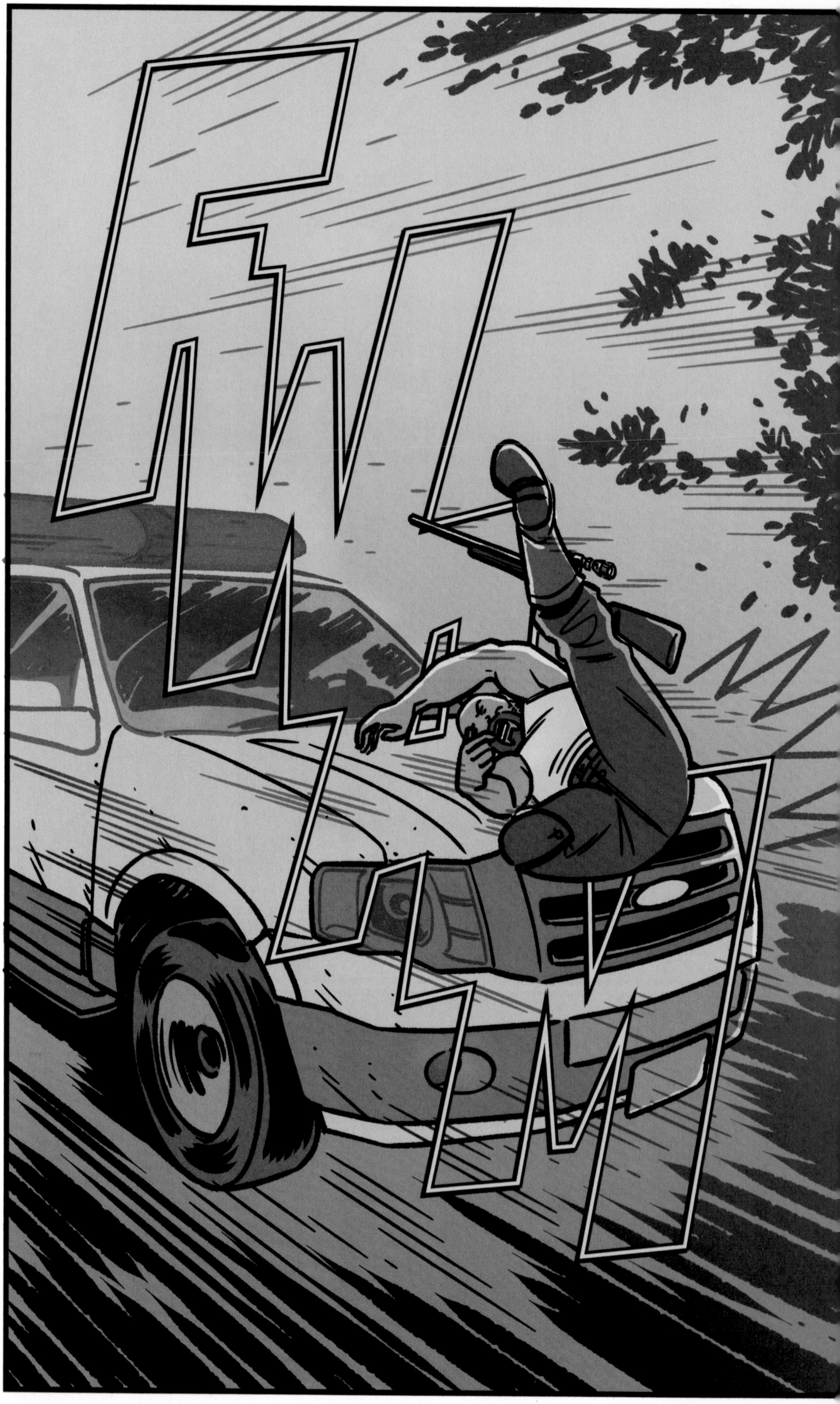

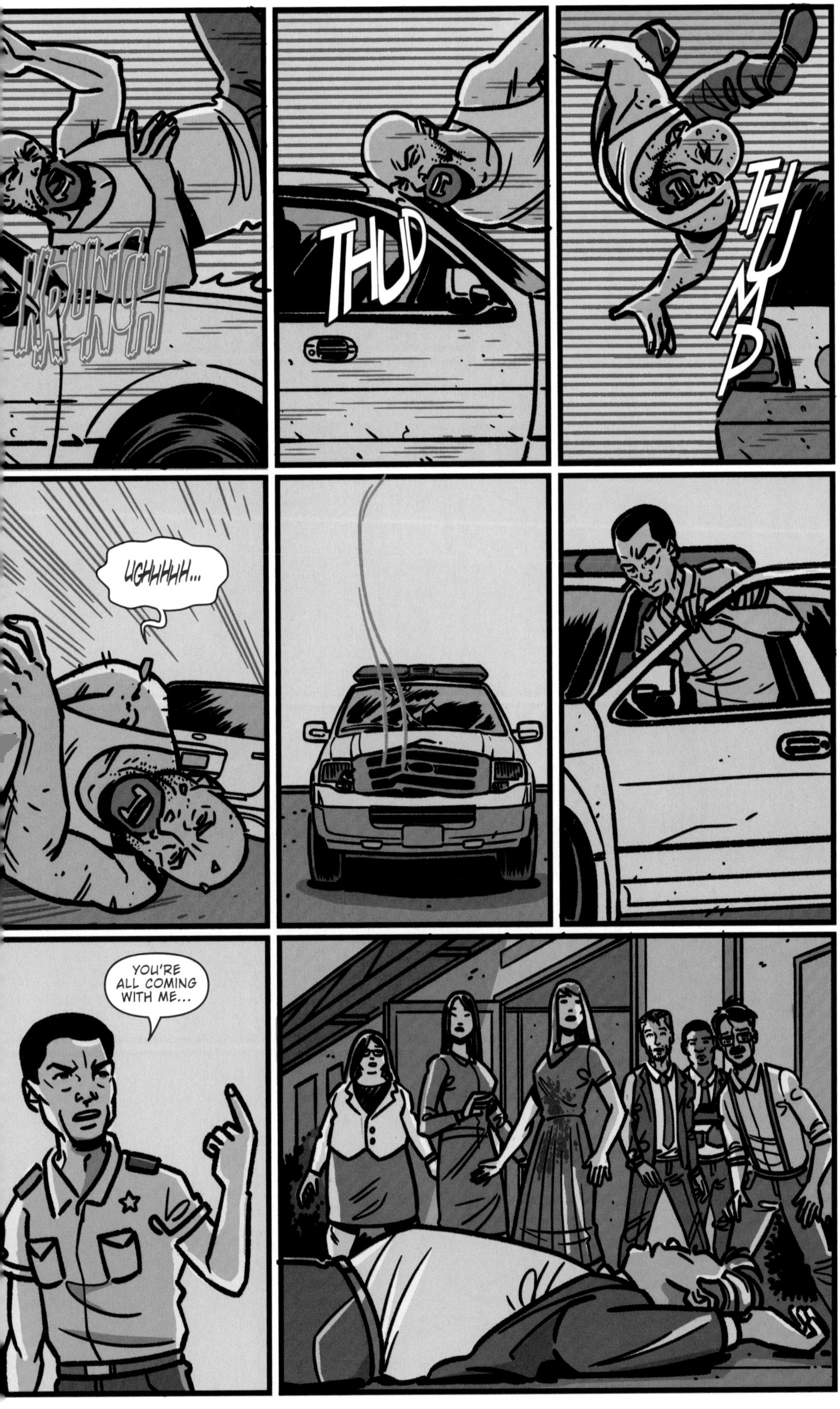
KRUNCH
THUD
THUMP
UGHHHHH...
YOU'RE ALL COMING WITH ME...

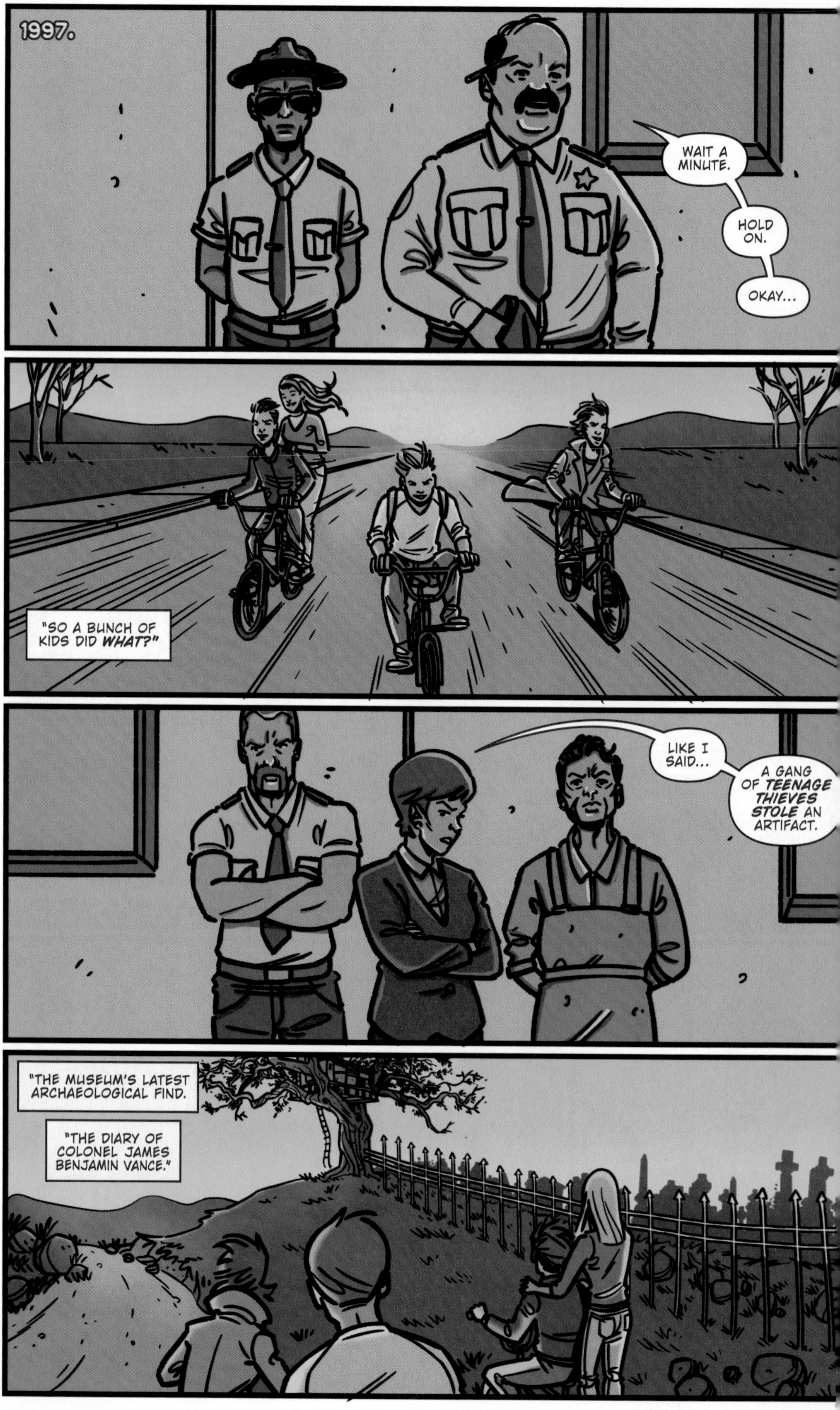
1997.
WAIT A MINUTE.
HOLD ON.
OKAY...
"SO A BUNCH OF KIDS DID WHAT?"
LIKE I SAID...
A GANG OF TEENAGE THIEVES STOLE AN ARTIFACT.
"THE MUSEUM'S LATEST ARCHAEOLOGICAL FIND.
"THE DIARY OF COLONEL JAMES BENJAMIN VANCE."

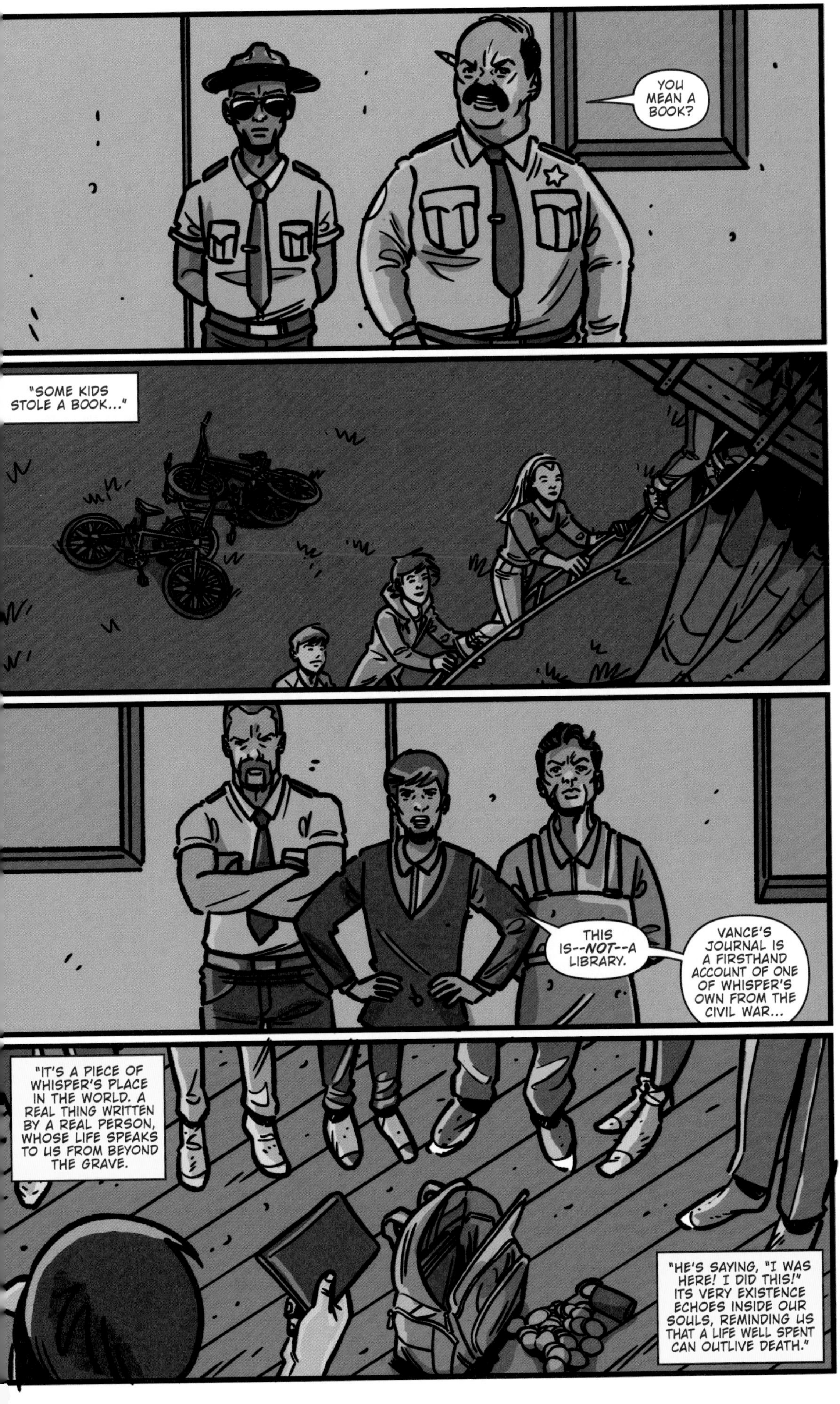

YOU MEAN A BOOK?
"SOME KIDS STOLE A BOOK..."
THIS IS--*NOT*--A LIBRARY.
VANCE'S JOURNAL IS A FIRSTHAND ACCOUNT OF ONE OF WHISPER'S OWN FROM THE CIVIL WAR...
"IT'S A PIECE OF WHISPER'S PLACE IN THE WORLD. A REAL THING WRITTEN BY A REAL PERSON, WHOSE LIFE SPEAKS TO US FROM BEYOND THE GRAVE.
"HE'S SAYING, "I WAS HERE! I DID THIS!" ITS VERY EXISTENCE ECHOES INSIDE OUR SOULS, REMINDING US THAT A LIFE WELL SPENT CAN OUTLIVE DEATH."

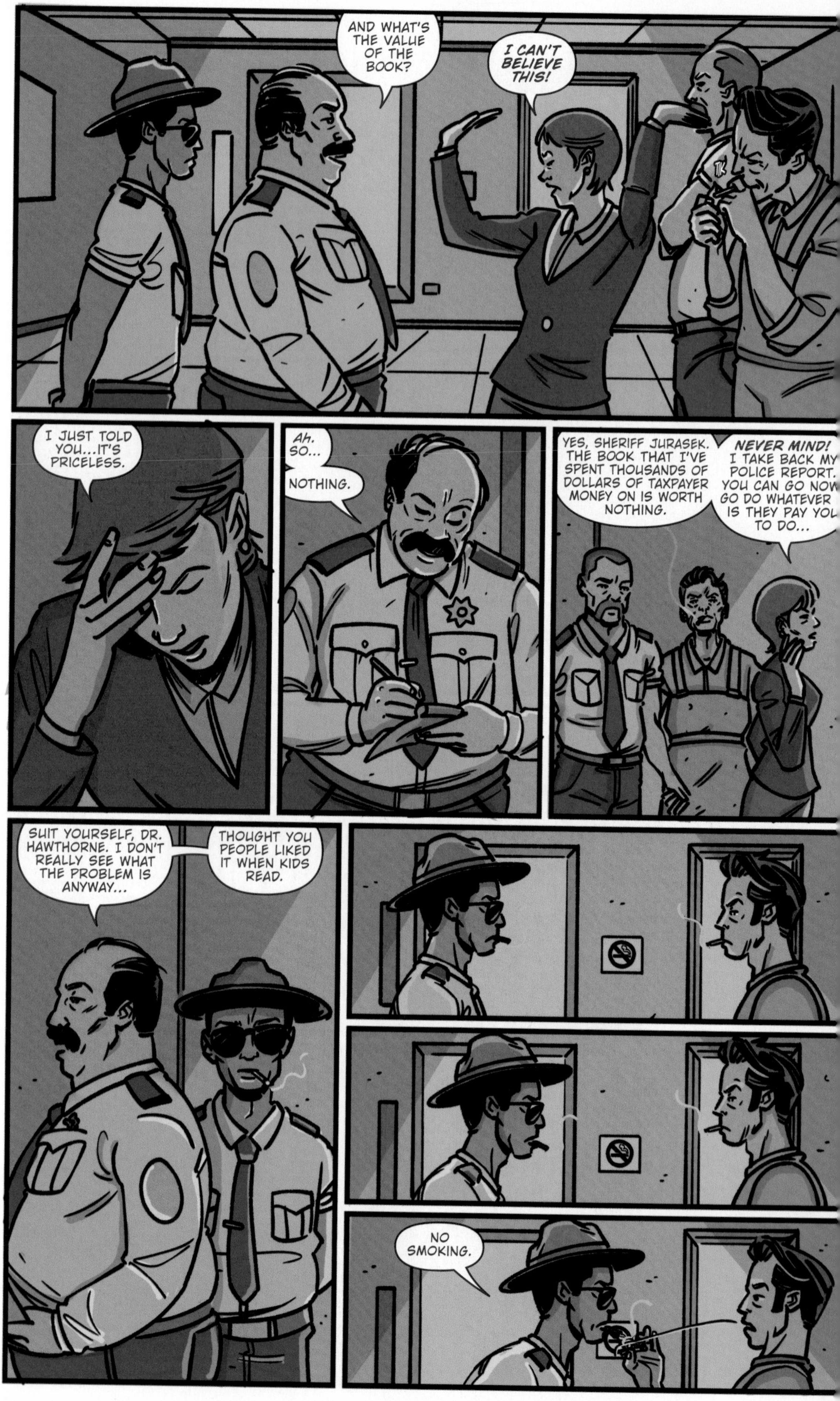
AND WHAT'S THE VALUE OF THE BOOK?
I CAN'T BELIEVE THIS!
I JUST TOLD YOU...IT'S PRICELESS.
Ah. SO...
NOTHING.
YES, SHERIFF JURASEK. THE BOOK THAT I'VE SPENT THOUSANDS OF DOLLARS OF TAXPAYER MONEY ON IS WORTH NOTHING.
NEVER MIND! I TAKE BACK MY POLICE REPORT. YOU CAN GO NOW GO DO WHATEVER IS THEY PAY YOU TO DO...
SUIT YOURSELF, DR. HAWTHORNE. I DON'T REALLY SEE WHAT THE PROBLEM IS ANYWAY...
THOUGHT YOU PEOPLE LIKED IT WHEN KIDS READ.
NO SMOKING.

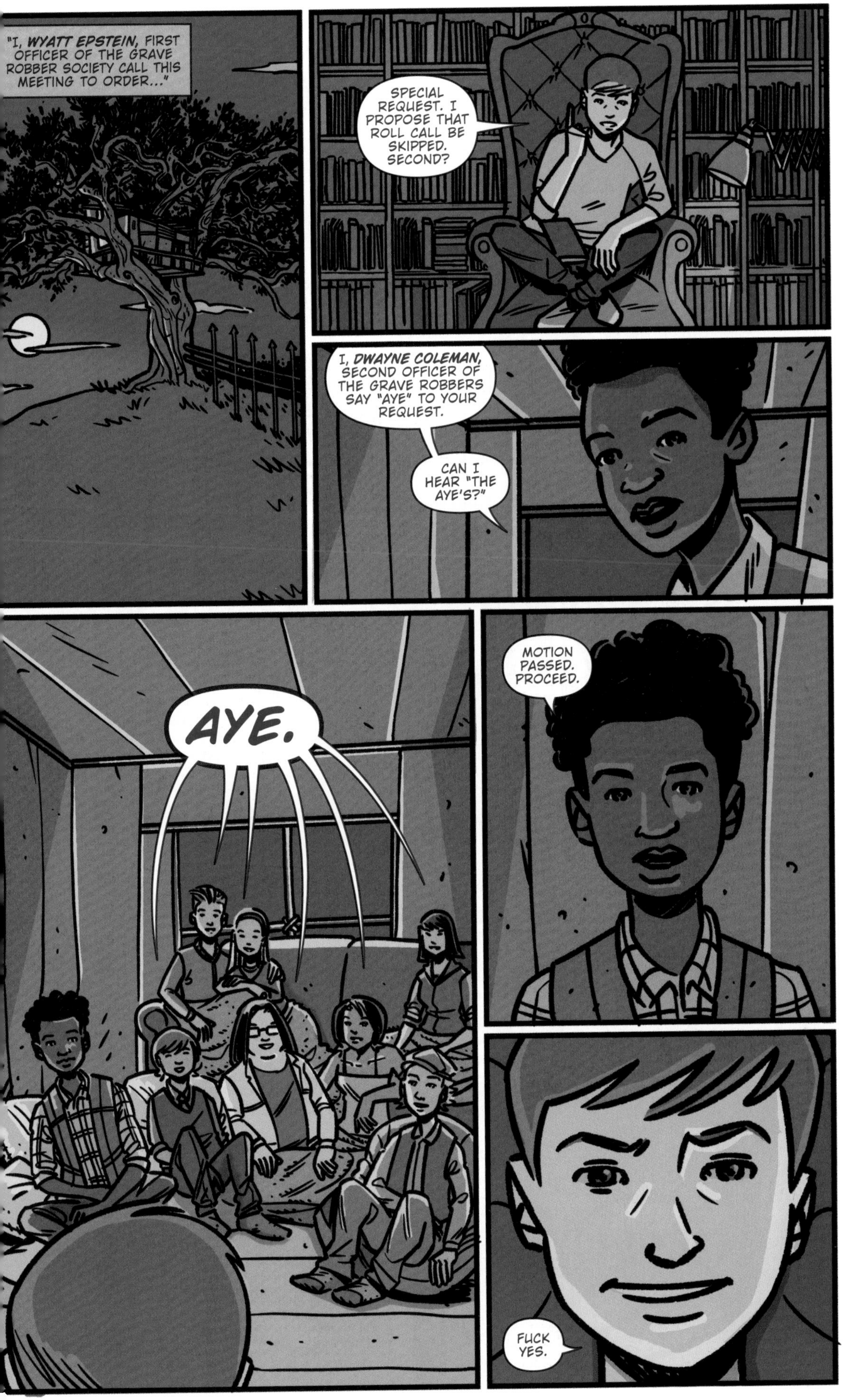
"I, WYATT EPSTEIN, FIRST OFFICER OF THE GRAVE ROBBER SOCIETY CALL THIS MEETING TO ORDER..."
SPECIAL REQUEST. I PROPOSE THAT ROLL CALL BE SKIPPED. SECOND?
I, DWAYNE COLEMAN, SECOND OFFICER OF THE GRAVE ROBBERS SAY "AYE" TO YOUR REQUEST.
CAN I HEAR "THE AYE'S?"
AYE.
MOTION PASSED. PROCEED.
FUCK YES.

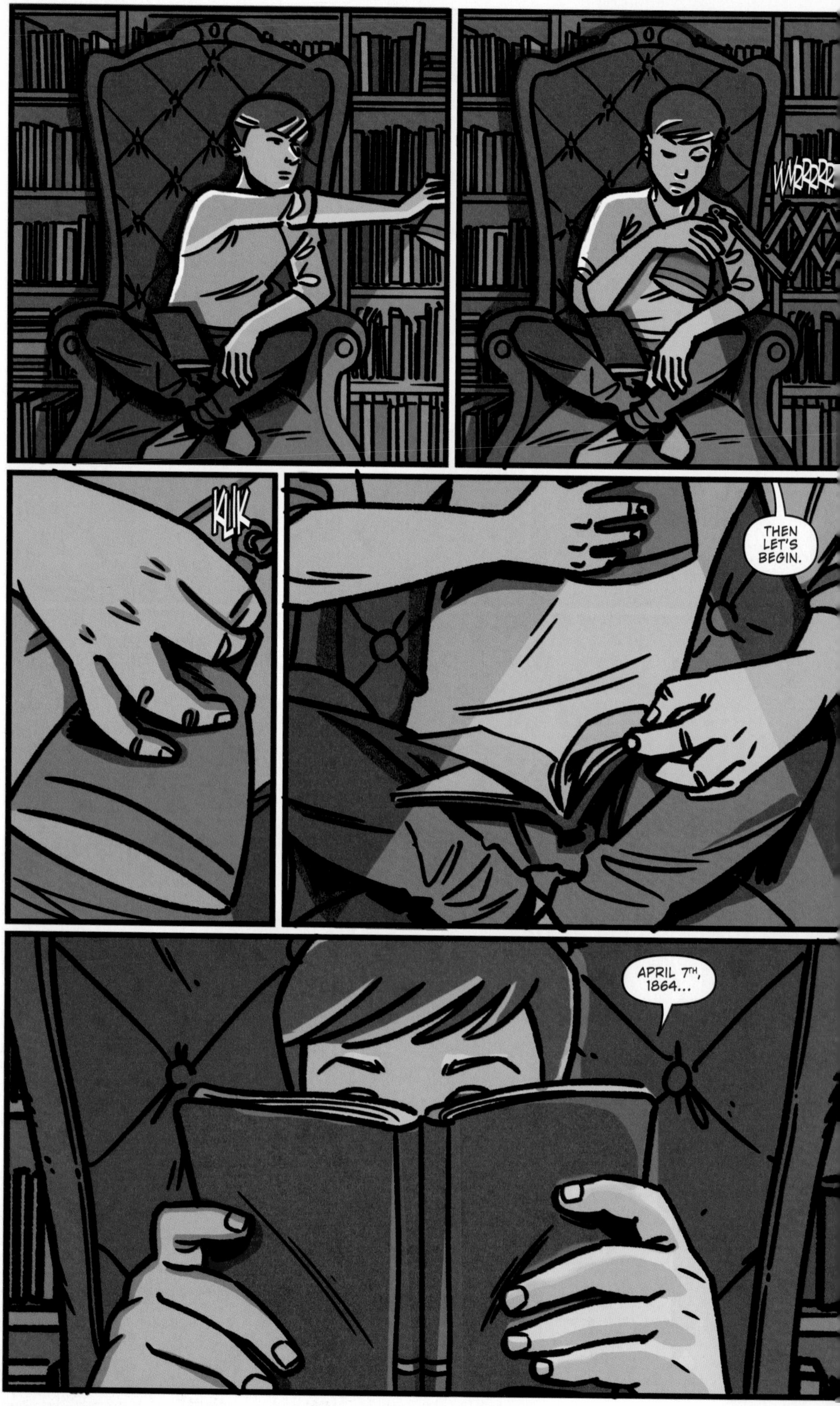
WWRRRR
KLIK
THEN LET'S BEGIN.
APRIL 7TH, 1864...

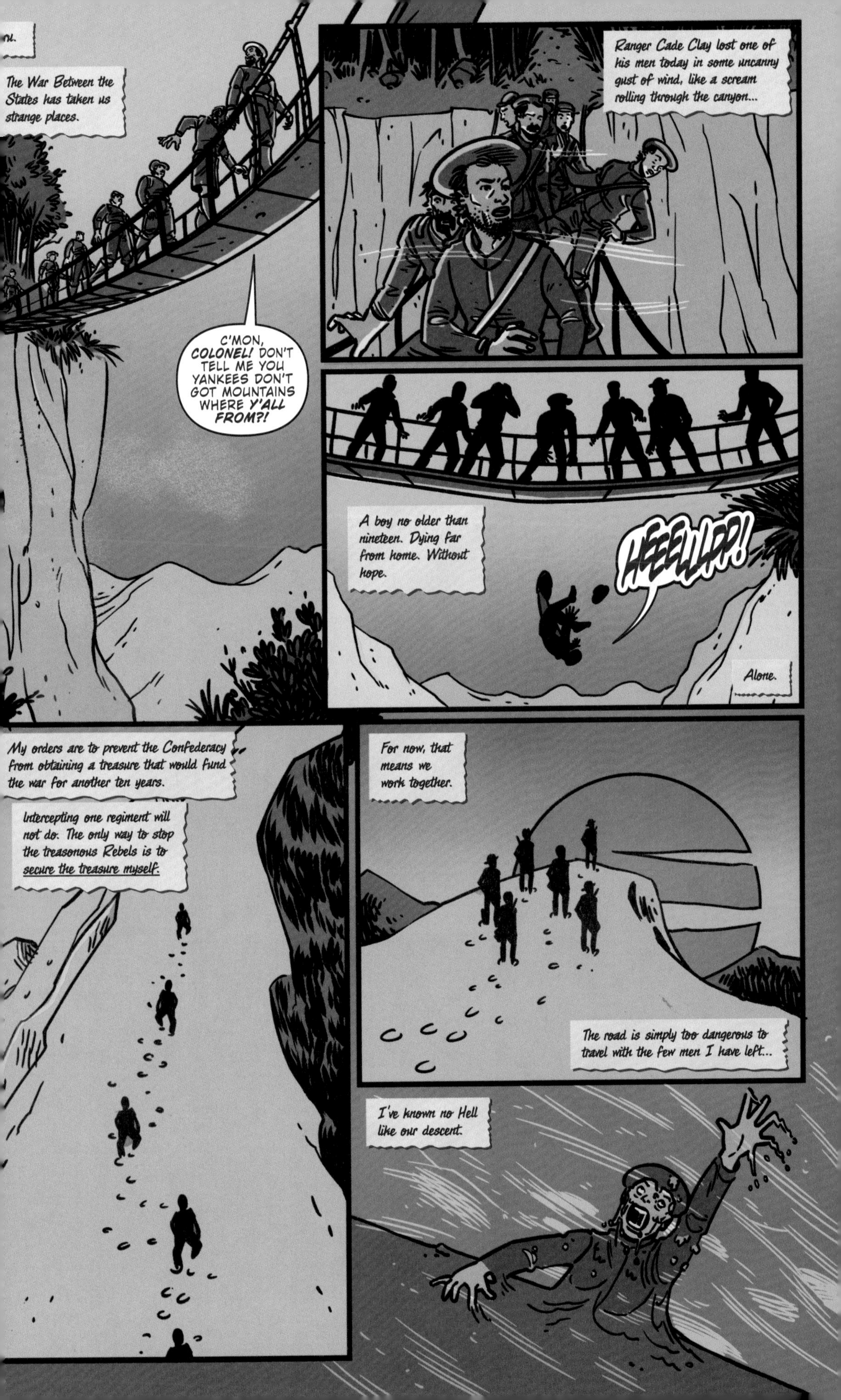

...n.
The War Between the States has taken us strange places.
Ranger Cade Clay lost one of his men today in some uncanny gust of wind, like a scream rolling through the canyon...
C'MON, COLONEL! DON'T TELL ME YOU YANKEES DON'T GOT MOUNTAINS WHERE Y'ALL FROM?!
A boy no older than nineteen. Dying far from home. Without hope.
HEEELLLP!
Alone.
My orders are to prevent the Confederacy from obtaining a treasure that would fund the war for another ten years.
Intercepting one regiment will not do. The only way to stop the treasonous Rebels is to secure the treasure myself.
For now, that means we work together.
The road is simply too dangerous to travel with the few men I have left...
I've known no Hell like our descent.

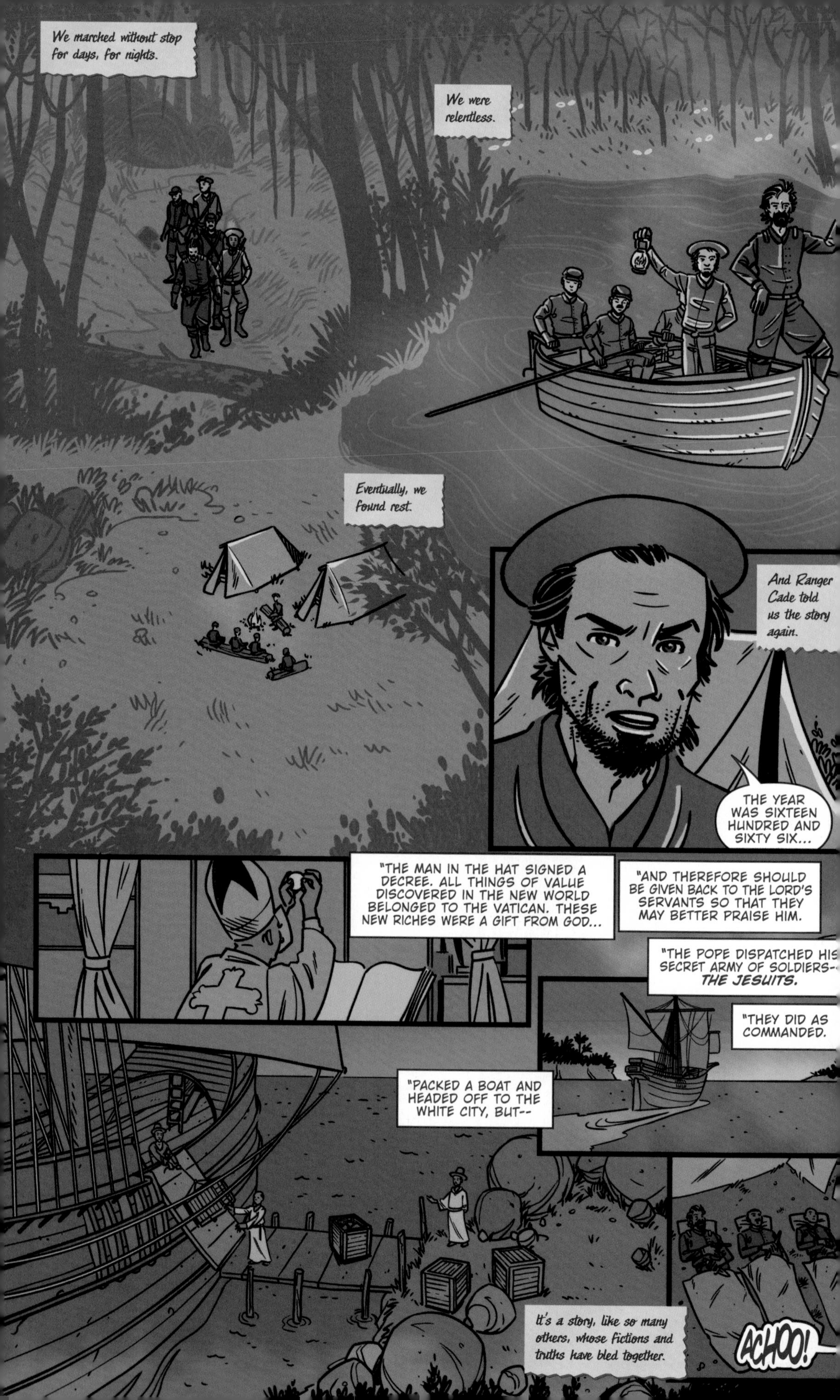

We marched without stop for days, for nights.
We were relentless.
Eventually, we found rest.
And Ranger Cade told us the story again.
THE YEAR WAS SIXTEEN HUNDRED AND SIXTY SIX...
"THE MAN IN THE HAT SIGNED A DECREE. ALL THINGS OF VALUE DISCOVERED IN THE NEW WORLD BELONGED TO THE VATICAN. THESE NEW RICHES WERE A GIFT FROM GOD...
"AND THEREFORE SHOULD BE GIVEN BACK TO THE LORD'S SERVANTS SO THAT THEY MAY BETTER PRAISE HIM.
"THE POPE DISPATCHED HIS SECRET ARMY OF SOLDIERS--*THE JESUITS.*
"THEY DID AS COMMANDED.
"PACKED A BOAT AND HEADED OFF TO THE WHITE CITY, BUT--
It's a story, like so many others, whose fictions and truths have bled together.
ACHOO!

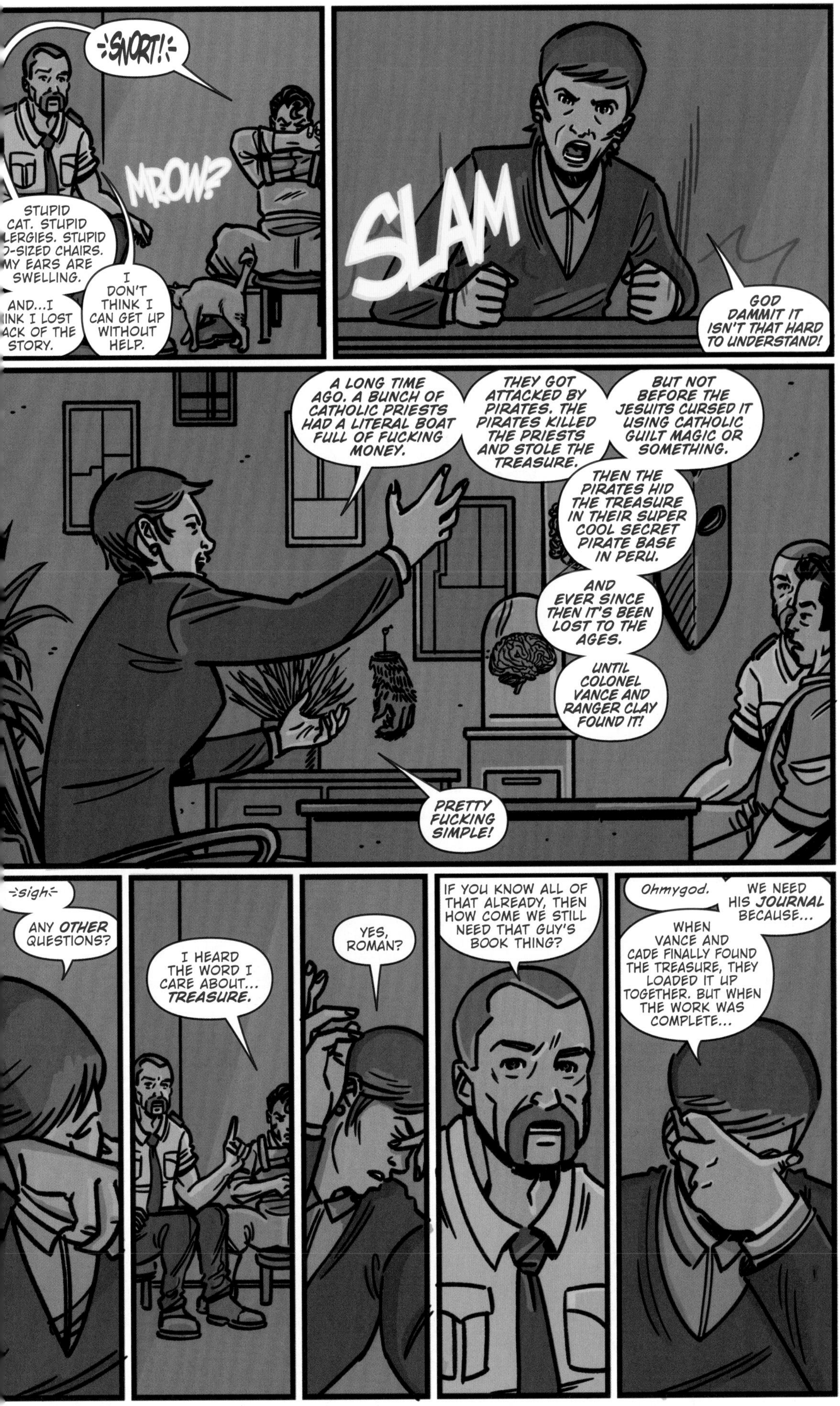

SNORT!
MROW?
STUPID CAT. STUPID LERGIES. STUPID -SIZED CHAIRS. MY EARS ARE SWELLING.
AND...I INK I LOST ACK OF THE STORY.
I DON'T THINK I CAN GET UP WITHOUT HELP.
SLAM
GOD DAMMIT IT ISN'T THAT HARD TO UNDERSTAND!
A LONG TIME AGO. A BUNCH OF CATHOLIC PRIESTS HAD A LITERAL BOAT FULL OF FUCKING MONEY.
THEY GOT ATTACKED BY PIRATES. THE PIRATES KILLED THE PRIESTS AND STOLE THE TREASURE.
BUT NOT BEFORE THE JESUITS CURSED IT USING CATHOLIC GUILT MAGIC OR SOMETHING.
THEN THE PIRATES HID THE TREASURE IN THEIR SUPER COOL SECRET PIRATE BASE IN PERU.
AND EVER SINCE THEN IT'S BEEN LOST TO THE AGES.
UNTIL COLONEL VANCE AND RANGER CLAY FOUND IT!
PRETTY FUCKING SIMPLE!
sigh
ANY OTHER QUESTIONS?
I HEARD THE WORD I CARE ABOUT... TREASURE.
YES, ROMAN?
IF YOU KNOW ALL OF THAT ALREADY, THEN HOW COME WE STILL NEED THAT GUY'S BOOK THING?
Ohmygod.
WE NEED HIS JOURNAL BECAUSE...
WHEN VANCE AND CADE FINALLY FOUND THE TREASURE, THEY LOADED IT UP TOGETHER. BUT WHEN THE WORK WAS COMPLETE...

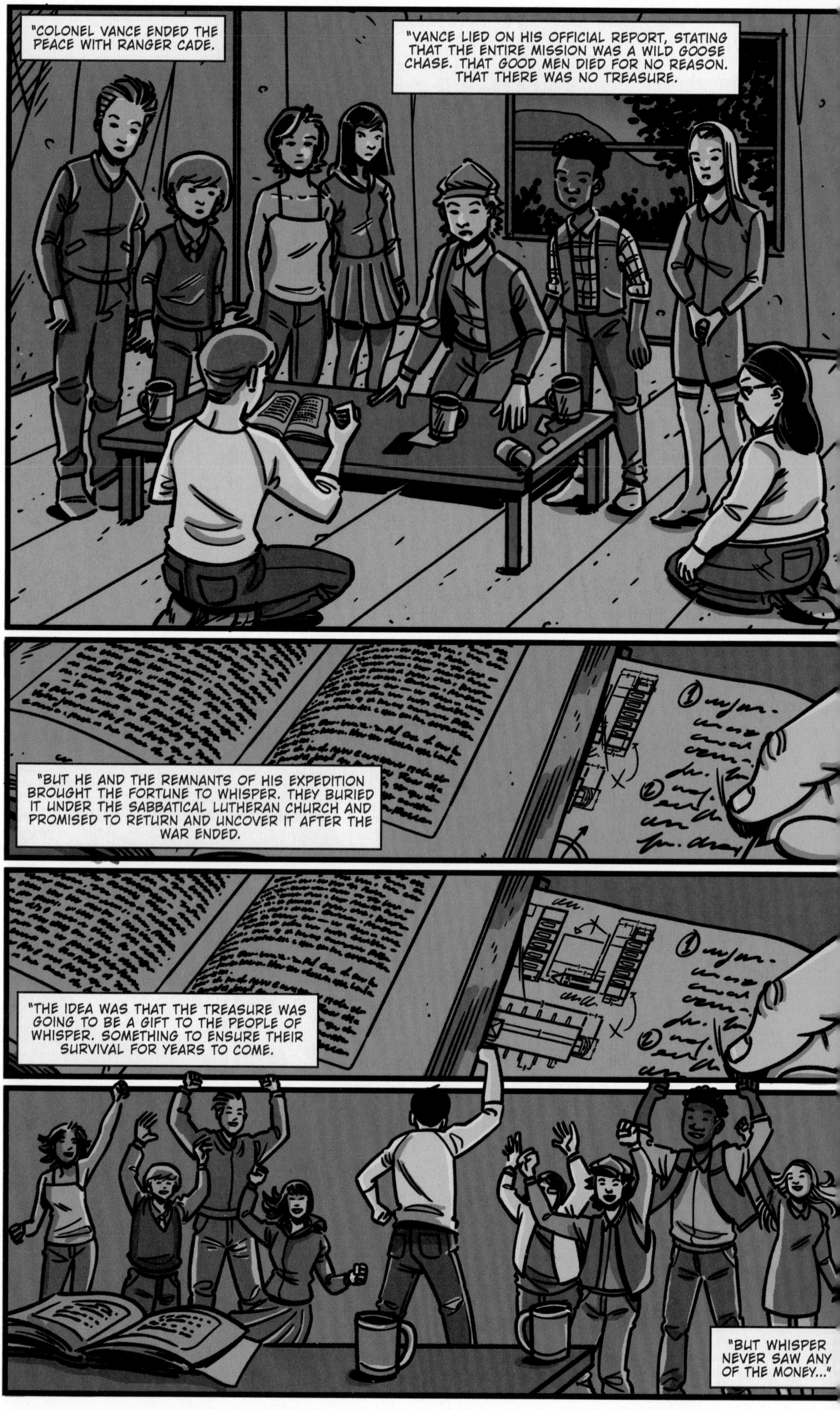
"COLONEL VANCE ENDED THE PEACE WITH RANGER CADE.
"VANCE LIED ON HIS OFFICIAL REPORT, STATING THAT THE ENTIRE MISSION WAS A WILD GOOSE CHASE. THAT GOOD MEN DIED FOR NO REASON. THAT THERE WAS NO TREASURE.
"BUT HE AND THE REMNANTS OF HIS EXPEDITION BROUGHT THE FORTUNE TO WHISPER. THEY BURIED IT UNDER THE SABBATICAL LUTHERAN CHURCH AND PROMISED TO RETURN AND UNCOVER IT AFTER THE WAR ENDED.
"THE IDEA WAS THAT THE TREASURE WAS GOING TO BE A GIFT TO THE PEOPLE OF WHISPER. SOMETHING TO ENSURE THEIR SURVIVAL FOR YEARS TO COME.
"BUT WHISPER NEVER SAW ANY OF THE MONEY..."

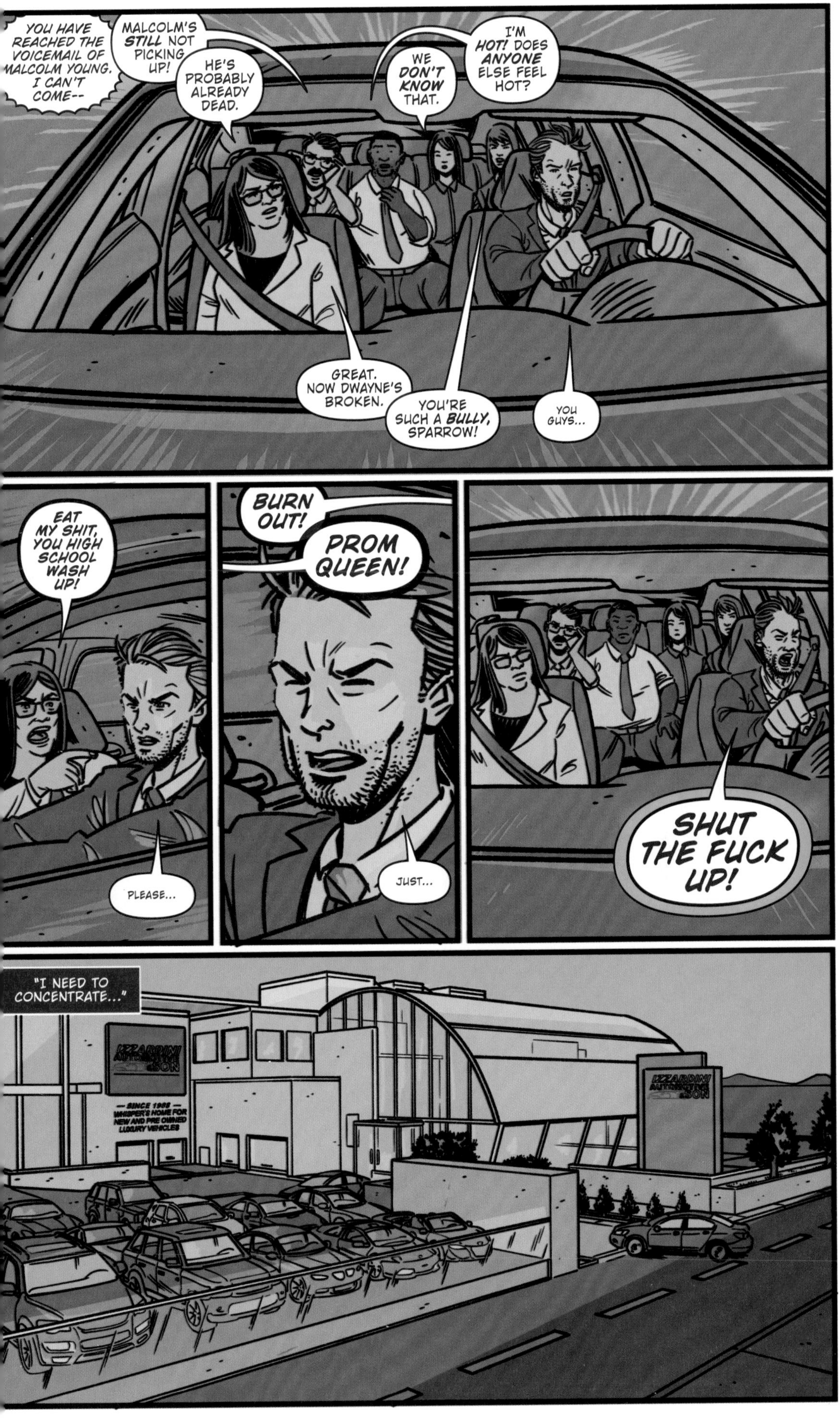
YOU HAVE REACHED THE VOICEMAIL OF MALCOLM YOUNG. I CAN'T COME--
MALCOLM'S STILL NOT PICKING UP!
HE'S PROBABLY ALREADY DEAD.
WE DON'T KNOW THAT.
I'M HOT! DOES ANYONE ELSE FEEL HOT?
GREAT. NOW DWAYNE'S BROKEN.
YOU'RE SUCH A BULLY, SPARROW!
YOU GUYS...
EAT MY SHIT, YOU HIGH SCHOOL WASH UP!
PLEASE...
BURN OUT!
PROM QUEEN!
JUST...
SHUT THE FUCK UP!
"I NEED TO CONCENTRATE..."
WHISPER'S HOME FOR NEW AND PRE OWNED LUXURY VEHICLES

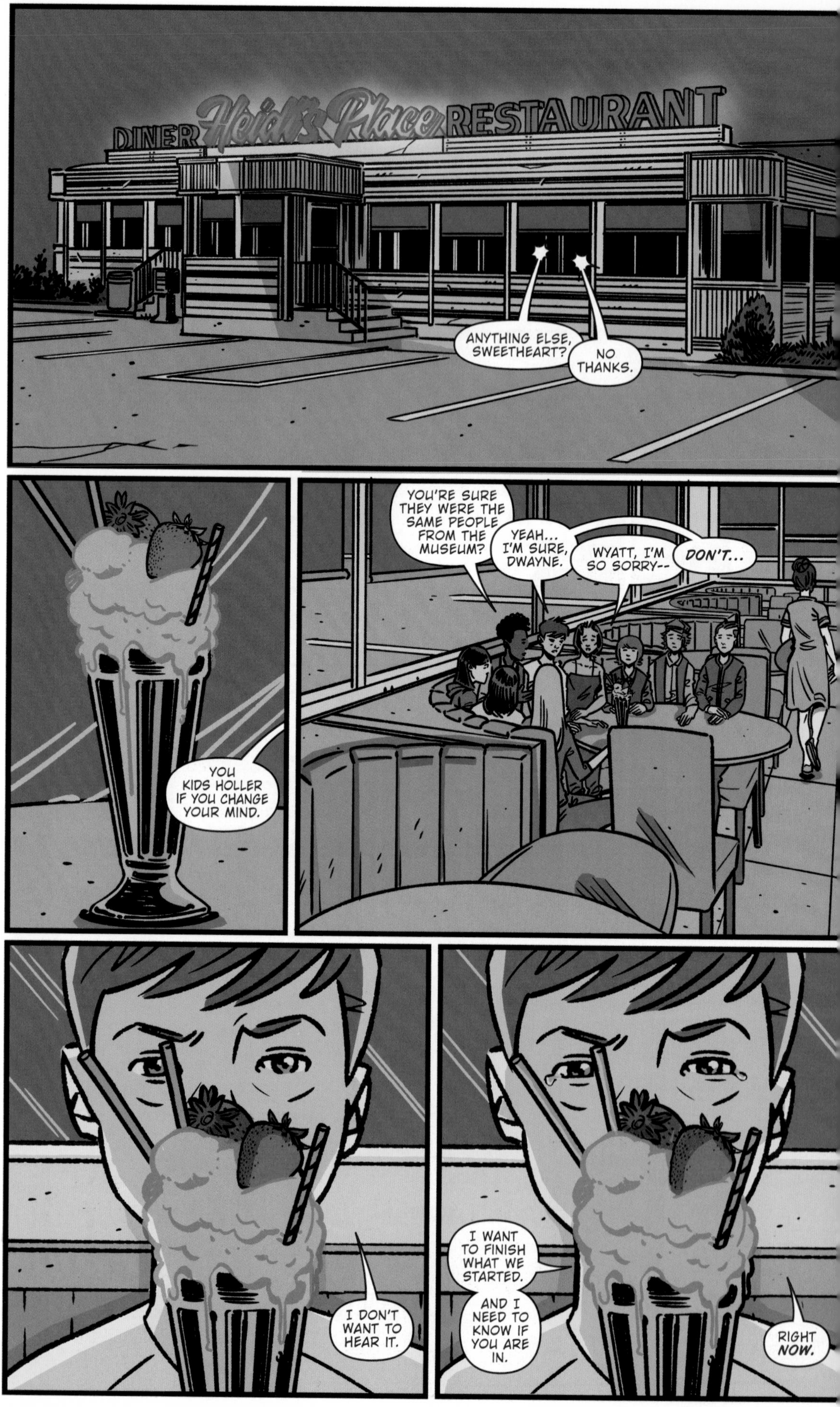
DINER Heidi's Place RESTAURANT
ANYTHING ELSE, SWEETHEART?
NO THANKS.
YOU KIDS HOLLER IF YOU CHANGE YOUR MIND.
YOU'RE SURE THEY WERE THE SAME PEOPLE FROM THE MUSEUM?
YEAH... I'M SURE, DWAYNE.
WYATT, I'M SO SORRY--
DON'T...
I DON'T WANT TO HEAR IT.
I WANT TO FINISH WHAT WE STARTED.
AND I NEED TO KNOW IF YOU ARE IN.
RIGHT NOW.

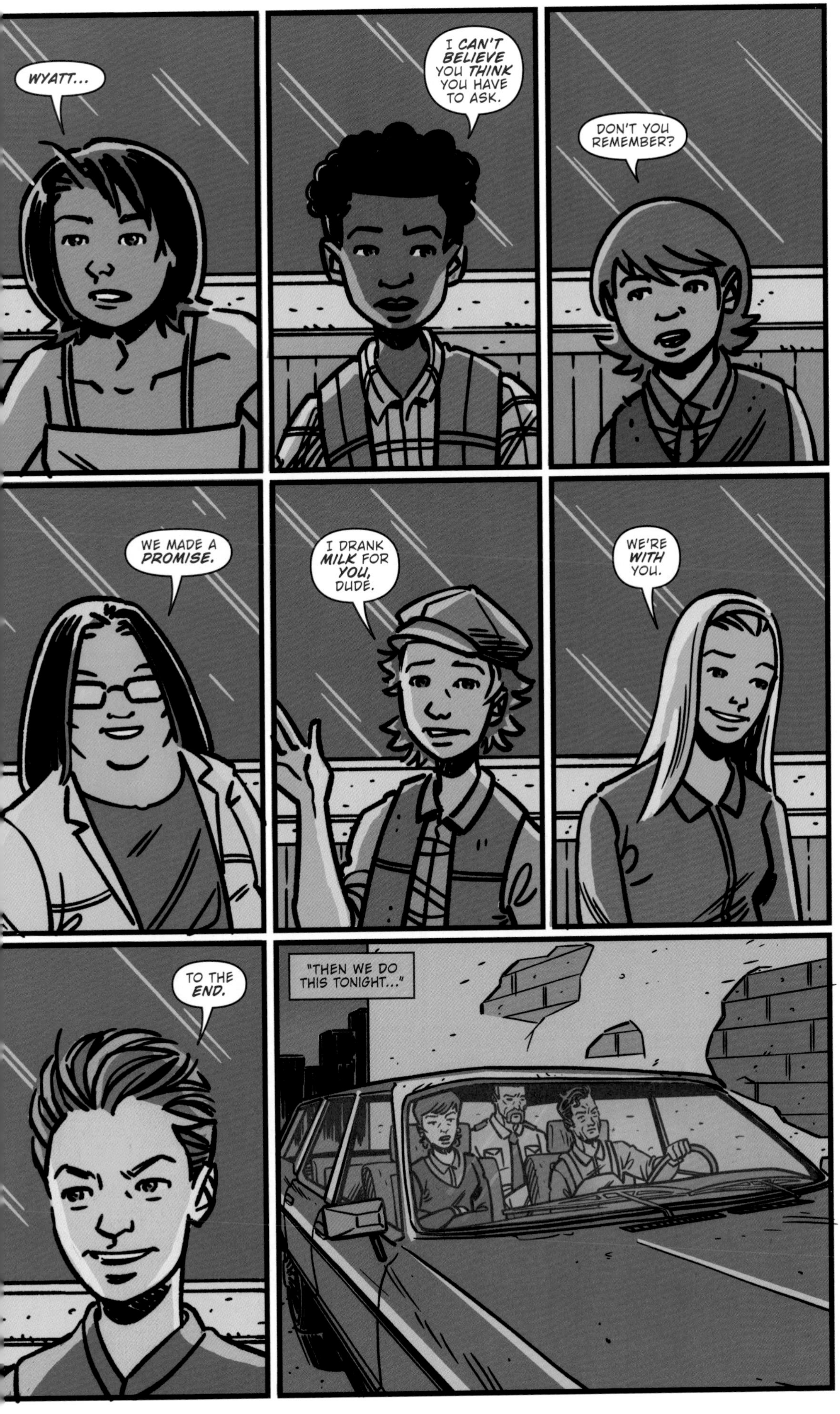
WYATT...
I CAN'T BELIEVE YOU THINK YOU HAVE TO ASK.
DON'T YOU REMEMBER?
WE MADE A PROMISE.
I DRANK MILK FOR YOU, DUDE.
WE'RE WITH YOU.
TO THE END.
"THEN WE DO THIS TONIGHT..."

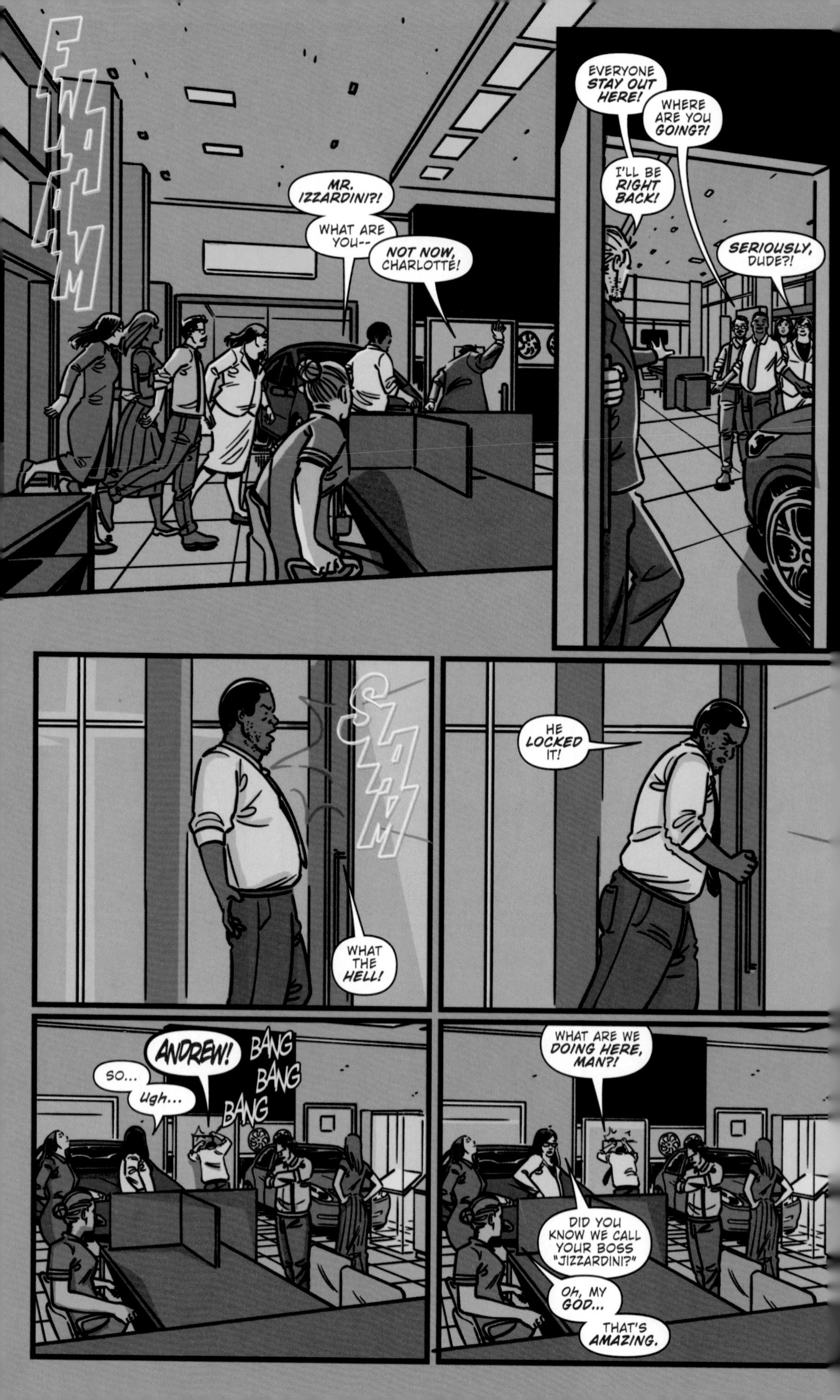

FWAM
MR. IZZARDINI?!
WHAT ARE YOU--
NOT NOW, CHARLOTTE!
EVERYONE STAY OUT HERE!
WHERE ARE YOU GOING?!
I'LL BE RIGHT BACK!
SERIOUSLY, DUDE?!
SLAM
WHAT THE HELL!
HE LOCKED IT!
SO...
Ugh...
ANDREW!
BANG
BANG
BANG
WHAT ARE WE DOING HERE, MAN?!
DID YOU KNOW WE CALL YOUR BOSS "JIZZARDINI?"
Oh, MY GOD...
THAT'S AMAZING.

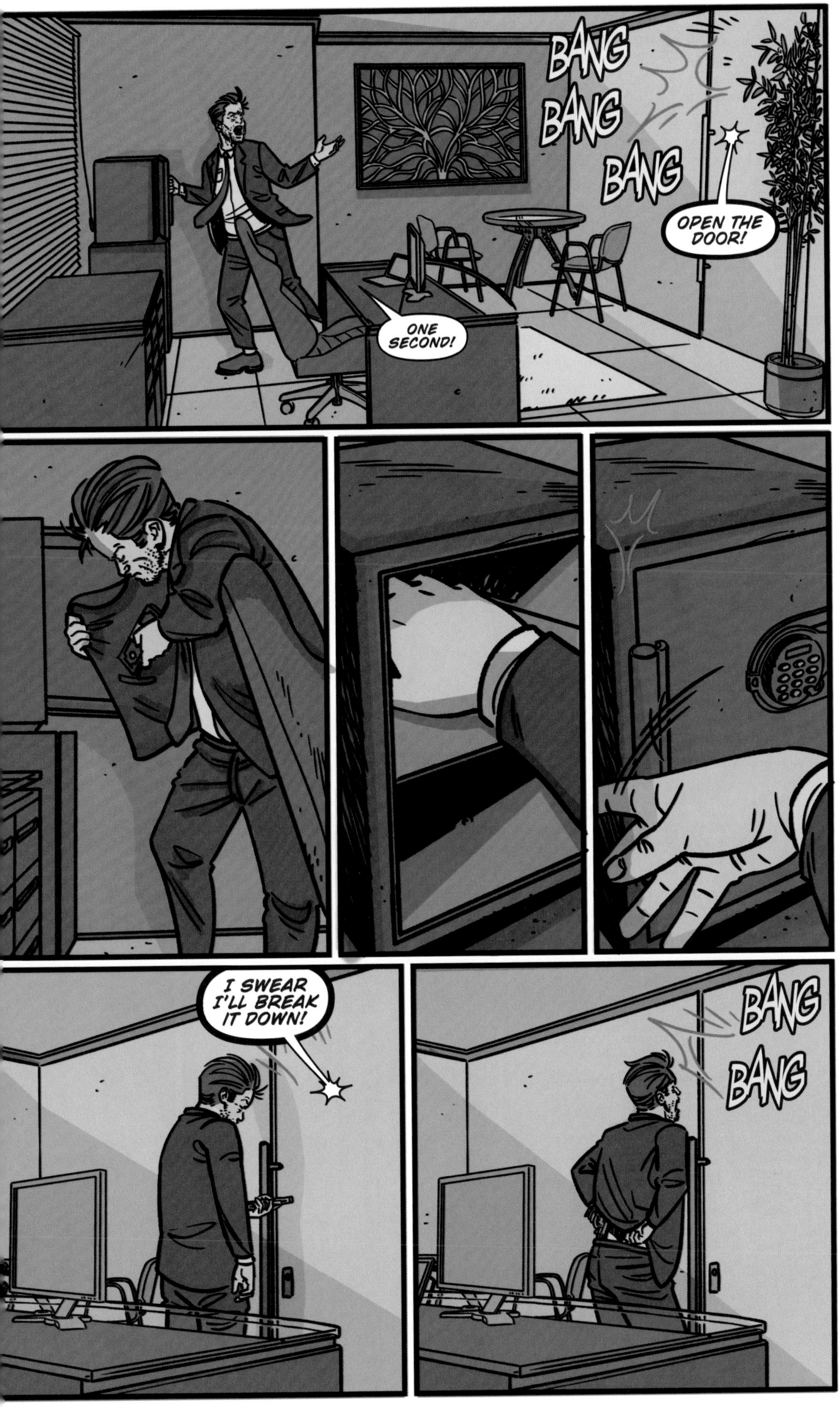
BANG
BANG
BANG
OPEN THE DOOR!
ONE SECOND!
I SWEAR I'LL BREAK IT DOWN!
BANG
BANG

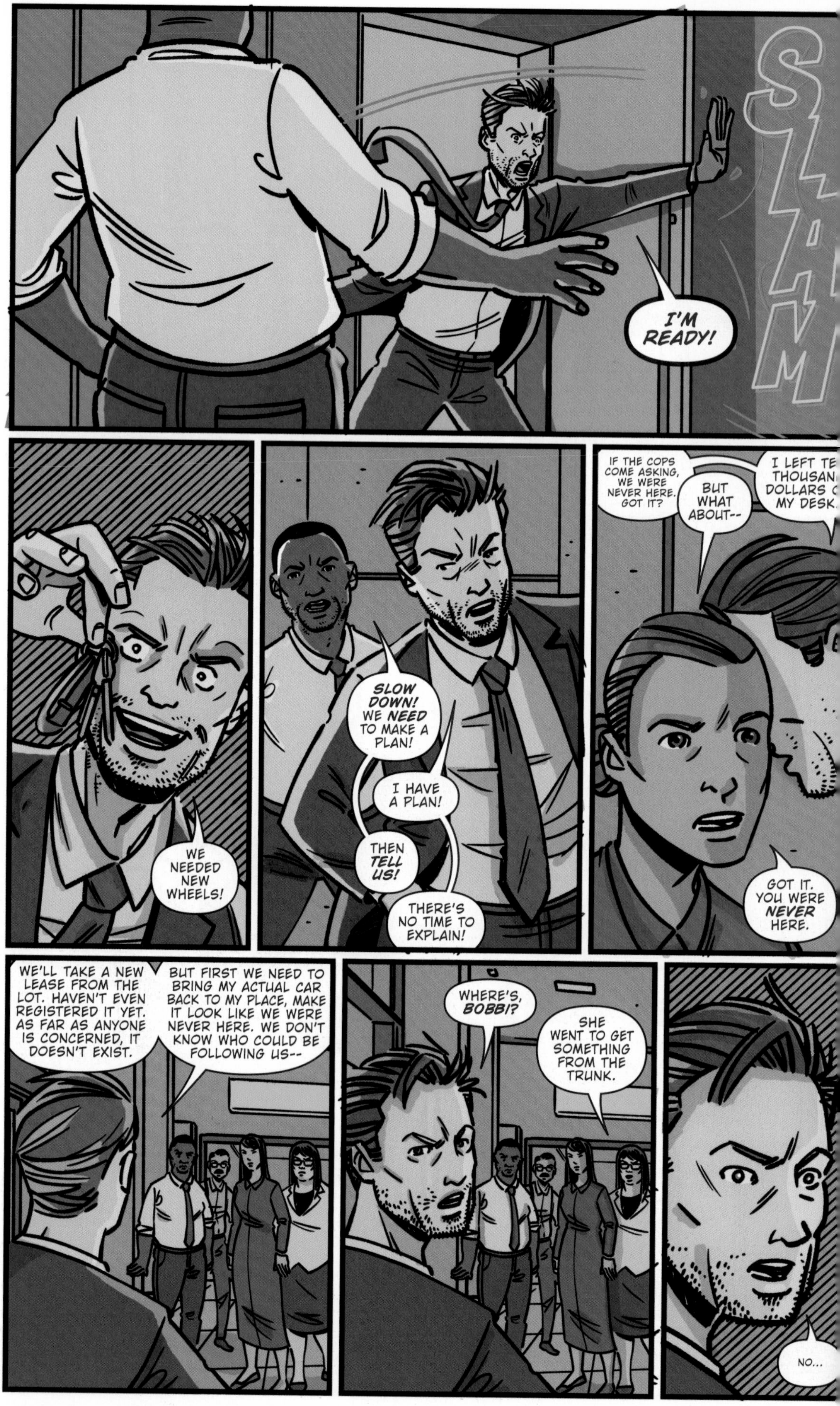
SLAM
I'M READY!
WE NEEDED NEW WHEELS!
SLOW DOWN! WE NEED TO MAKE A PLAN!
I HAVE A PLAN!
THEN TELL US!
THERE'S NO TIME TO EXPLAIN!
IF THE COPS COME ASKING, WE WERE NEVER HERE. GOT IT?
BUT WHAT ABOUT--
I LEFT TE THOUSAN DOLLARS O MY DESK.
GOT IT. YOU WERE NEVER HERE.
WE'LL TAKE A NEW LEASE FROM THE LOT. HAVEN'T EVEN REGISTERED IT YET. AS FAR AS ANYONE IS CONCERNED, IT DOESN'T EXIST.
BUT FIRST WE NEED TO BRING MY ACTUAL CAR BACK TO MY PLACE, MAKE IT LOOK LIKE WE WERE NEVER HERE. WE DON'T KNOW WHO COULD BE FOLLOWING US--
WHERE'S, BOBBI?
SHE WENT TO GET SOMETHING FROM THE TRUNK.
NO...

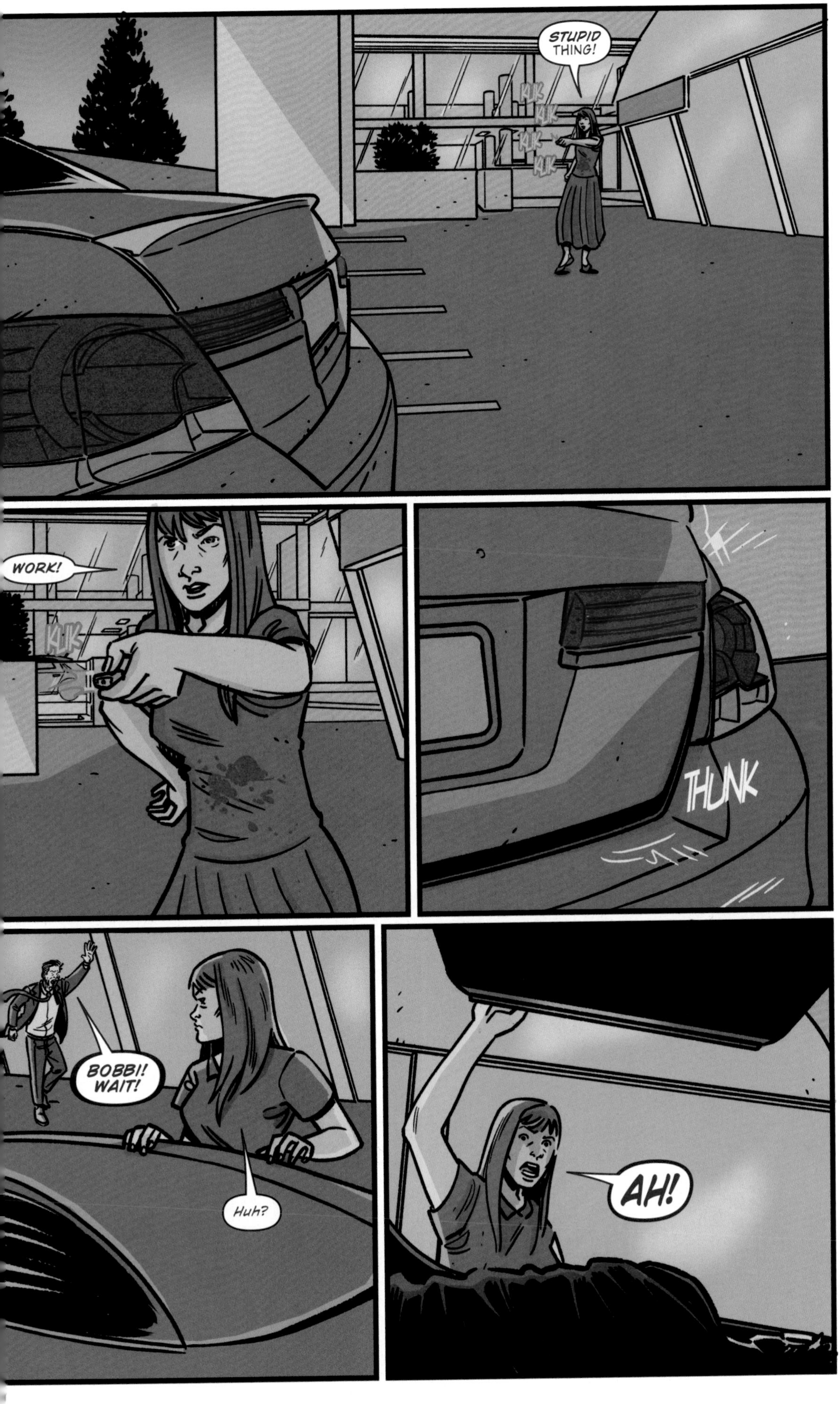
STUPID THING!
KLIK
KLIK
KLIK
KLIK
WORK!
KLIK
THUNK
BOBBI! WAIT!
Huh?
AH!

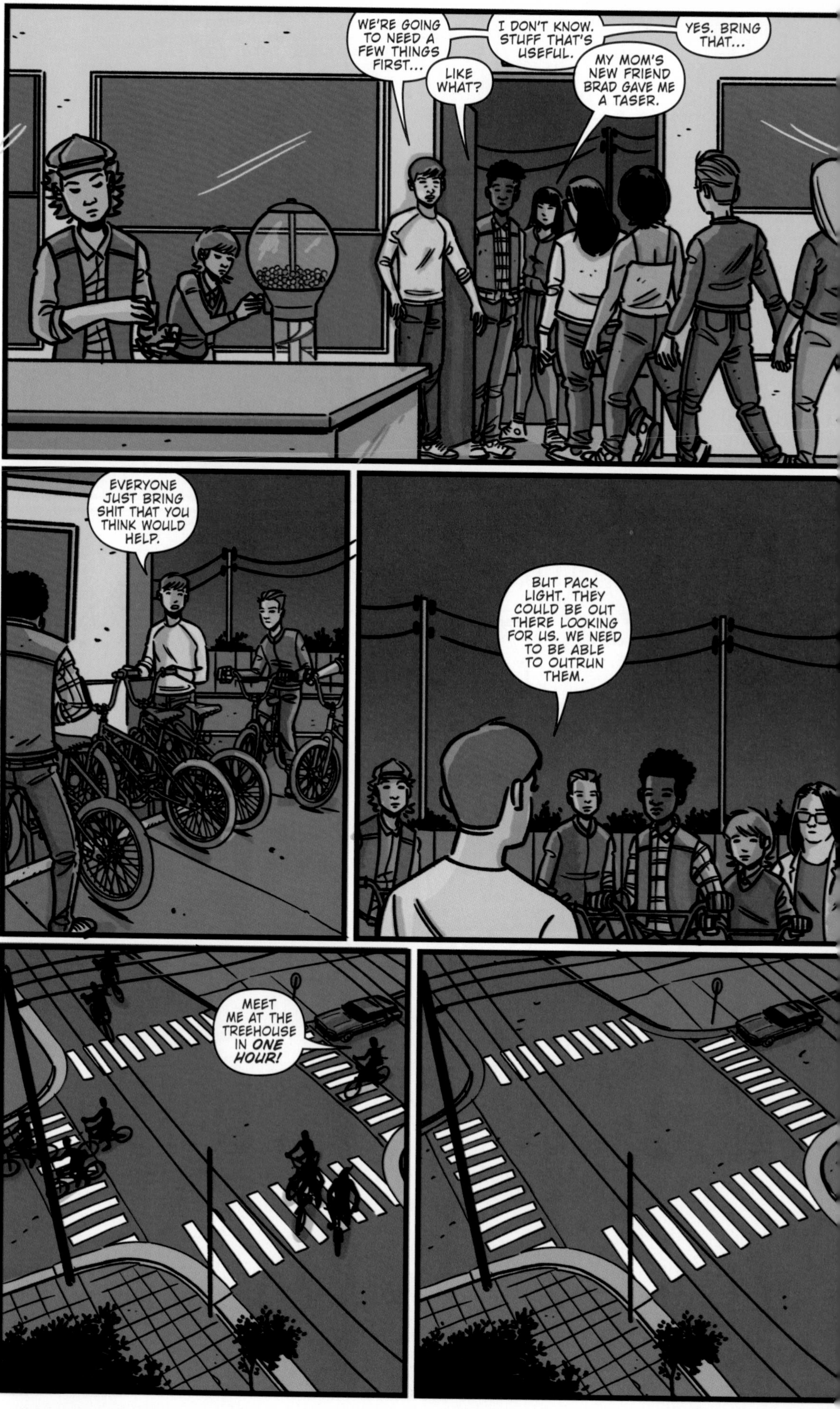

WE'RE GOING TO NEED A FEW THINGS FIRST...
LIKE WHAT?
I DON'T KNOW. STUFF THAT'S USEFUL.
MY MOM'S NEW FRIEND BRAD GAVE ME A TASER.
YES. BRING THAT...
EVERYONE JUST BRING SHIT THAT YOU THINK WOULD HELP.
BUT PACK LIGHT. THEY COULD BE OUT THERE LOOKING FOR US. WE NEED TO BE ABLE TO OUTRUN THEM.
MEET ME AT THE TREEHOUSE IN ONE HOUR!

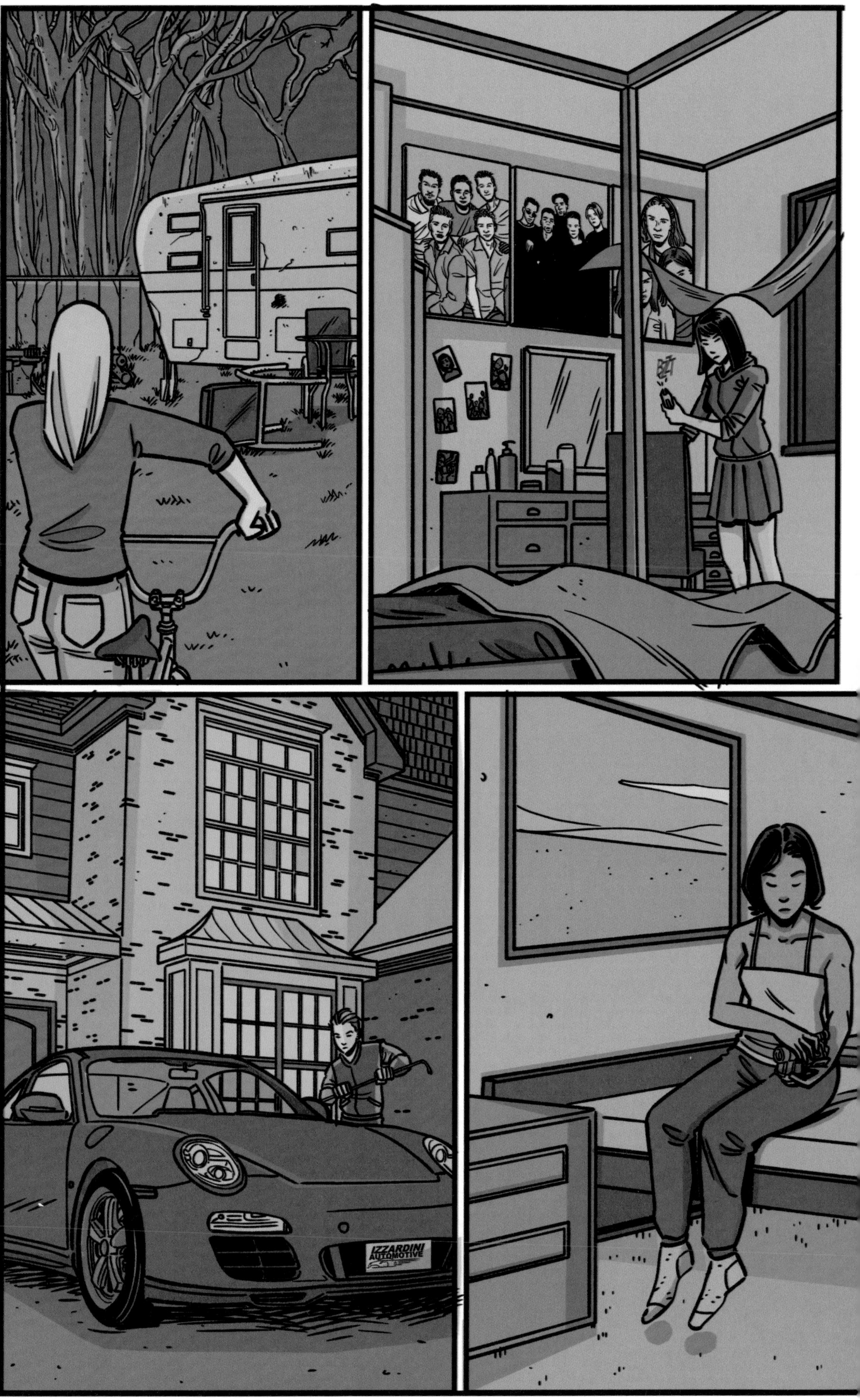

BZZT
IZZARDINI AUTOMOTIVE

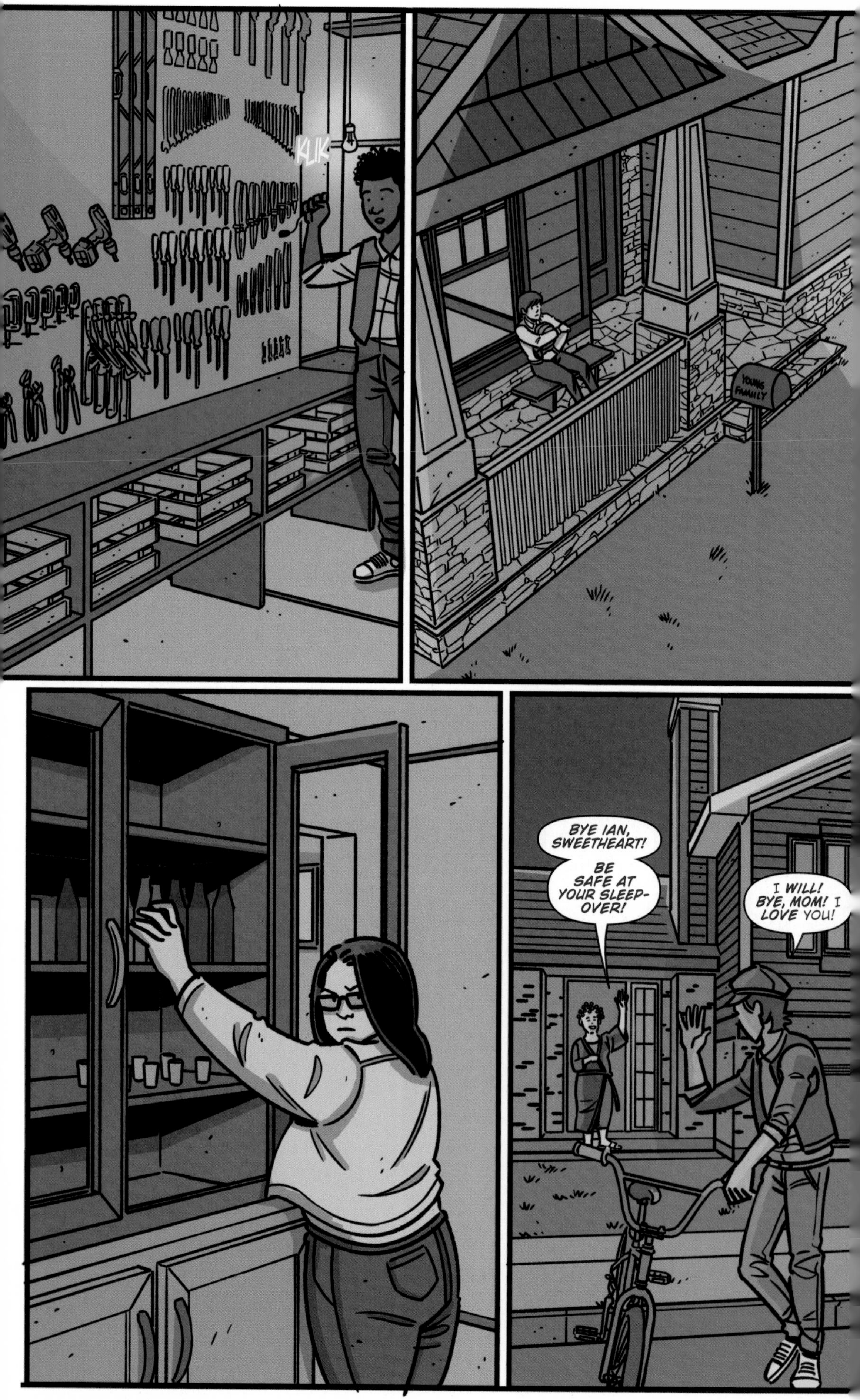
KLIK
YOUNG FAMILY
BYE IAN, SWEETHEART!
BE SAFE AT YOUR SLEEP-OVER!
I WILL! BYE, MOM! I LOVE YOU!

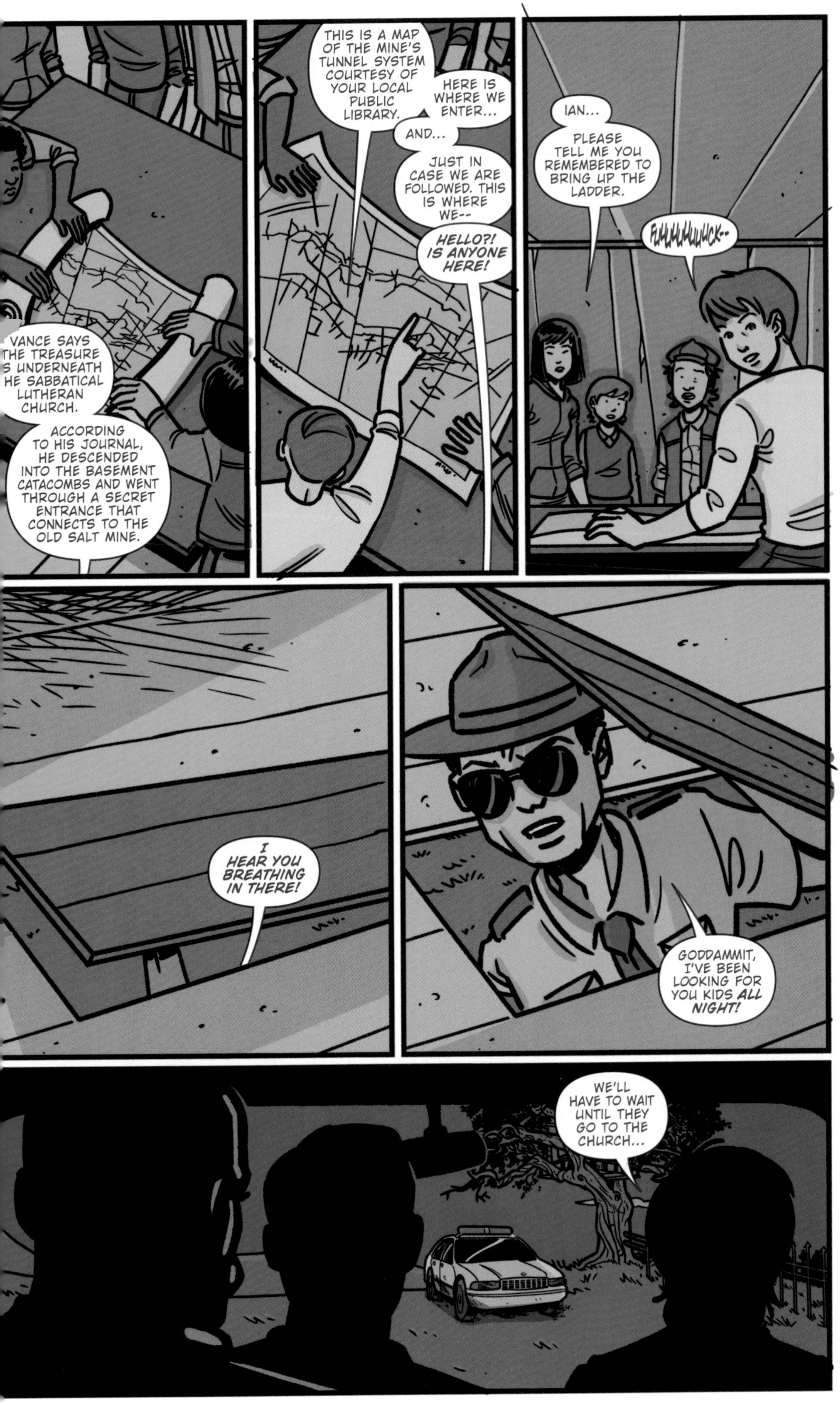

VANCE SAYS THE TREASURE S UNDERNEATH HE SABBATICAL LUTHERAN CHURCH.
ACCORDING TO HIS JOURNAL, HE DESCENDED INTO THE BASEMENT CATACOMBS AND WENT THROUGH A SECRET ENTRANCE THAT CONNECTS TO THE OLD SALT MINE.
THIS IS A MAP OF THE MINE'S TUNNEL SYSTEM COURTESY OF YOUR LOCAL PUBLIC LIBRARY.
HERE IS WHERE WE ENTER...
AND...
JUST IN CASE WE ARE FOLLOWED. THIS IS WHERE WE--
HELLO?! IS ANYONE HERE!
IAN...
PLEASE TELL ME YOU REMEMBERED TO BRING UP THE LADDER.
FUUUUUUUUCK--
I HEAR YOU BREATHING IN THERE!
GODDAMMIT, I'VE BEEN LOOKING FOR YOU KIDS ALL NIGHT!
WE'LL HAVE TO WAIT UNTIL THEY GO TO THE CHURCH...

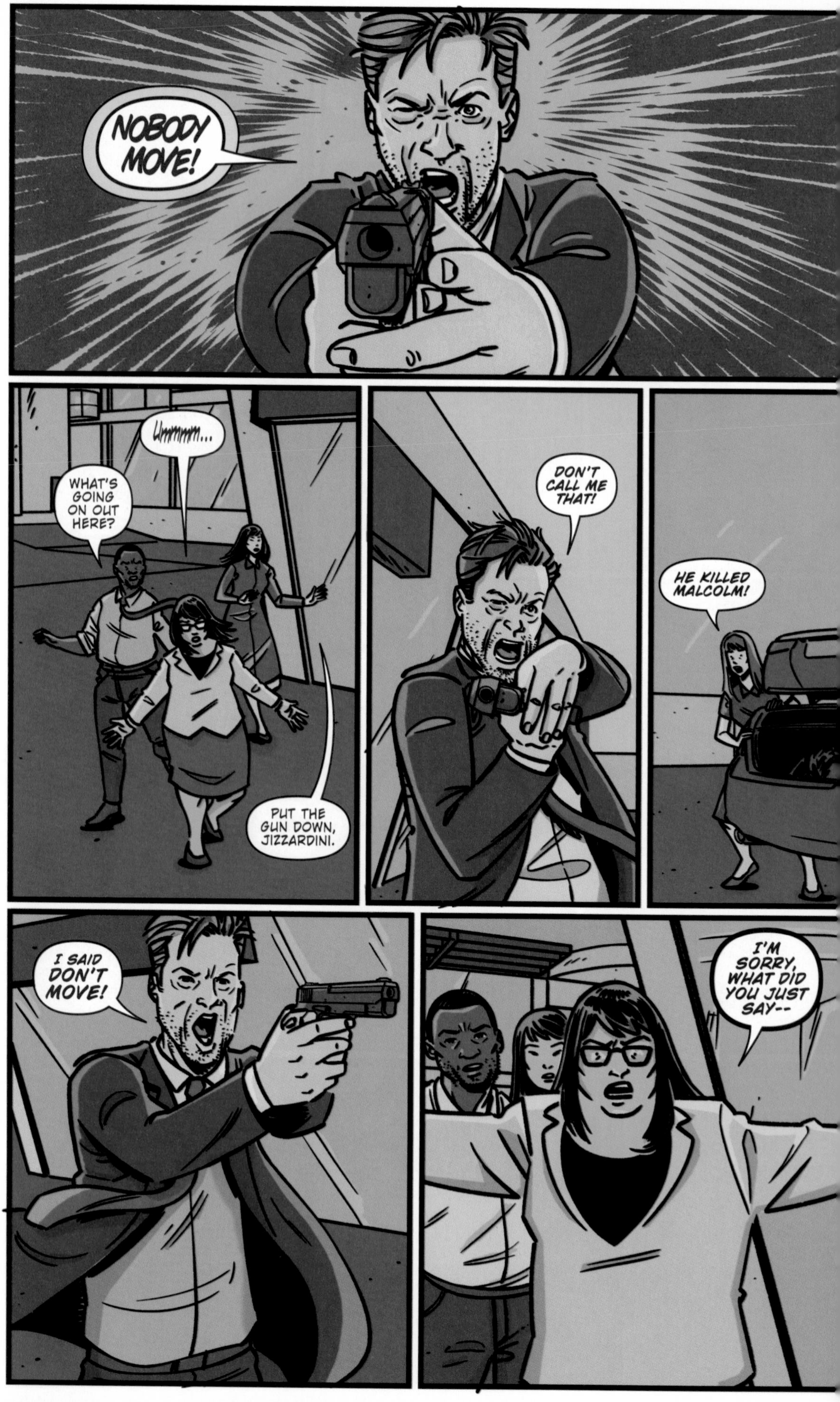

NOBODY MOVE!
WHAT'S GOING ON OUT HERE?
Ummmm...
PUT THE GUN DOWN, JIZZARDINI.
DON'T CALL ME THAT!
HE KILLED MALCOLM!
I SAID DON'T MOVE!
I'M SORRY, WHAT DID YOU JUST SAY--

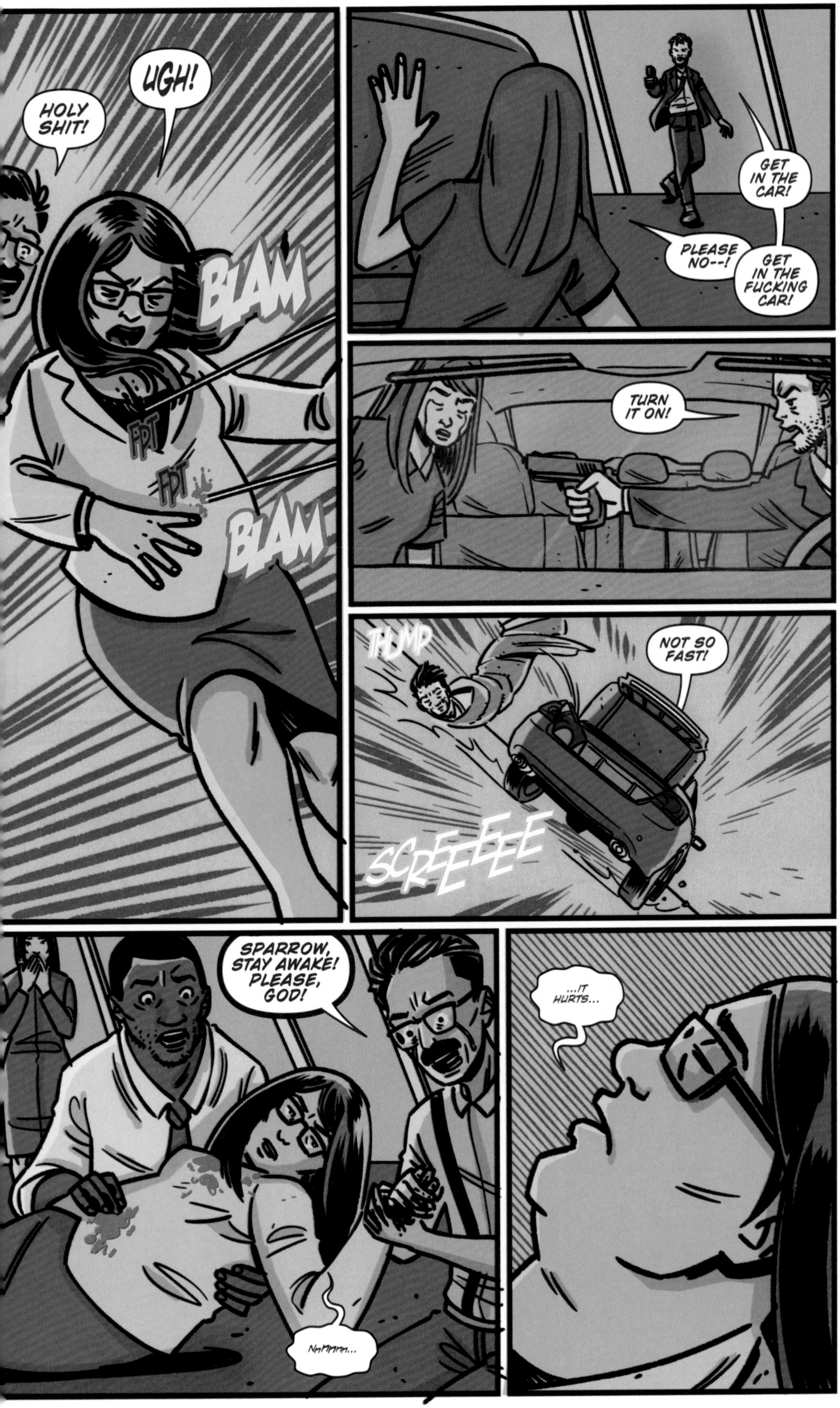
HOLY SHIT!
UGH!
BLAM
FPT
FPT
BLAM
GET IN THE CAR!
PLEASE NO--!
GET IN THE FUCKING CAR!
TURN IT ON!
THUMP
NOT SO FAST!
SCREEEEEE
SPARROW, STAY AWAKE! PLEASE, GOD!
NnMmmm...
...IT HURTS...

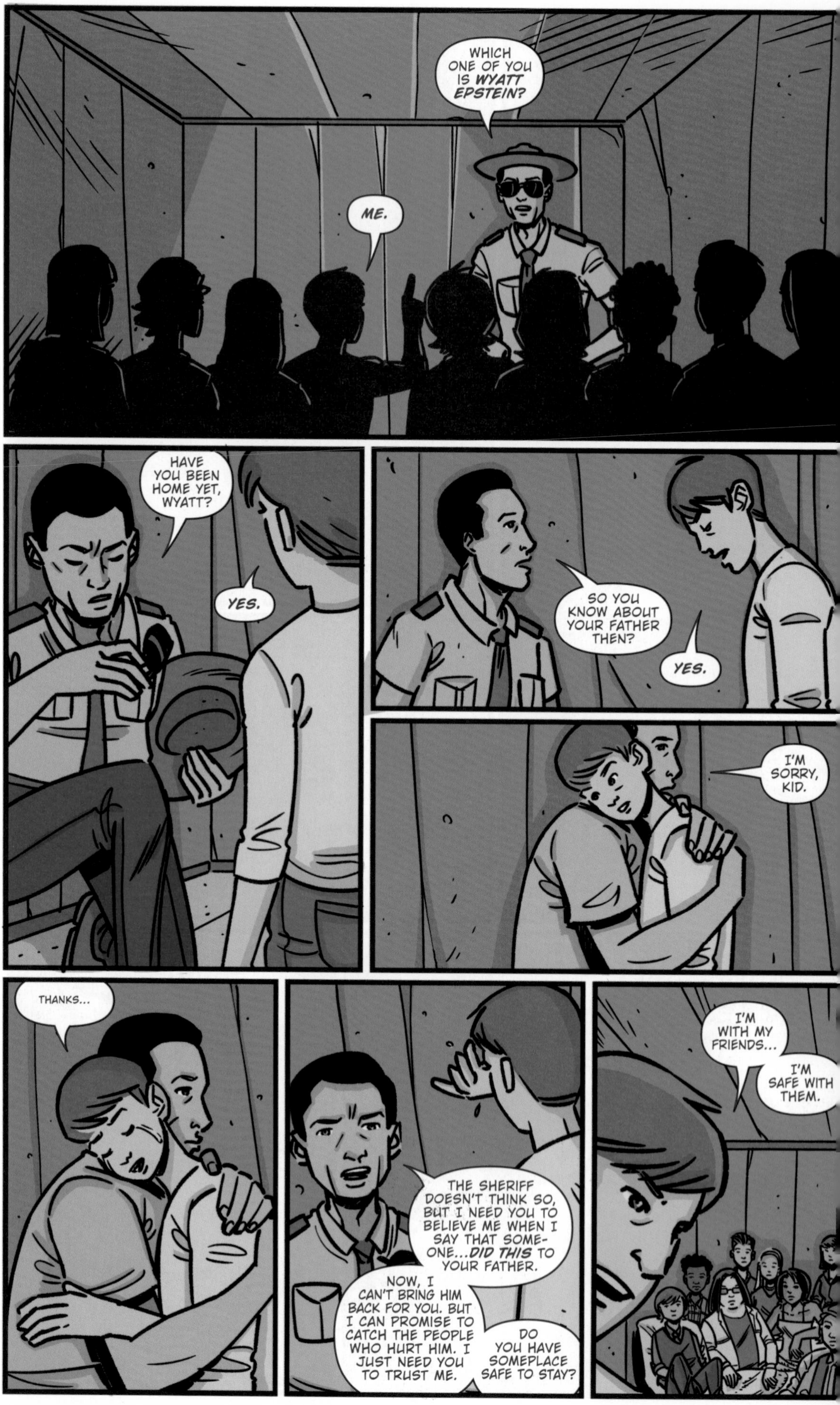
WHICH ONE OF YOU IS WYATT EPSTEIN?
ME.
HAVE YOU BEEN HOME YET, WYATT?
YES.
SO YOU KNOW ABOUT YOUR FATHER THEN?
YES.
I'M SORRY, KID.
THANKS...
THE SHERIFF DOESN'T THINK SO, BUT I NEED YOU TO BELIEVE ME WHEN I SAY THAT SOME-ONE...DID THIS TO YOUR FATHER.
NOW, I CAN'T BRING HIM BACK FOR YOU. BUT I CAN PROMISE TO CATCH THE PEOPLE WHO HURT HIM. I JUST NEED YOU TO TRUST ME.
DO YOU HAVE SOMEPLACE SAFE TO STAY?
I'M WITH MY FRIENDS...
I'M SAFE WITH THEM.

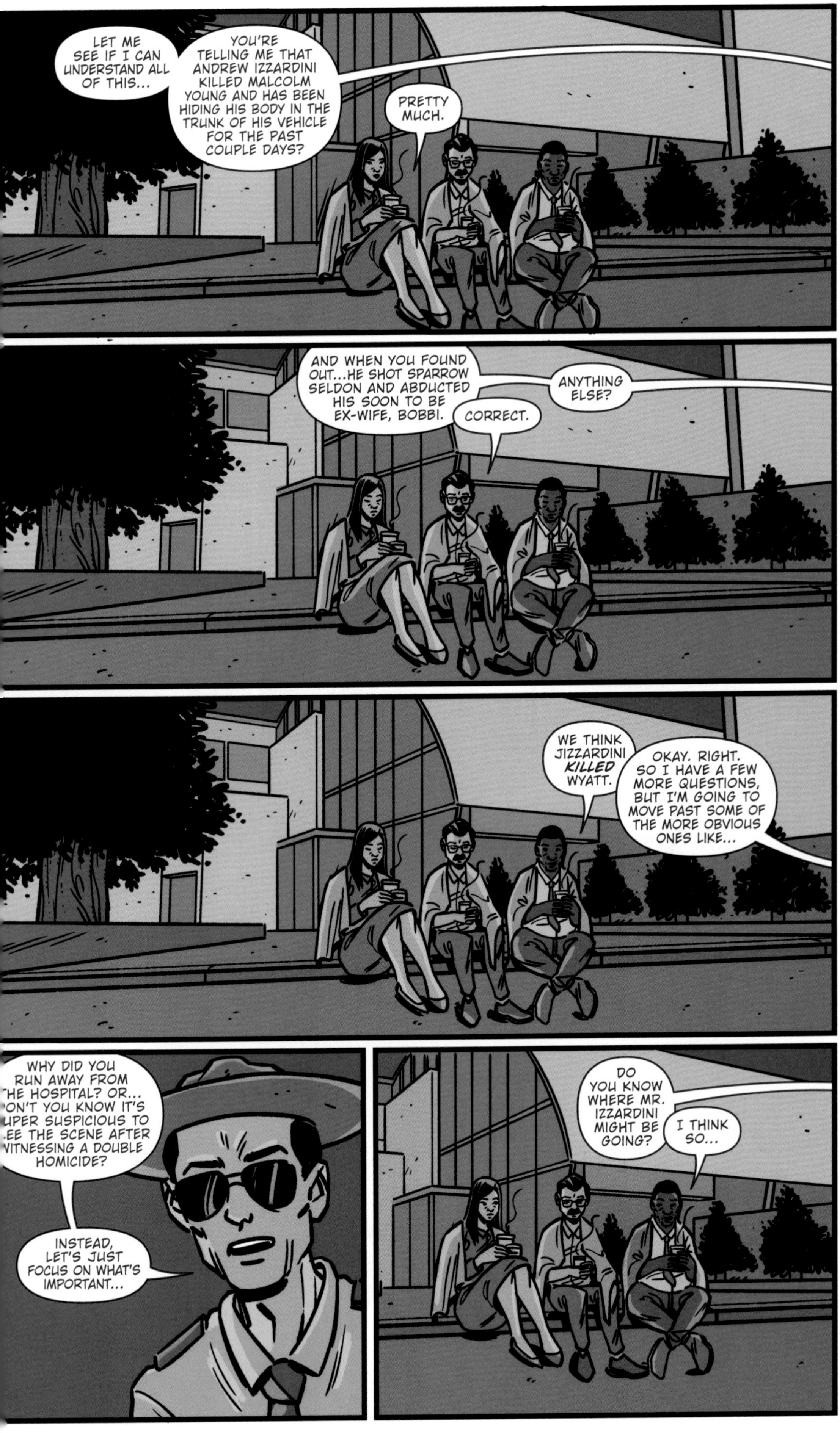

LET ME SEE IF I CAN UNDERSTAND ALL OF THIS...
YOU'RE TELLING ME THAT ANDREW IZZARDINI KILLED MALCOLM YOUNG AND HAS BEEN HIDING HIS BODY IN THE TRUNK OF HIS VEHICLE FOR THE PAST COUPLE DAYS?
PRETTY MUCH.
AND WHEN YOU FOUND OUT...HE SHOT SPARROW SELDON AND ABDUCTED HIS SOON TO BE EX-WIFE, BOBBI.
CORRECT.
ANYTHING ELSE?
WE THINK JIZZARDINI KILLED WYATT.
OKAY. RIGHT. SO I HAVE A FEW MORE QUESTIONS, BUT I'M GOING TO MOVE PAST SOME OF THE MORE OBVIOUS ONES LIKE...
WHY DID YOU RUN AWAY FROM THE HOSPITAL? OR... DON'T YOU KNOW IT'S SUPER SUSPICIOUS TO FLEE THE SCENE AFTER WITNESSING A DOUBLE HOMICIDE?
INSTEAD, LET'S JUST FOCUS ON WHAT'S IMPORTANT...
DO YOU KNOW WHERE MR. IZZARDINI MIGHT BE GOING?
I THINK SO...

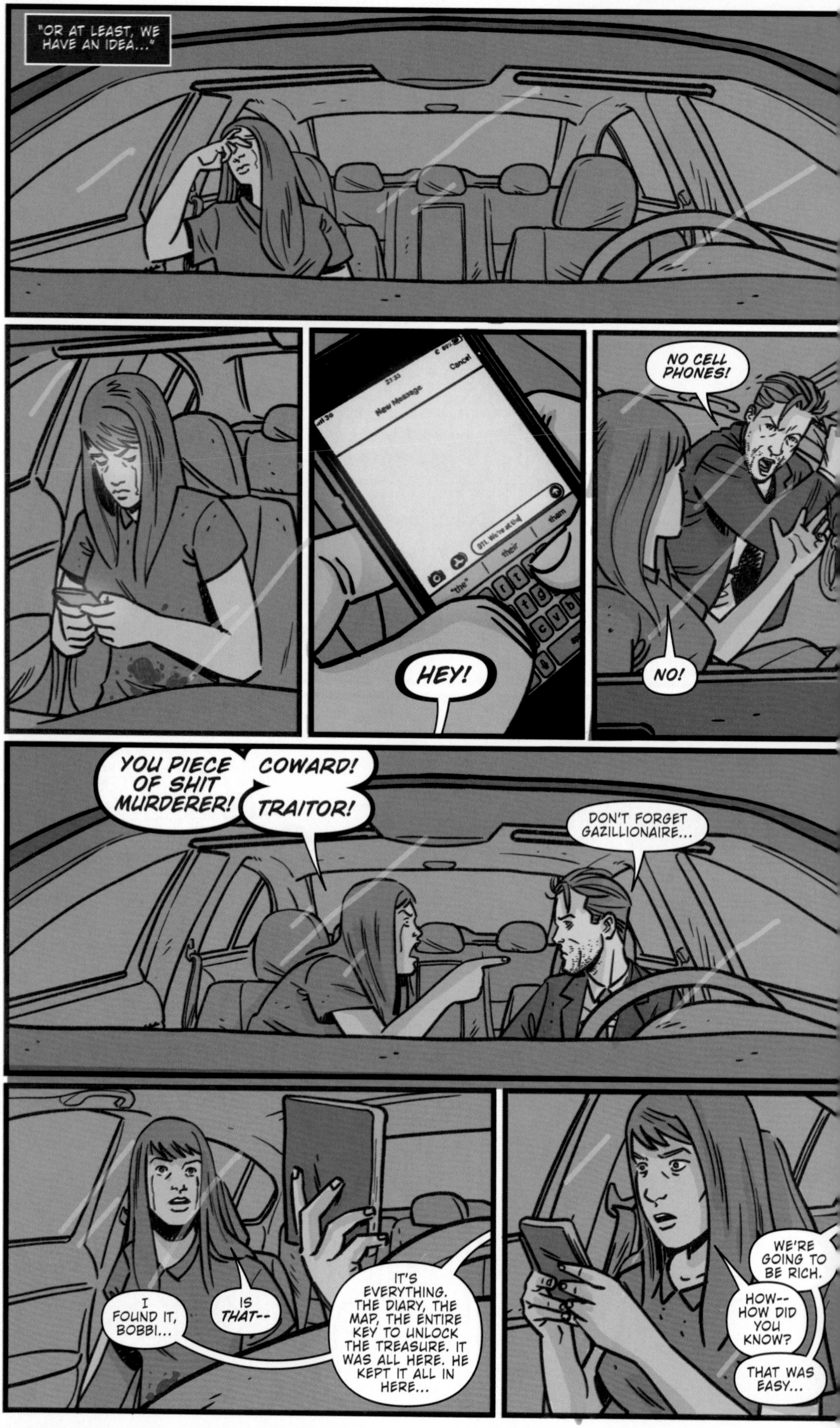
"OR AT LEAST, WE HAVE AN IDEA..."
NO CELL PHONES!
HEY!
NO!
YOU PIECE OF SHIT MURDERER!
COWARD!
TRAITOR!
DON'T FORGET GAZILLIONAIRE...
I FOUND IT, BOBBI...
IS THAT--
IT'S EVERYTHING. THE DIARY, THE MAP, THE ENTIRE KEY TO UNLOCK THE TREASURE. IT WAS ALL HERE. HE KEPT IT ALL IN HERE...
WE'RE GOING TO BE RICH.
HOW-- HOW DID YOU KNOW?
THAT WAS EASY...

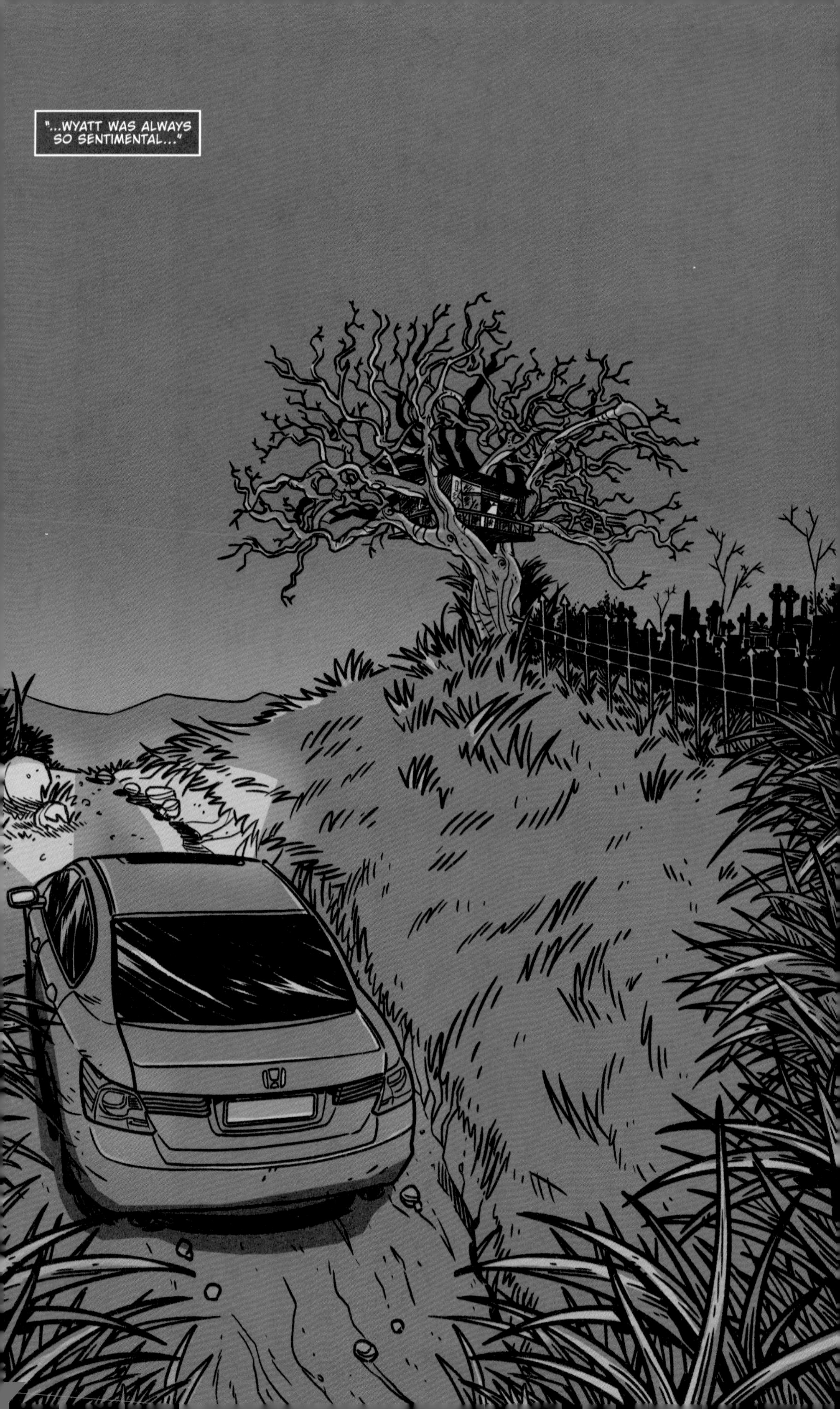
"...WYATT WAS ALWAYS SO SENTIMENTAL..."

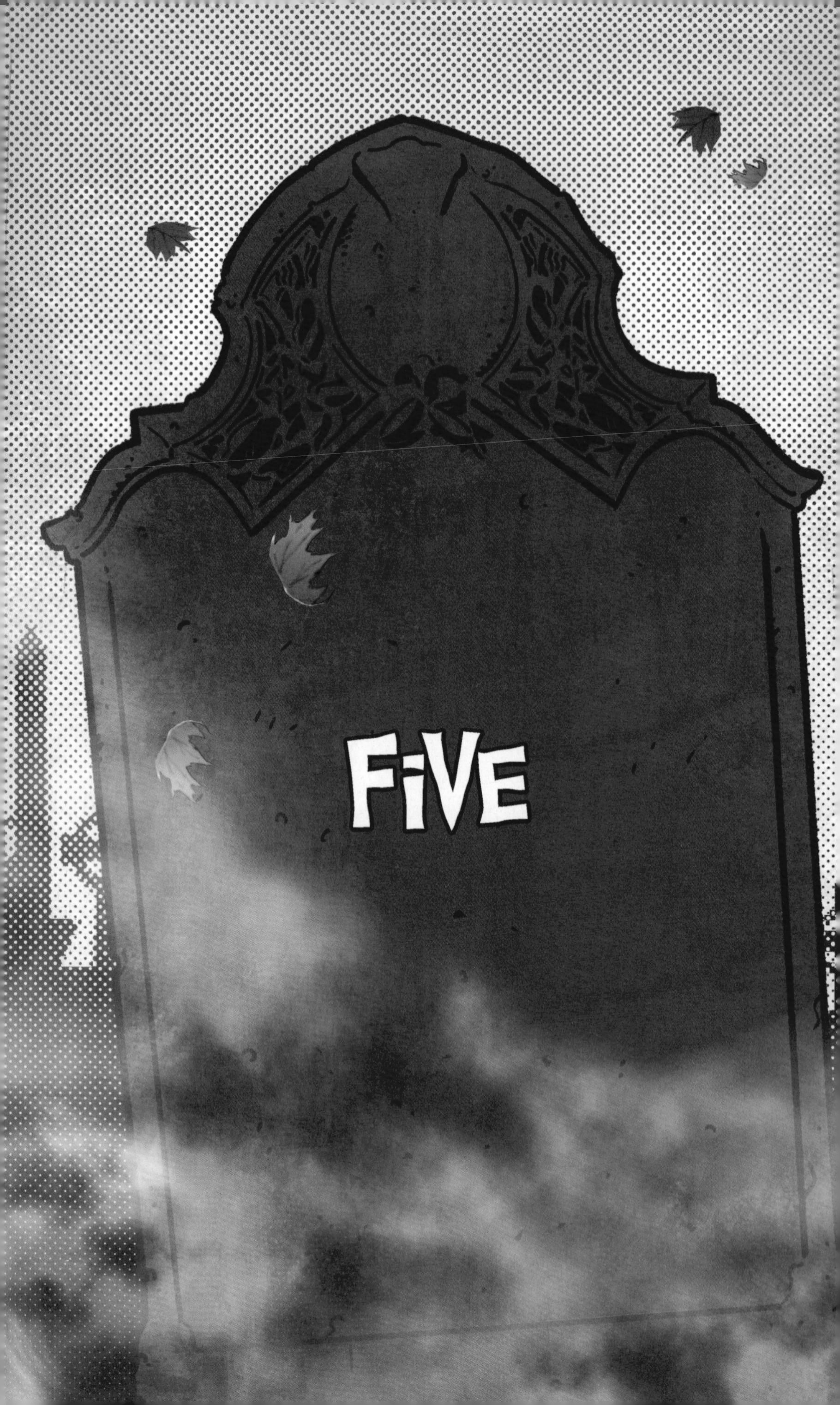
FIVE

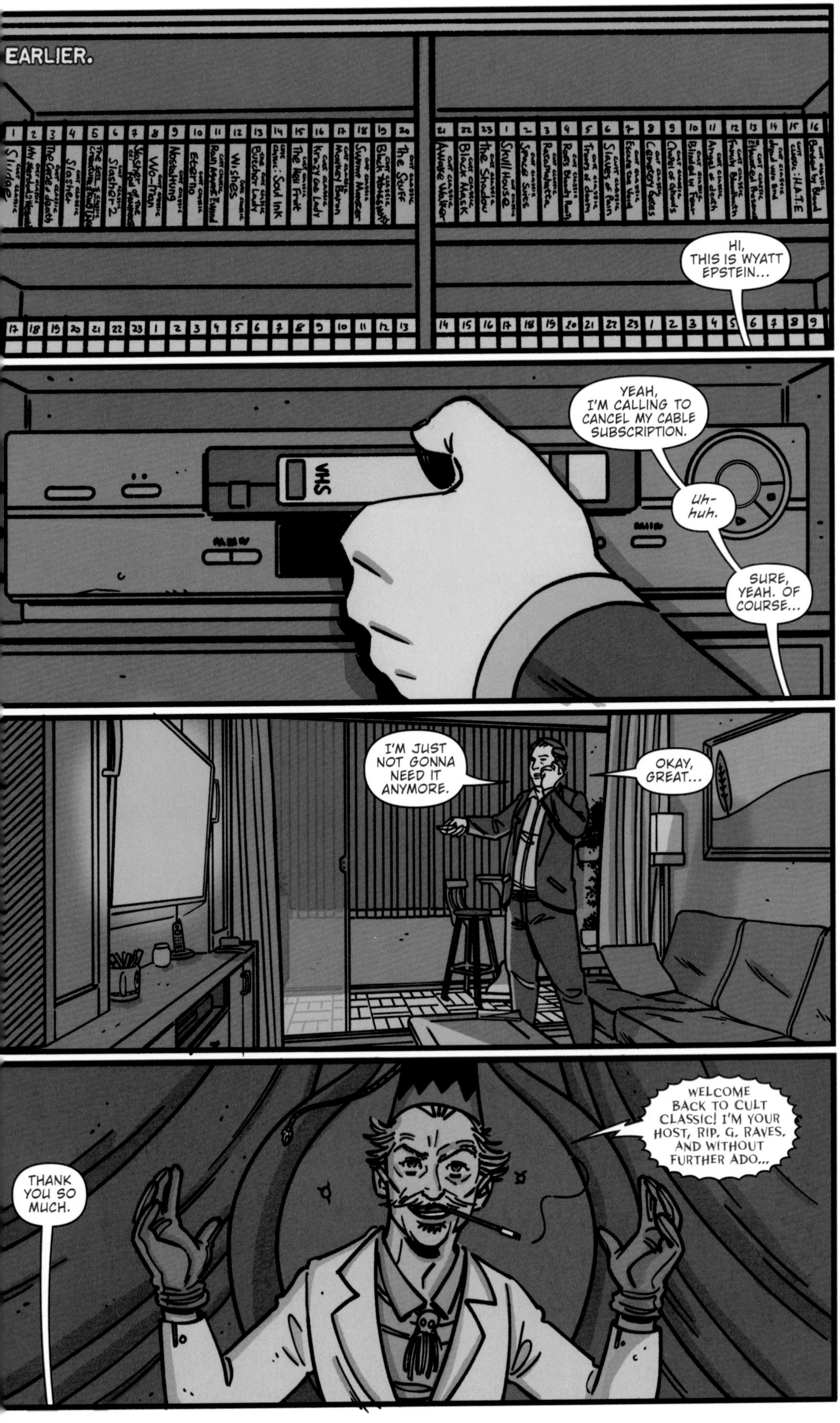
EARLIER.
HI, THIS IS WYATT EPSTEIN...
YEAH, I'M CALLING TO CANCEL MY CABLE SUBSCRIPTION.
UH-HUH.
SURE, YEAH. OF COURSE...
VHS
I'M JUST NOT GONNA NEED IT ANYMORE.
OKAY, GREAT...
WELCOME BACK TO CULT CLASSIC! I'M YOUR HOST, RIP. G. RAVES. AND WITHOUT FURTHER ADO...
THANK YOU SO MUCH.

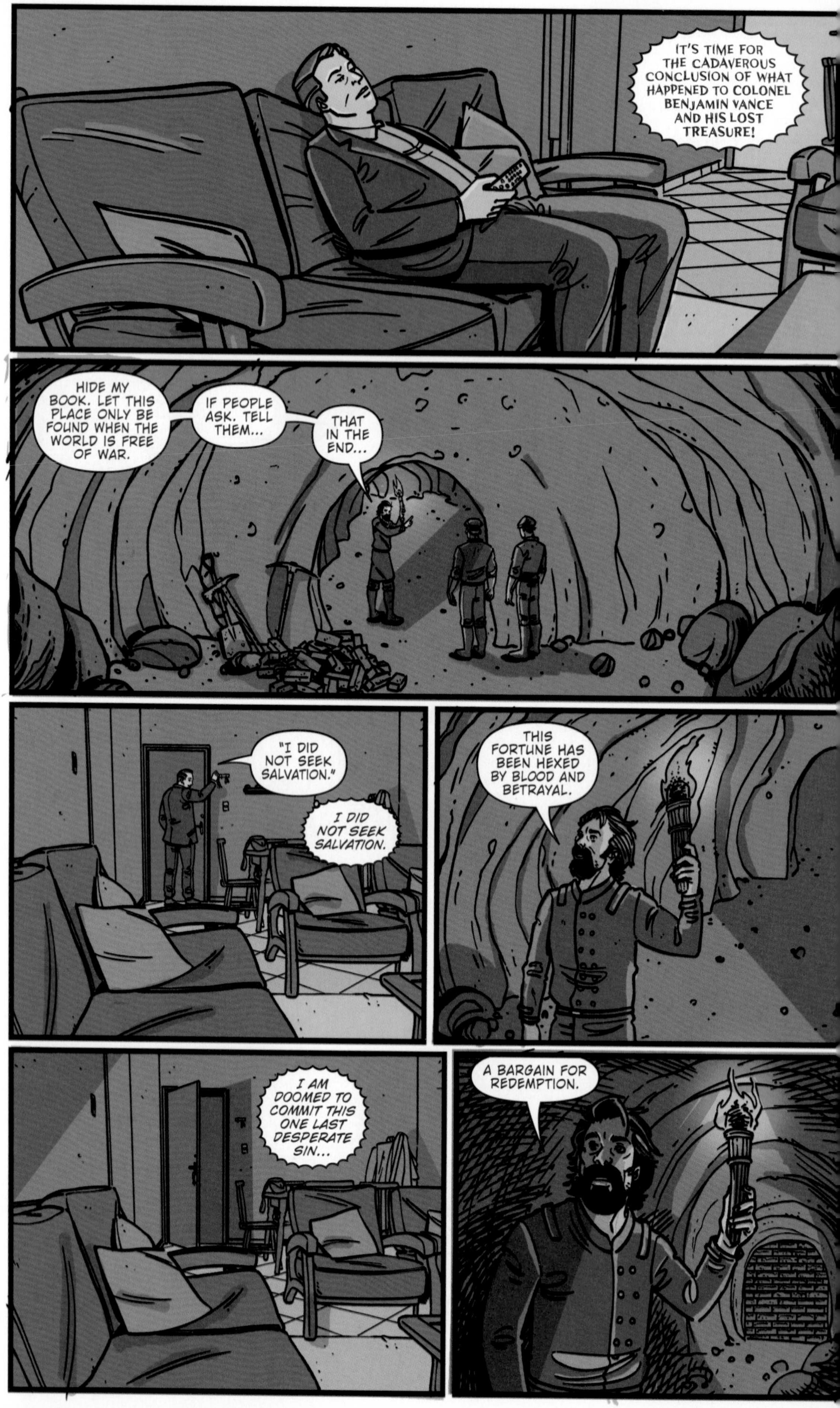
IT'S TIME FOR THE CADAVEROUS CONCLUSION OF WHAT HAPPENED TO COLONEL BENJAMIN VANCE AND HIS LOST TREASURE!
HIDE MY BOOK. LET THIS PLACE ONLY BE FOUND WHEN THE WORLD IS FREE OF WAR.
IF PEOPLE ASK, TELL THEM...
THAT IN THE END...
"I DID NOT SEEK SALVATION."
I DID NOT SEEK SALVATION.
THIS FORTUNE HAS BEEN HEXED BY BLOOD AND BETRAYAL.
I AM DOOMED TO COMMIT THIS ONE LAST DESPERATE SIN...
A BARGAIN FOR REDEMPTION.

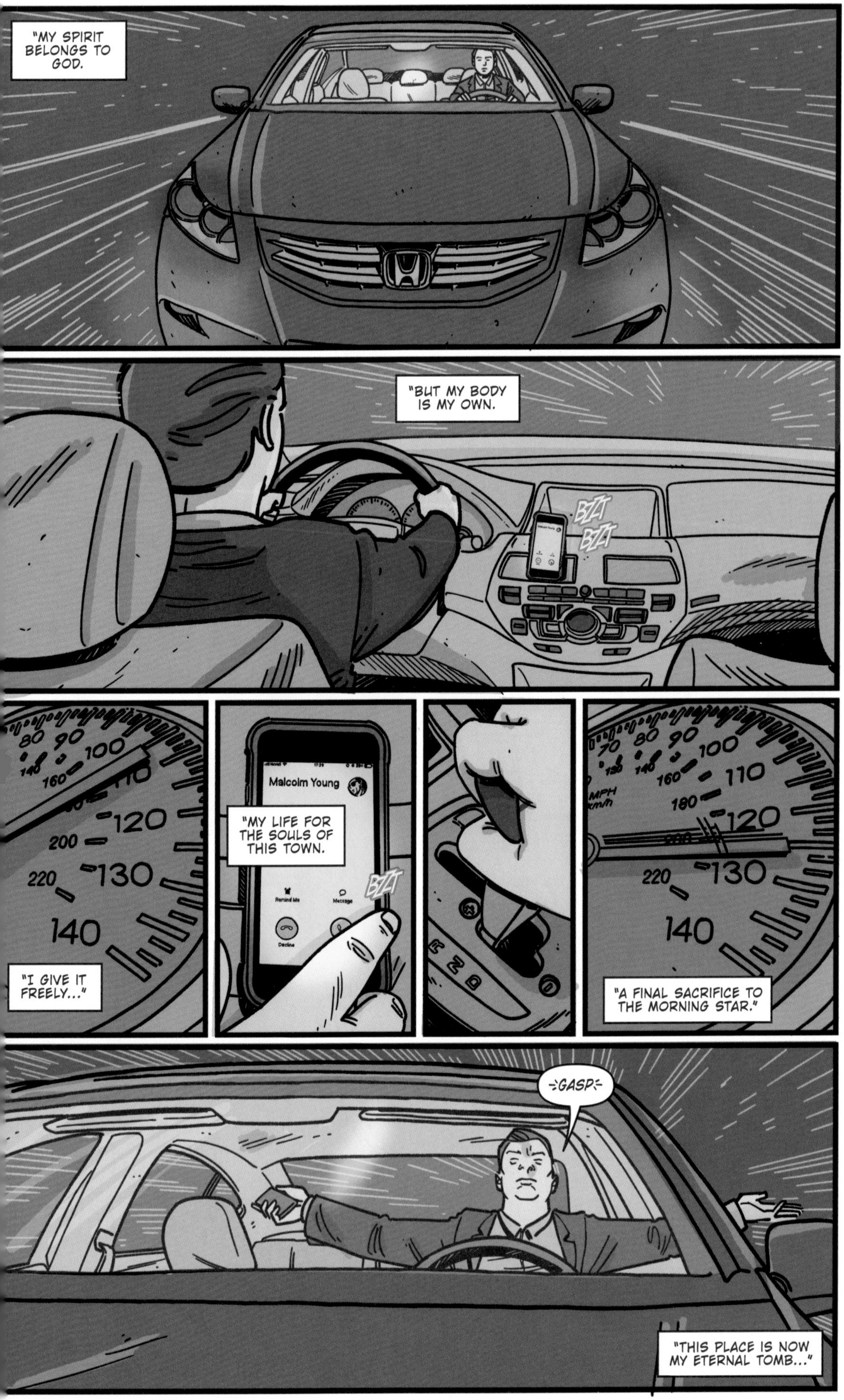
"MY SPIRIT BELONGS TO GOD.
"BUT MY BODY IS MY OWN.
BZZT
BZZT
"I GIVE IT FREELY..."
Malcolm Young
"MY LIFE FOR THE SOULS OF THIS TOWN.
BZZT
"A FINAL SACRIFICE TO THE MORNING STAR."
GASP
"THIS PLACE IS NOW MY ETERNAL TOMB..."

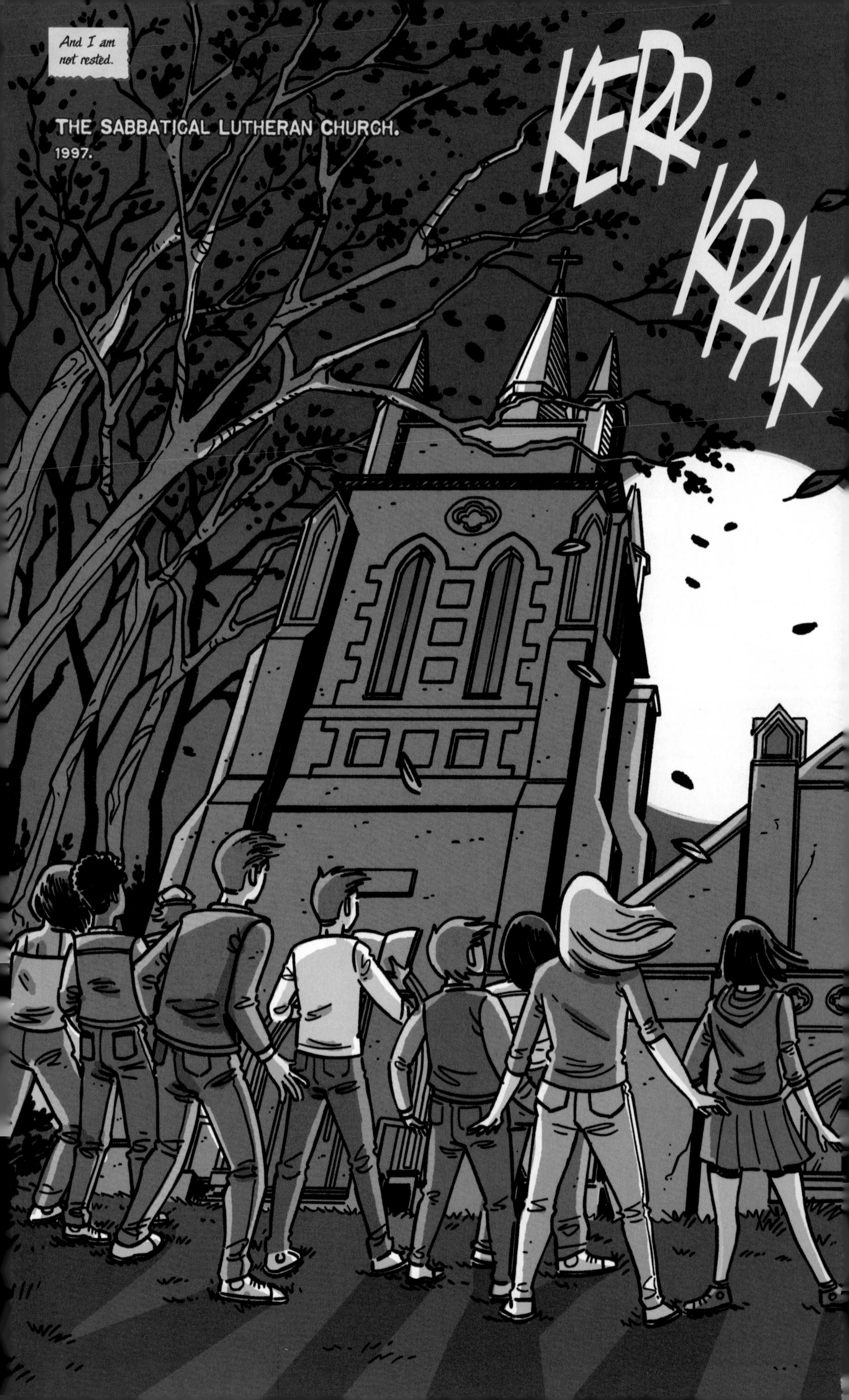
And I am not rested.
THE SABBATICAL LUTHERAN CHURCH.
1997.
KERR
KRAK

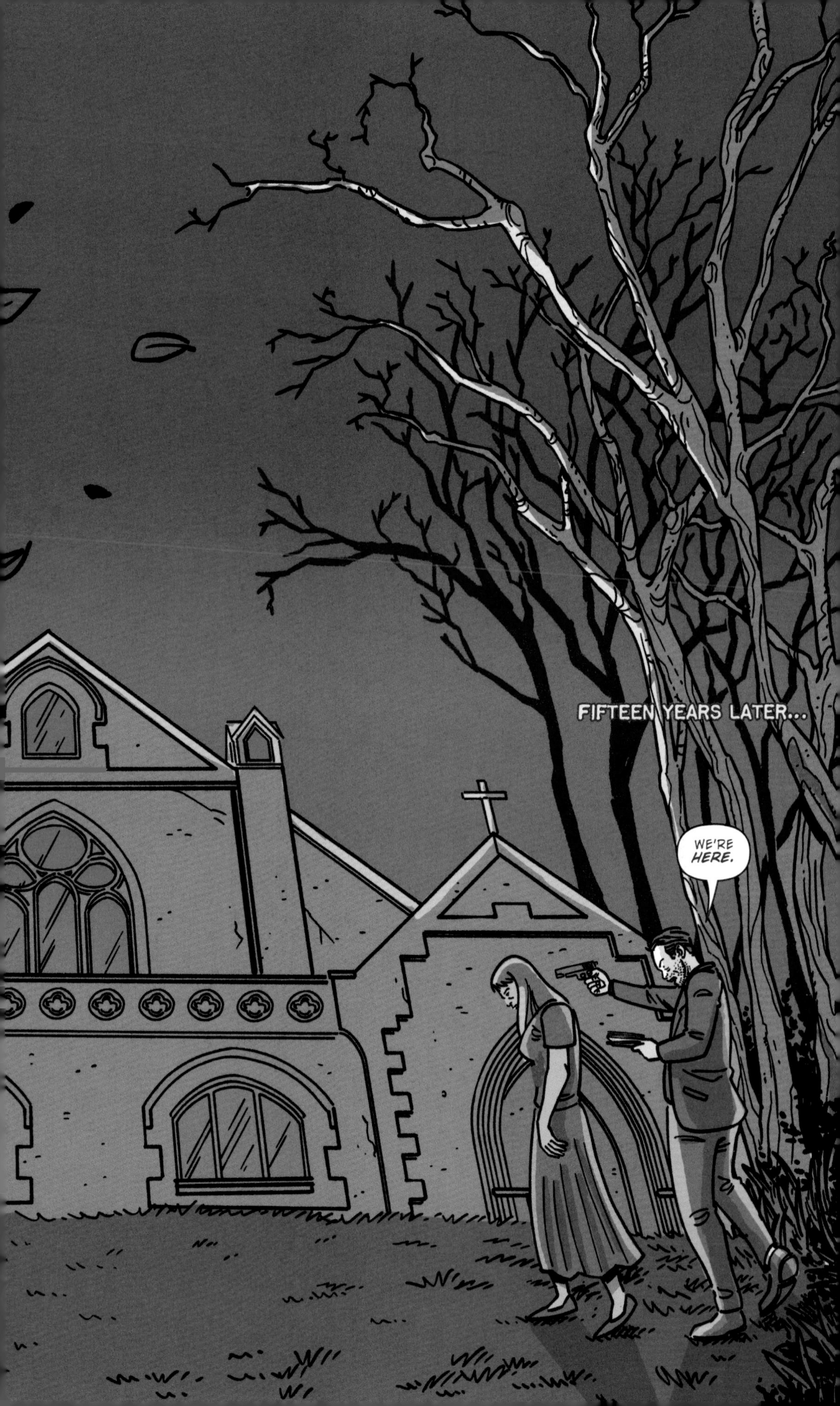
FIFTEEN YEARS LATER...
WE'RE *HERE.*

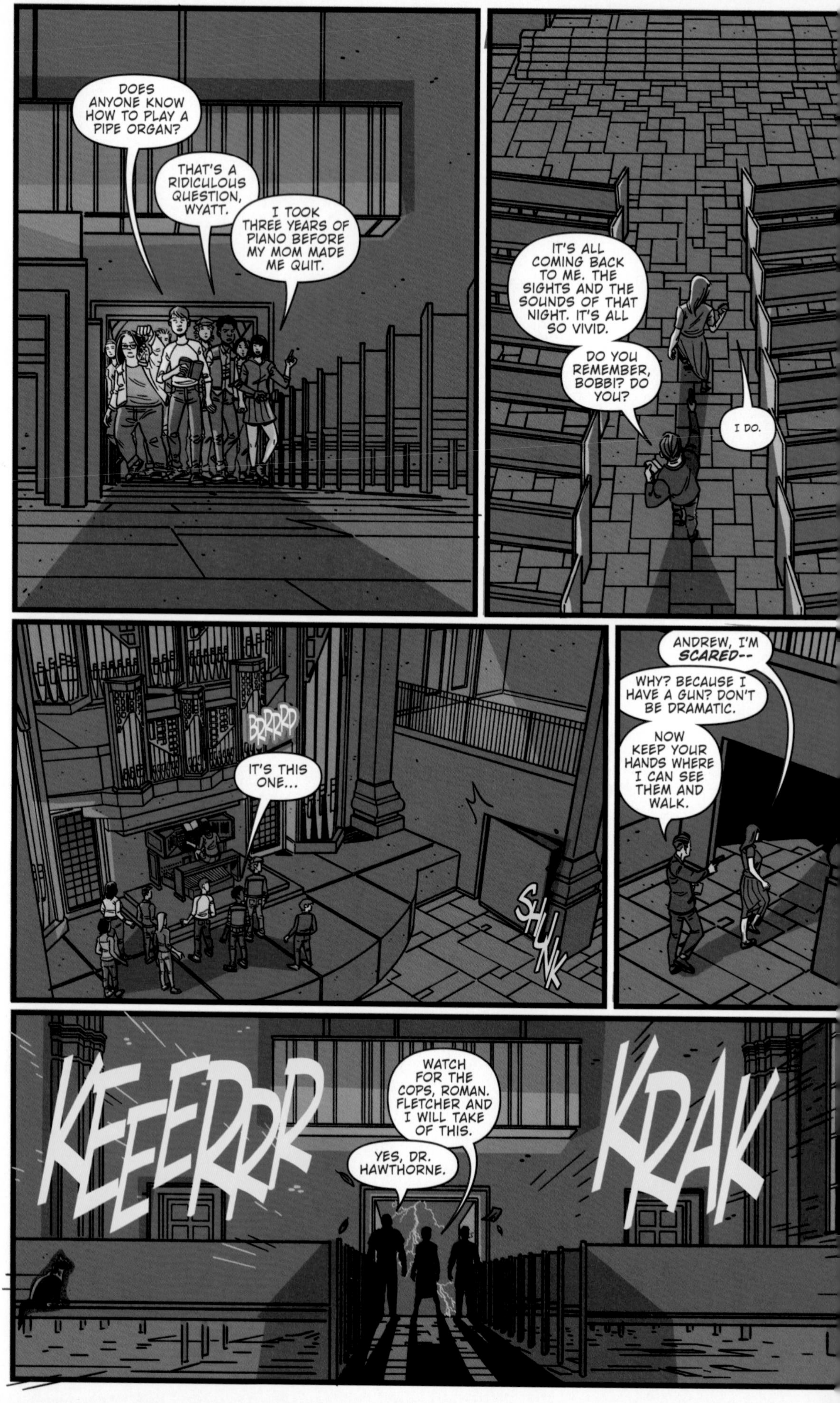
DOES ANYONE KNOW HOW TO PLAY A PIPE ORGAN?
THAT'S A RIDICULOUS QUESTION, WYATT.
I TOOK THREE YEARS OF PIANO BEFORE MY MOM MADE ME QUIT.
IT'S ALL COMING BACK TO ME. THE SIGHTS AND THE SOUNDS OF THAT NIGHT. IT'S ALL SO VIVID.
DO YOU REMEMBER, BOBBI? DO YOU?
I DO.
BRRRRP
IT'S THIS ONE...
SHUNK
ANDREW, I'M *SCARED--*
WHY? BECAUSE I HAVE A GUN? DON'T BE DRAMATIC.
NOW KEEP YOUR HANDS WHERE I CAN SEE THEM AND WALK.
KEEERRR
WATCH FOR THE COPS, ROMAN. FLETCHER AND I WILL TAKE OF THIS.
YES, DR. HAWTHORNE.
KRAK

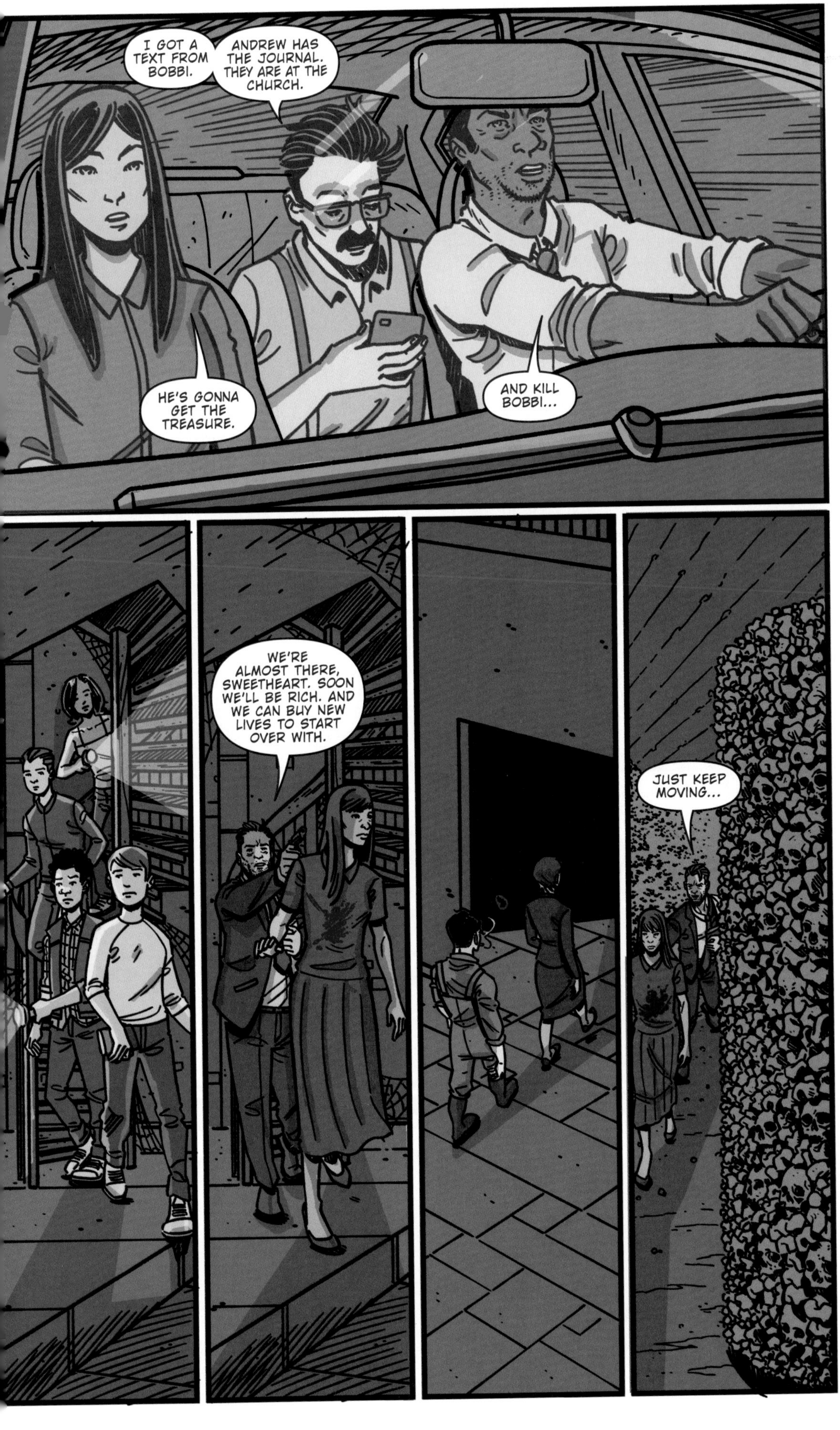
I GOT A TEXT FROM BOBBI.
ANDREW HAS THE JOURNAL. THEY ARE AT THE CHURCH.
HE'S GONNA GET THE TREASURE.
AND KILL BOBBI...
WE'RE ALMOST THERE, SWEETHEART. SOON WE'LL BE RICH. AND WE CAN BUY NEW LIVES TO START OVER WITH.
JUST KEEP MOVING...

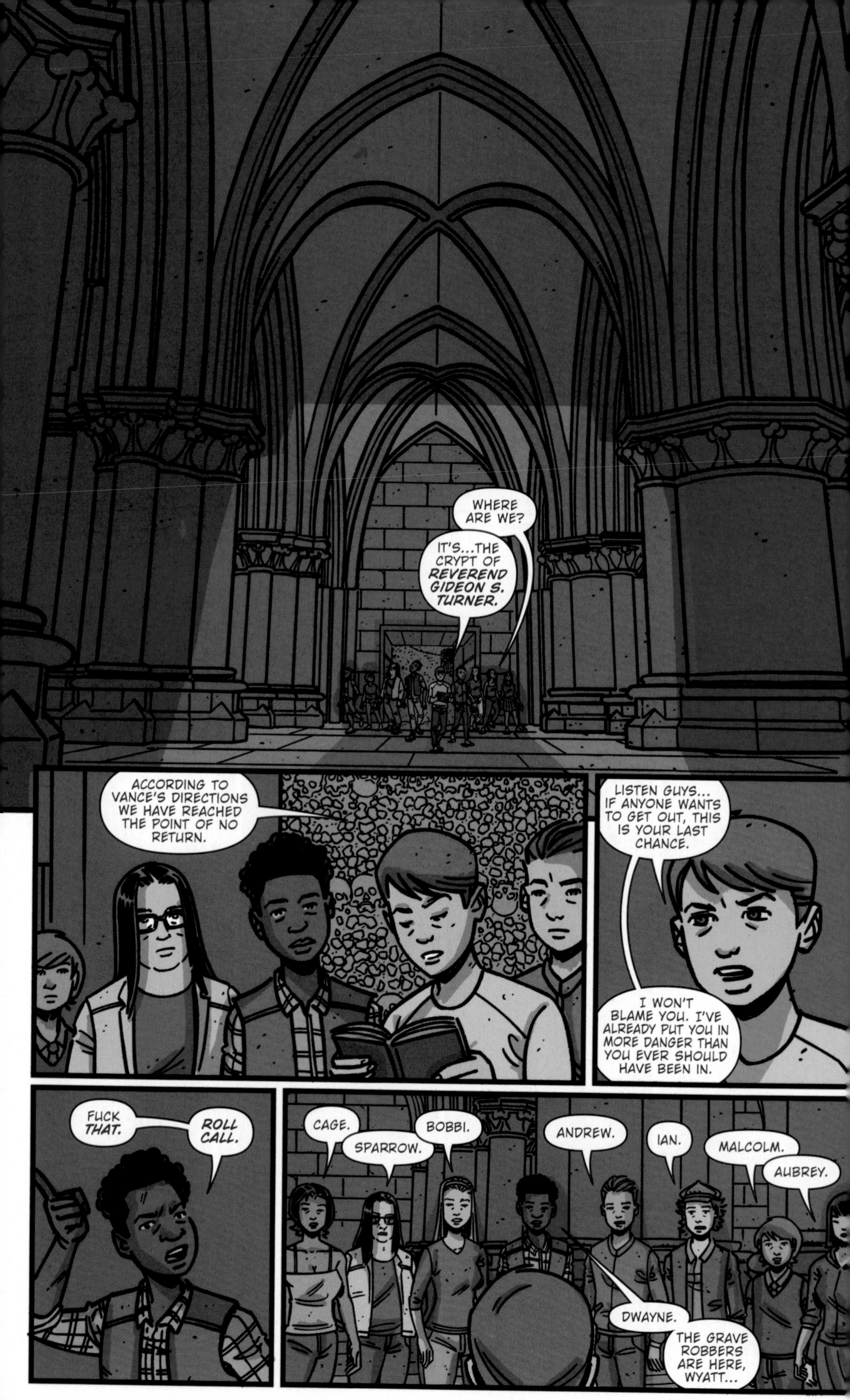
WHERE ARE WE?
IT'S...THE CRYPT OF *REVEREND GIDEON S. TURNER.*
ACCORDING TO VANCE'S DIRECTIONS WE HAVE REACHED THE POINT OF NO RETURN.
LISTEN GUYS... IF ANYONE WANTS TO GET OUT, THIS IS YOUR LAST CHANCE.
I WON'T BLAME YOU. I'VE ALREADY PUT YOU IN MORE DANGER THAN YOU EVER SHOULD HAVE BEEN IN.
FUCK *THAT.*
ROLL CALL.
CAGE.
SPARROW.
BOBBI.
ANDREW.
IAN.
MALCOLM.
AUBREY.
DWAYNE.
THE GRAVE ROBBERS ARE HERE, WYATT...

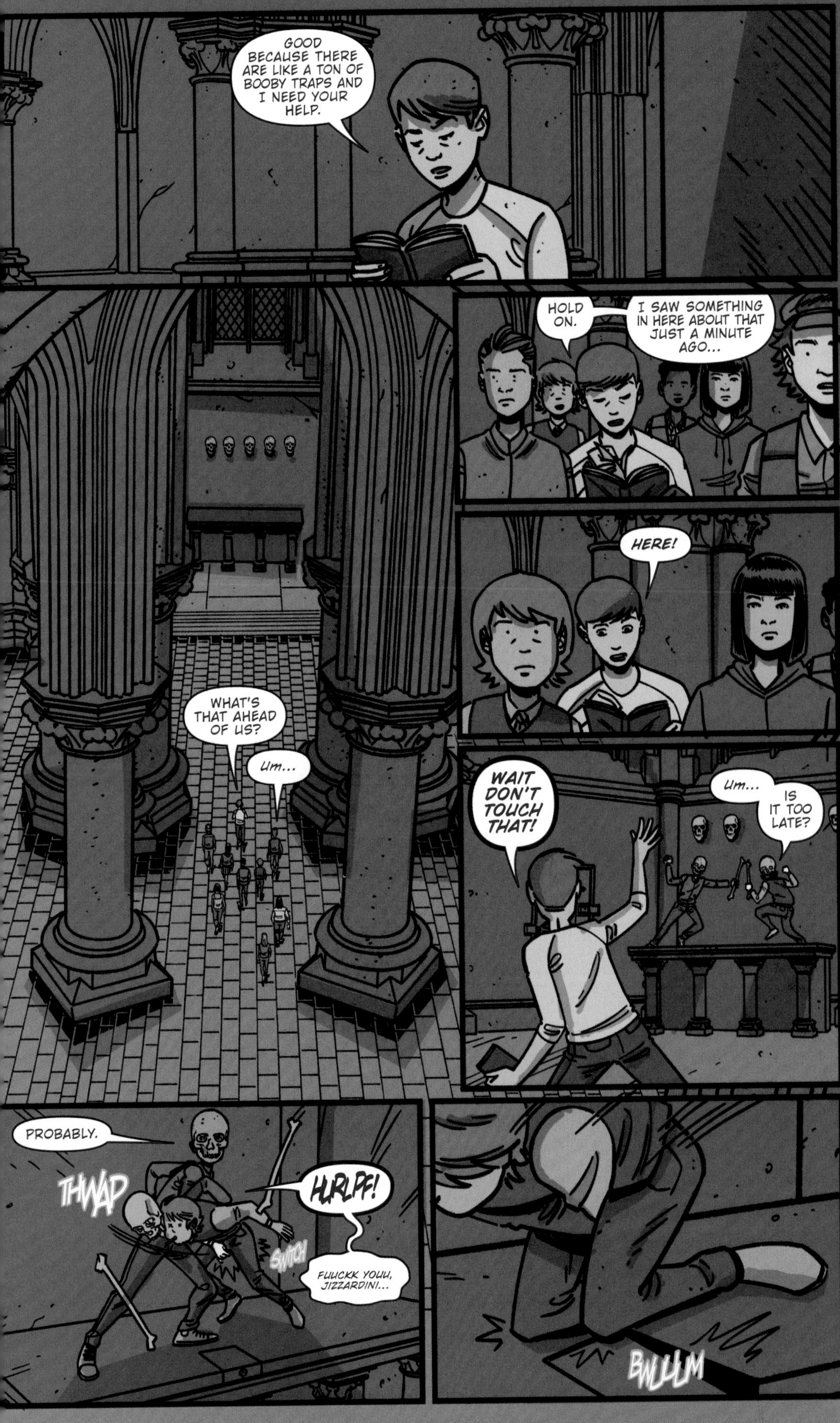
GOOD BECAUSE THERE ARE LIKE A TON OF BOOBY TRAPS AND I NEED YOUR HELP.
WHAT'S THAT AHEAD OF US?
Um...
HOLD ON.
I SAW SOMETHING IN HERE ABOUT THAT JUST A MINUTE AGO...
HERE!
WAIT DON'T TOUCH THAT!
Um...
IS IT TOO LATE?
PROBABLY.
THWAP
HURLPF!
SWITCH
FUUCKK YOUU, JIZZARDINI...
BWUUUM

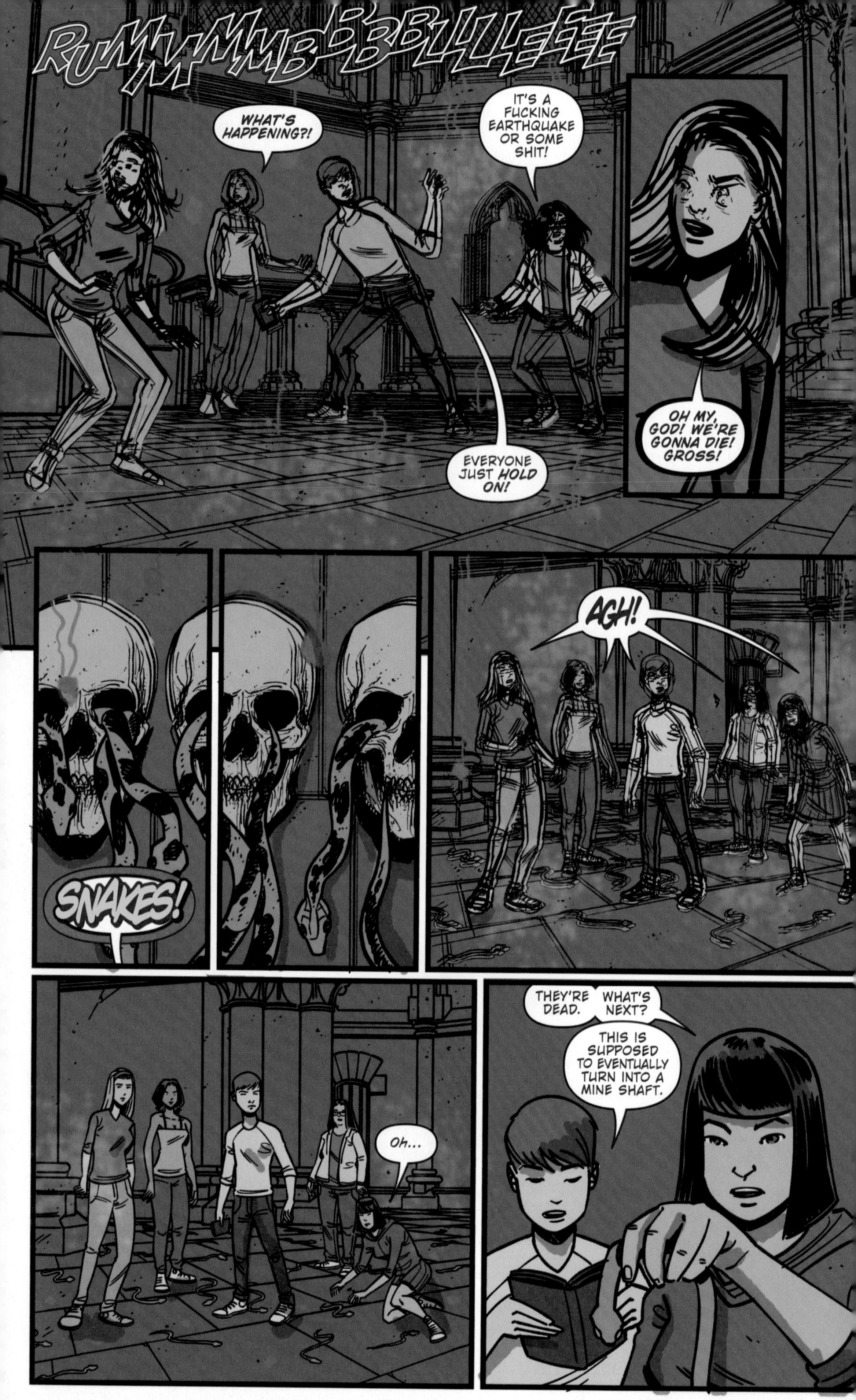
RUMMMMMBBBBLLLEEE
WHAT'S HAPPENING?!
IT'S A FUCKING EARTHQUAKE OR SOME SHIT!
EVERYONE JUST HOLD ON!
OH MY, GOD! WE'RE GONNA DIE! GROSS!
SNAKES!
AGH!
Oh...
THEY'RE DEAD.
WHAT'S NEXT?
THIS IS SUPPOSED TO EVENTUALLY TURN INTO A MINE SHAFT.

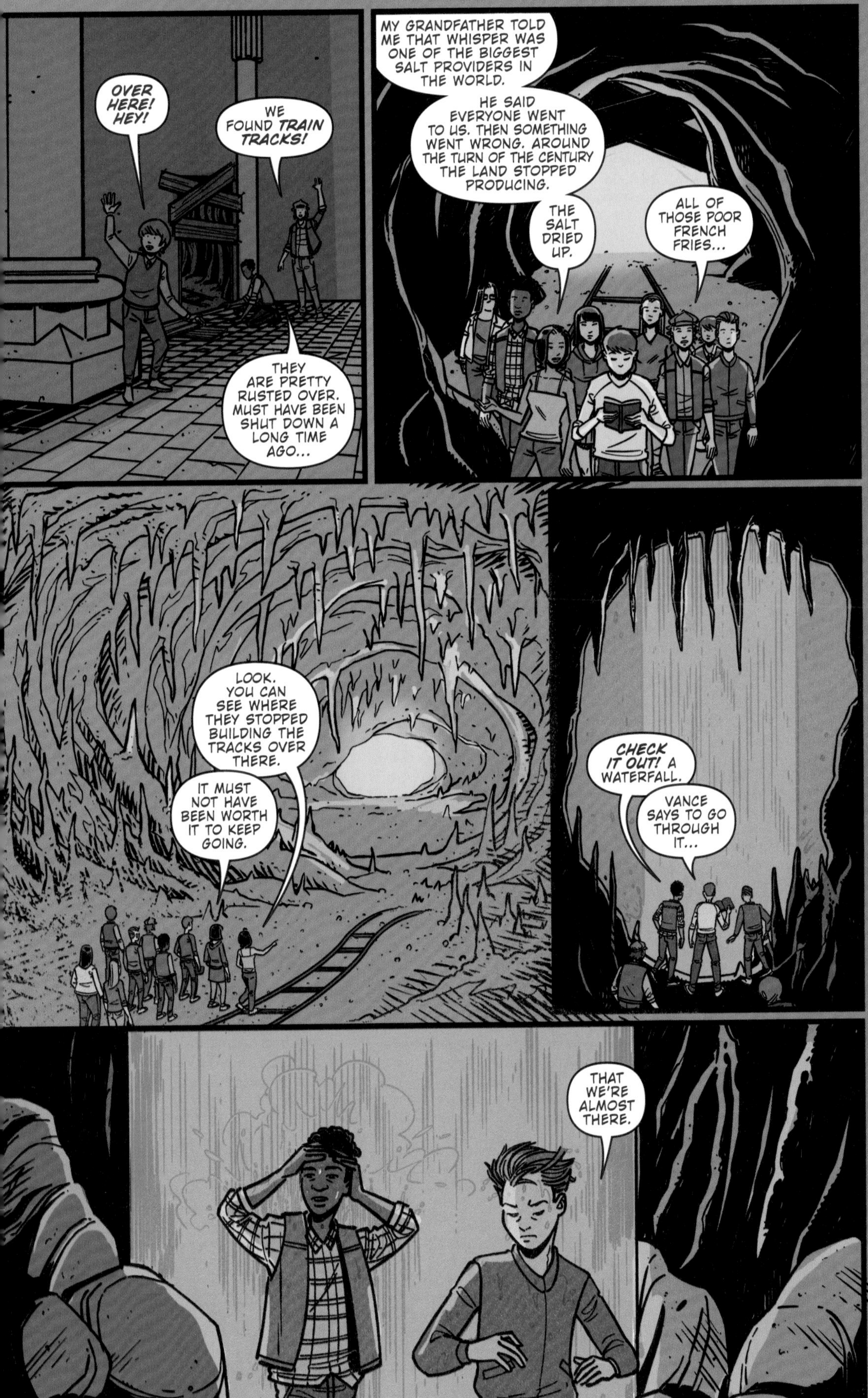
OVER HERE! HEY!
WE FOUND TRAIN TRACKS!
THEY ARE PRETTY RUSTED OVER. MUST HAVE BEEN SHUT DOWN A LONG TIME AGO...
MY GRANDFATHER TOLD ME THAT WHISPER WAS ONE OF THE BIGGEST SALT PROVIDERS IN THE WORLD.
HE SAID EVERYONE WENT TO US. THEN SOMETHING WENT WRONG. AROUND THE TURN OF THE CENTURY THE LAND STOPPED PRODUCING.
THE SALT DRIED UP.
ALL OF THOSE POOR FRENCH FRIES...
LOOK. YOU CAN SEE WHERE THEY STOPPED BUILDING THE TRACKS OVER THERE.
IT MUST NOT HAVE BEEN WORTH IT TO KEEP GOING.
CHECK IT OUT! A WATERFALL.
VANCE SAYS TO GO THROUGH IT...
THAT WE'RE ALMOST THERE.

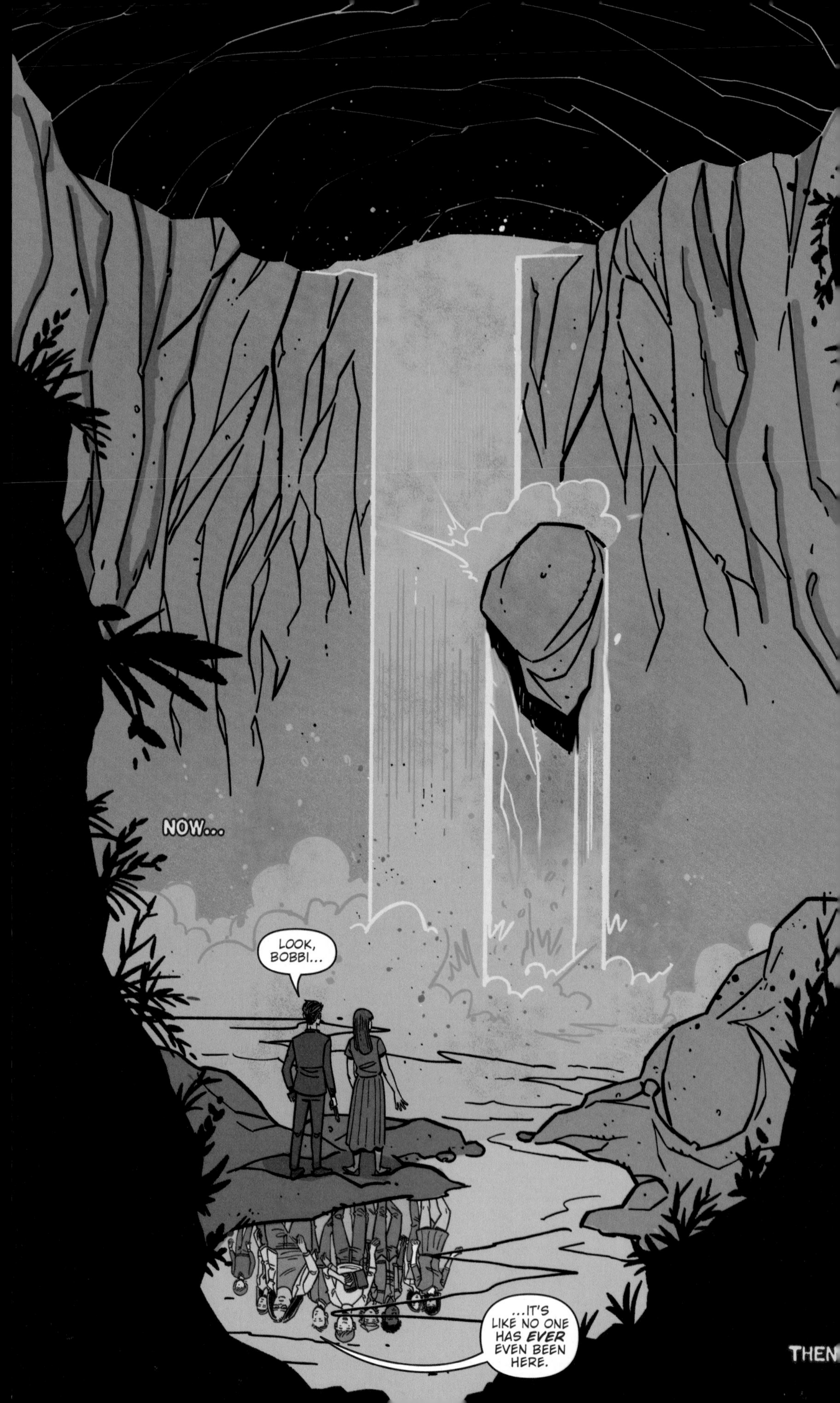
NOW...
LOOK, BOBBI...
...IT'S LIKE NO ONE HAS EVER EVEN BEEN HERE.
THEN

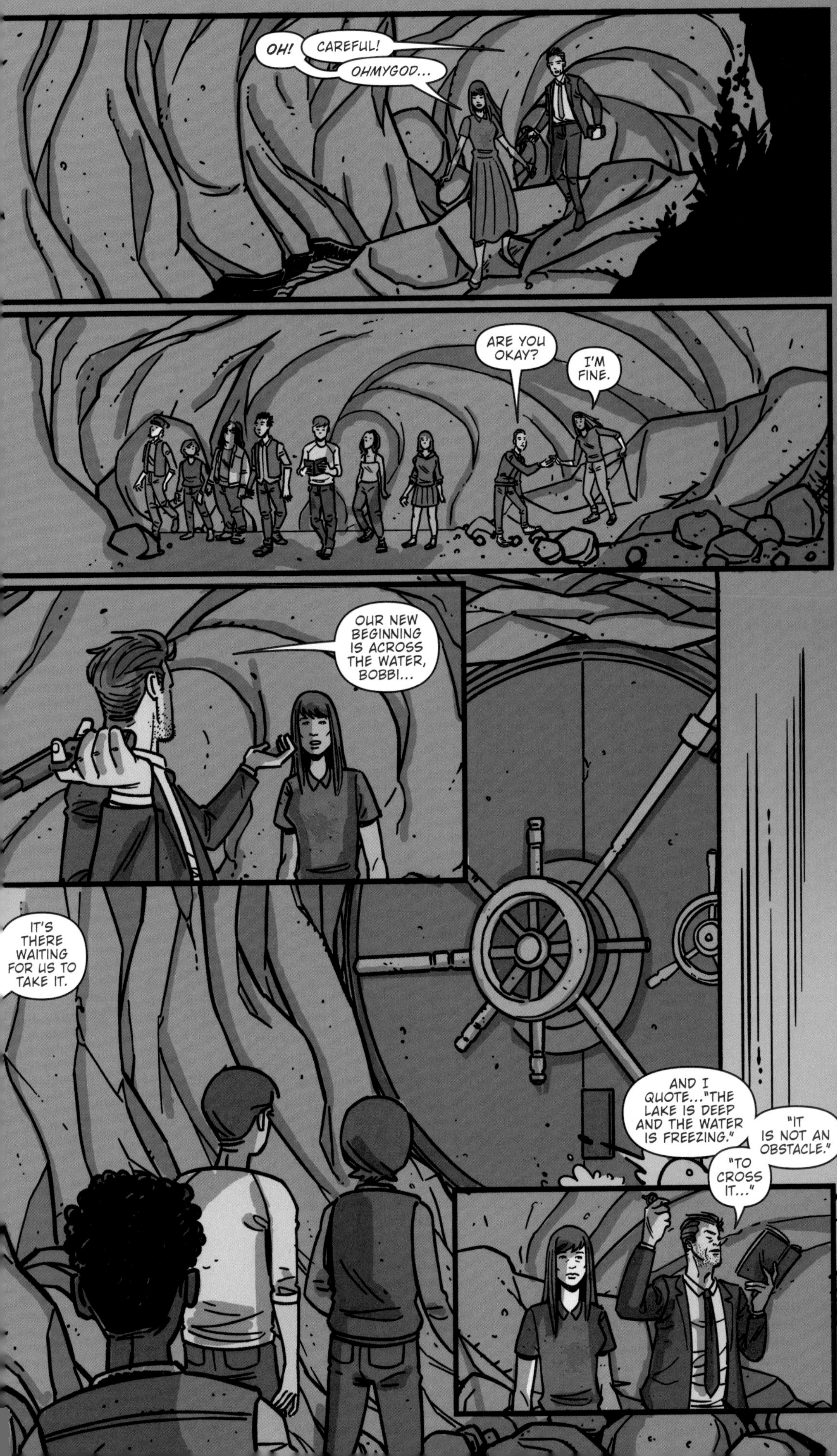
OH!
CAREFUL!
OHMYGOD...
ARE YOU OKAY?
I'M FINE.
OUR NEW BEGINNING IS ACROSS THE WATER, BOBBI...
IT'S THERE WAITING FOR US TO TAKE IT.
AND I QUOTE..."THE LAKE IS DEEP AND THE WATER IS FREEZING."
"TO CROSS IT..."
"IT IS NOT AN OBSTACLE."

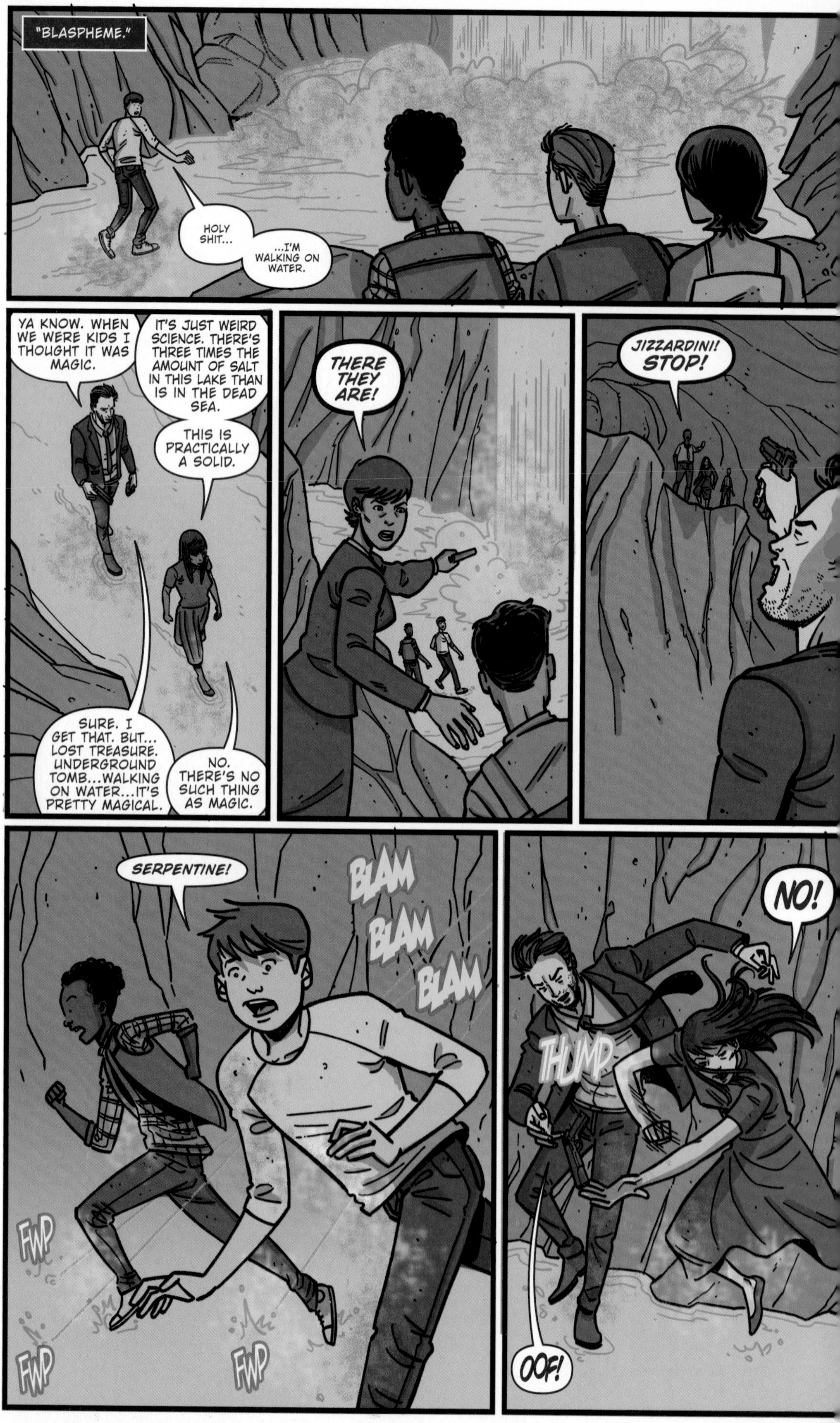
"BLASPHEME."
HOLY SHIT...
...I'M WALKING ON WATER.
YA KNOW. WHEN WE WERE KIDS I THOUGHT IT WAS MAGIC.
IT'S JUST WEIRD SCIENCE. THERE'S THREE TIMES THE AMOUNT OF SALT IN THIS LAKE THAN IS IN THE DEAD SEA.
THIS IS PRACTICALLY A SOLID.
SURE. I GET THAT. BUT... LOST TREASURE. UNDERGROUND TOMB...WALKING ON WATER...IT'S PRETTY MAGICAL.
NO. THERE'S NO SUCH THING AS MAGIC.
THERE THEY ARE!
JIZZARDINI! STOP!
SERPENTINE!
BLAM
BLAM
BLAM
FWP
FWP
FWP
NO!
THUMP
OOF!

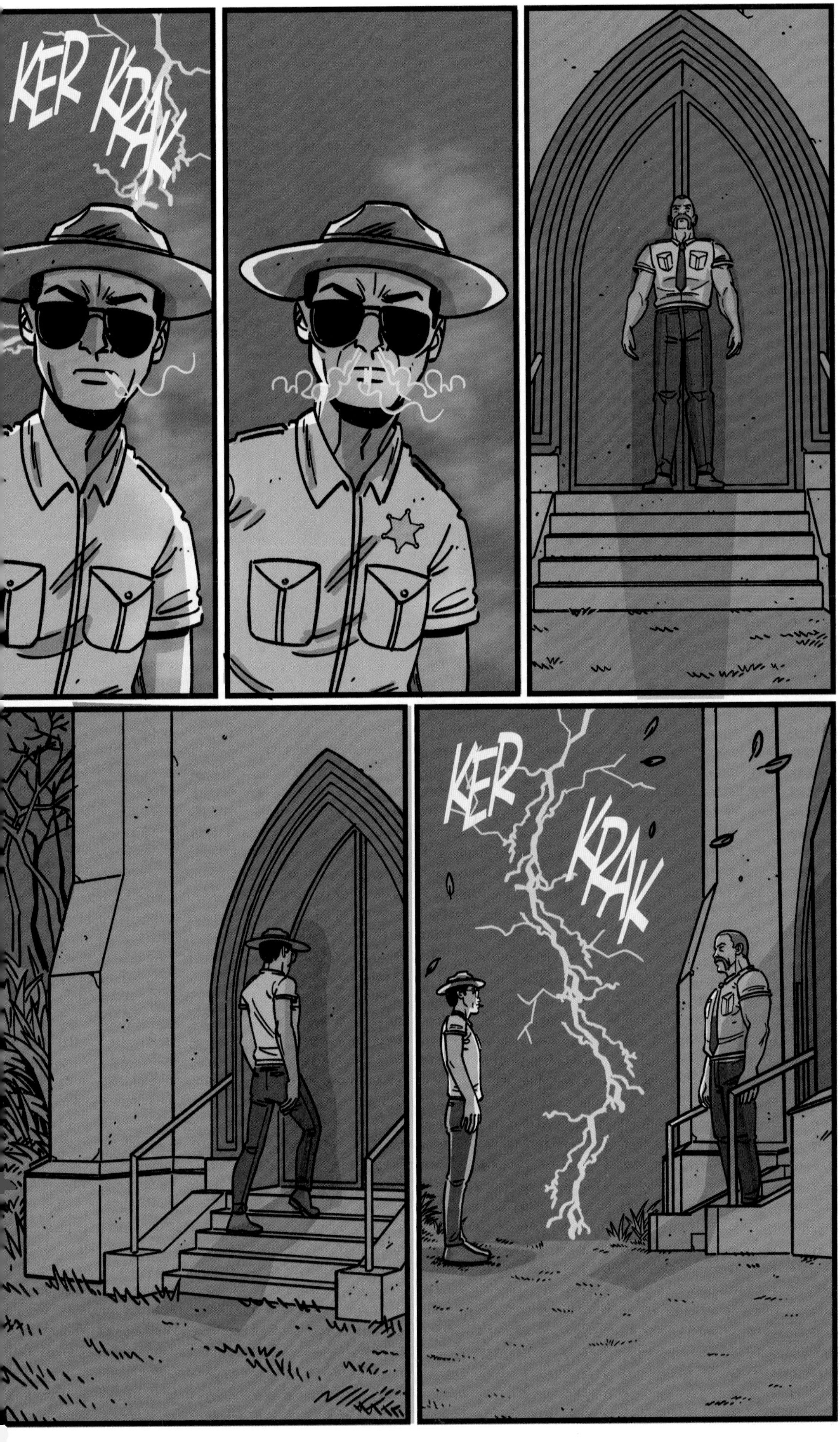
KER KRAK
KER
KRAK

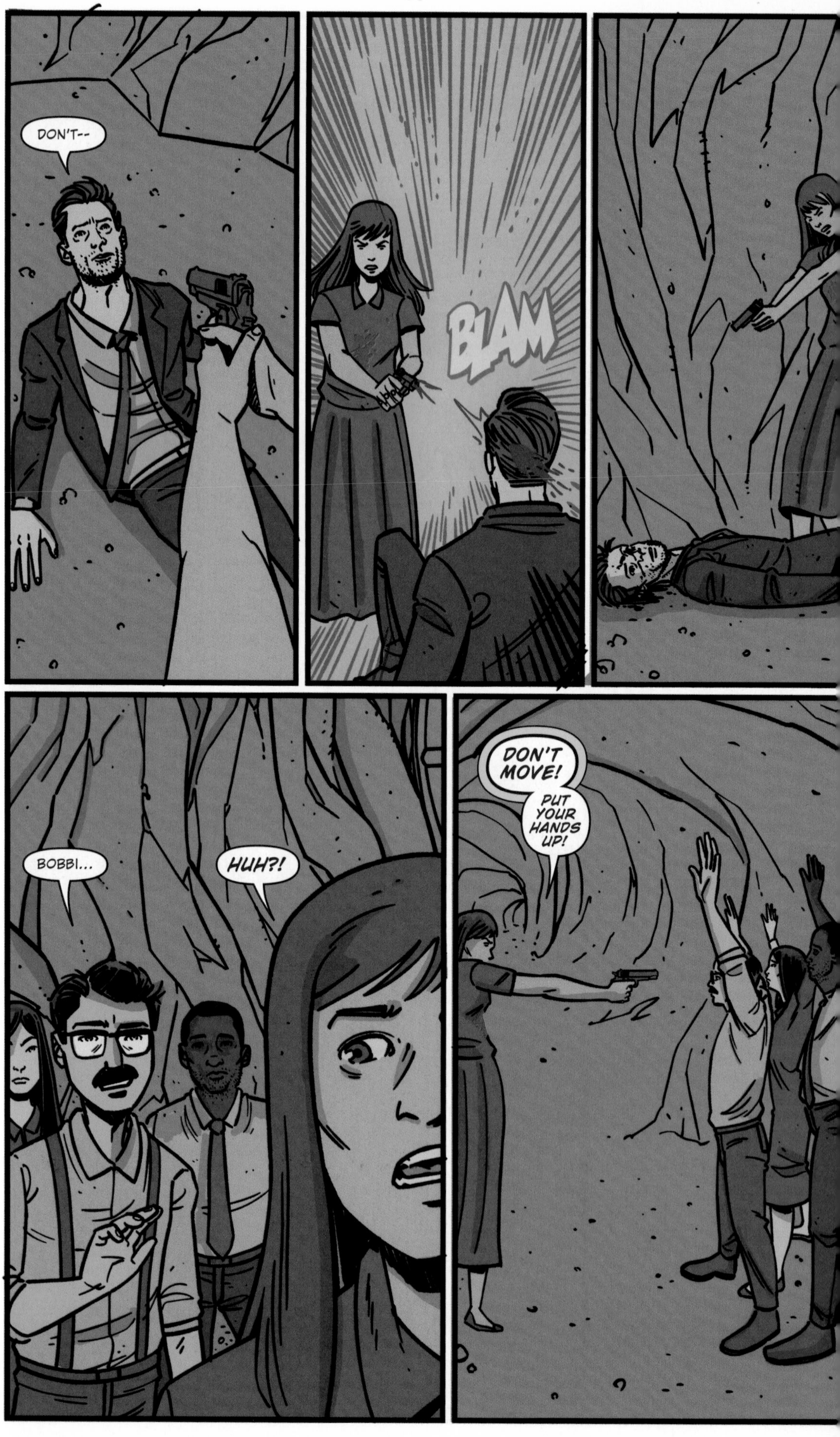
DON'T--
BLAM
BOBBI...
HUH?!
DON'T MOVE!
PUT YOUR HANDS UP!

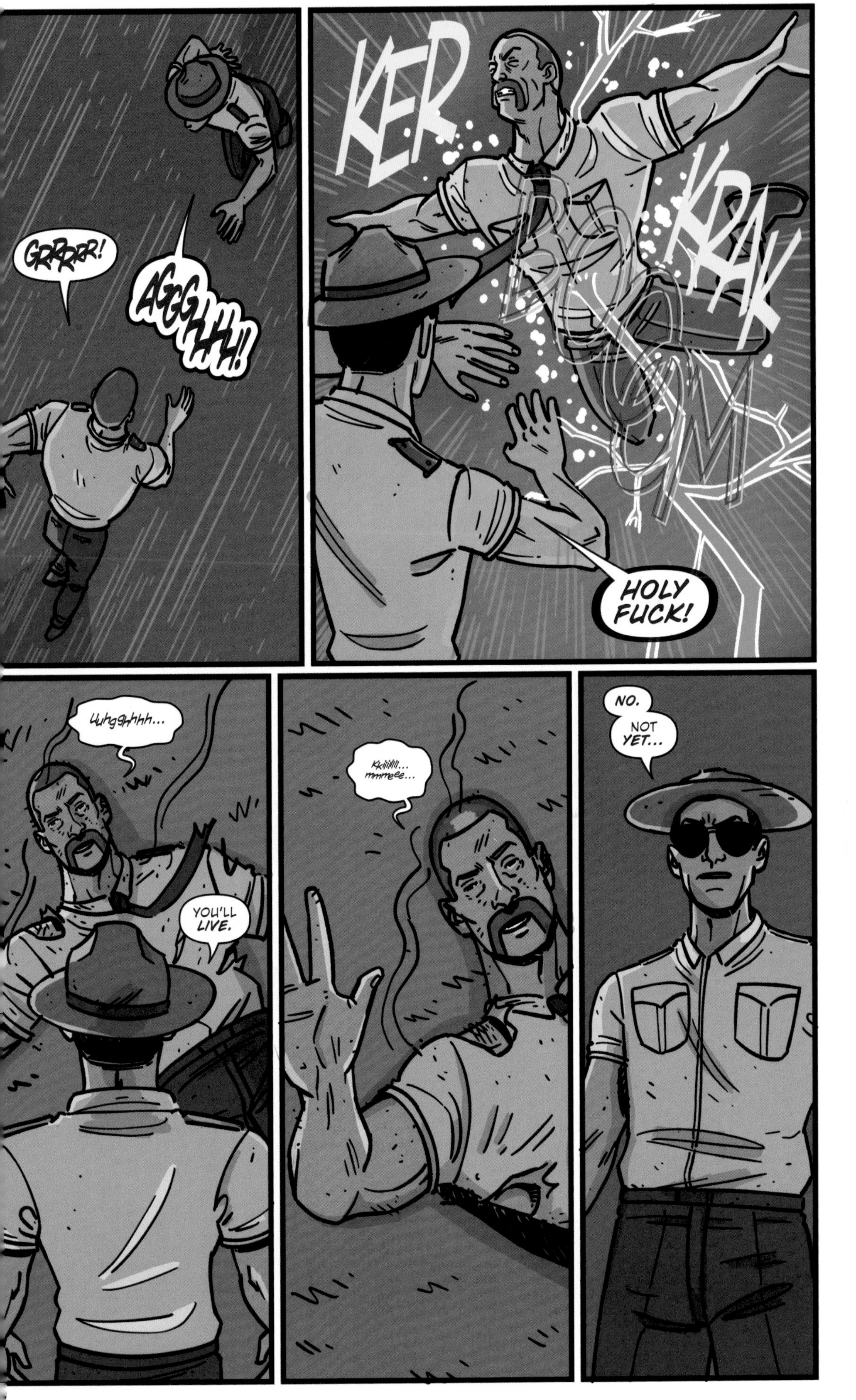
GRRRRR!
AGGGHHHH!!
KER
BOOOOM
KRAK
HOLY FUCK!
Uuhgghhhh...
YOU'LL LIVE.
Kkiiillll... mmmeee...
NO.
NOT YET...

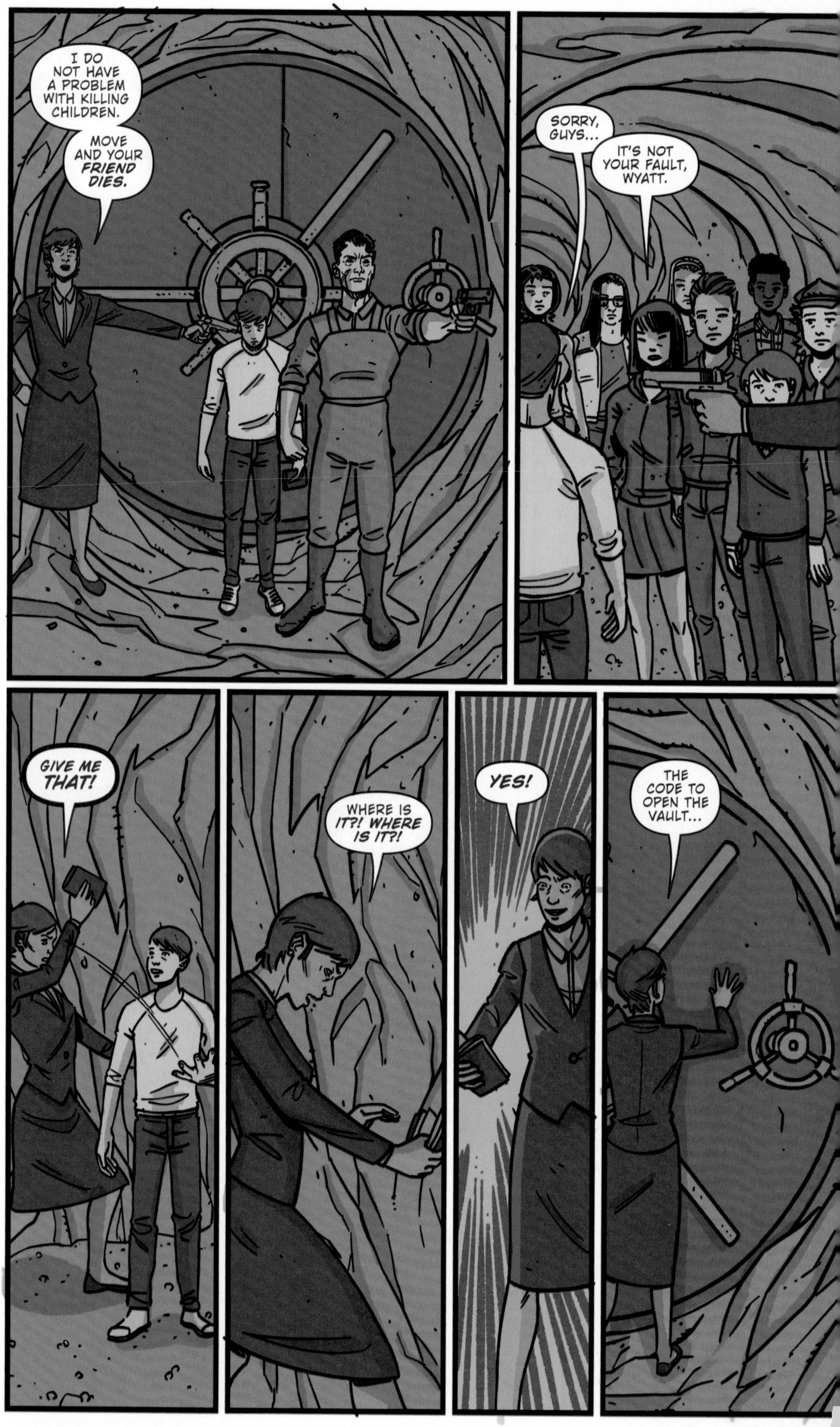
I DO NOT HAVE A PROBLEM WITH KILLING CHILDREN.
MOVE AND YOUR *FRIEND DIES.*
SORRY, GUYS...
IT'S NOT YOUR FAULT, WYATT.
GIVE ME THAT!
WHERE IS *IT?! WHERE IS IT?!*
YES!
THE CODE TO OPEN THE VAULT...

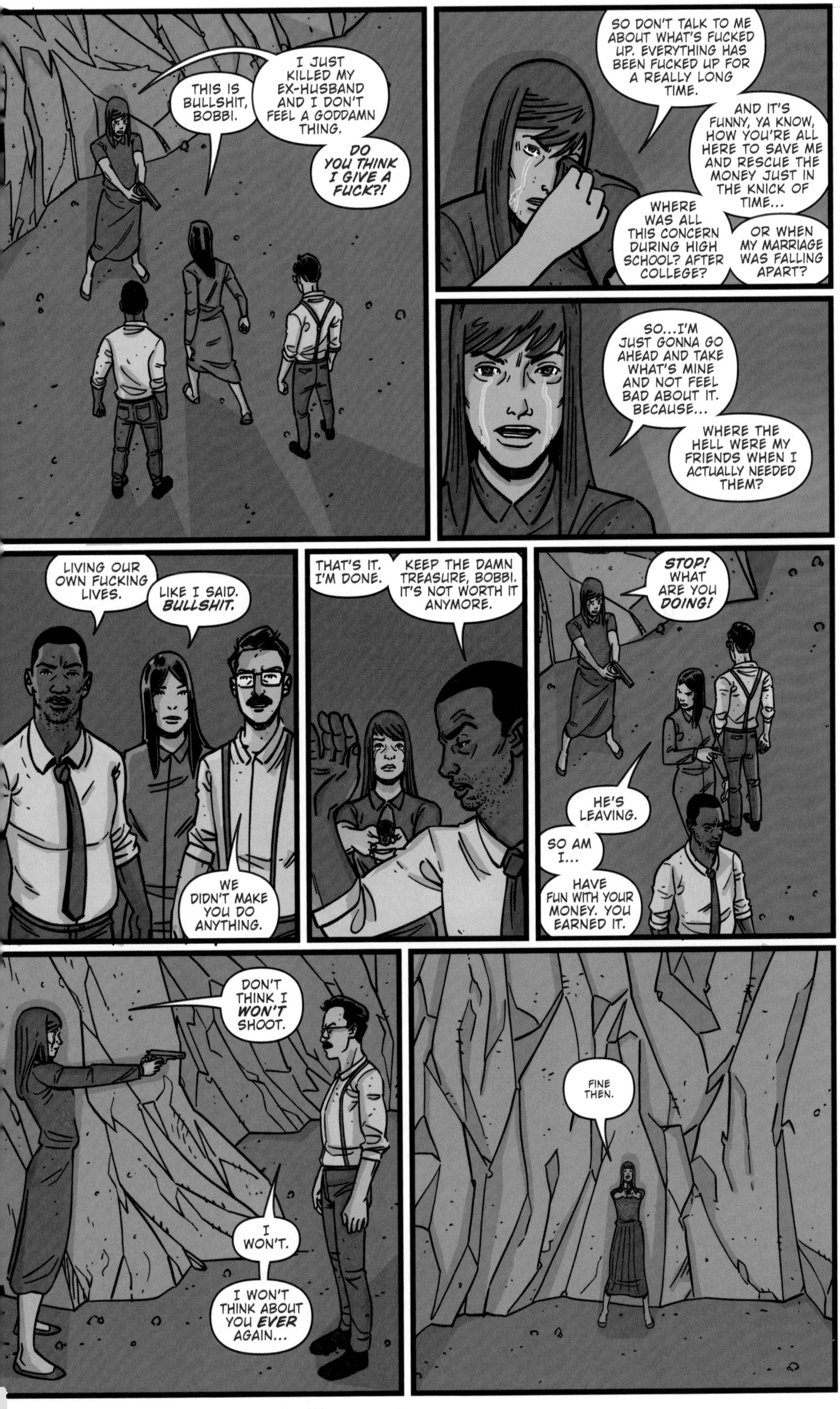

THIS IS BULLSHIT, BOBBI.
I JUST KILLED MY EX-HUSBAND AND I DON'T FEEL A GODDAMN THING.
DO YOU THINK I GIVE A FUCK?!
SO DON'T TALK TO ME ABOUT WHAT'S FUCKED UP. EVERYTHING HAS BEEN FUCKED UP FOR A REALLY LONG TIME.
AND IT'S FUNNY, YA KNOW, HOW YOU'RE ALL HERE TO SAVE ME AND RESCUE THE MONEY JUST IN THE KNICK OF TIME...
WHERE WAS ALL THIS CONCERN DURING HIGH SCHOOL? AFTER COLLEGE?
OR WHEN MY MARRIAGE WAS FALLING APART?
SO...I'M JUST GONNA GO AHEAD AND TAKE WHAT'S MINE AND NOT FEEL BAD ABOUT IT. BECAUSE...
WHERE THE HELL WERE MY FRIENDS WHEN I ACTUALLY NEEDED THEM?
LIVING OUR OWN FUCKING LIVES.
LIKE I SAID. BULLSHIT.
WE DIDN'T MAKE YOU DO ANYTHING.
THAT'S IT. I'M DONE.
KEEP THE DAMN TREASURE, BOBBI. IT'S NOT WORTH IT ANYMORE.
STOP! WHAT ARE YOU DOING!
HE'S LEAVING.
SO AM I...
HAVE FUN WITH YOUR MONEY. YOU EARNED IT.
DON'T THINK I WON'T SHOOT.
I WON'T.
I WON'T THINK ABOUT YOU EVER AGAIN...
FINE THEN.

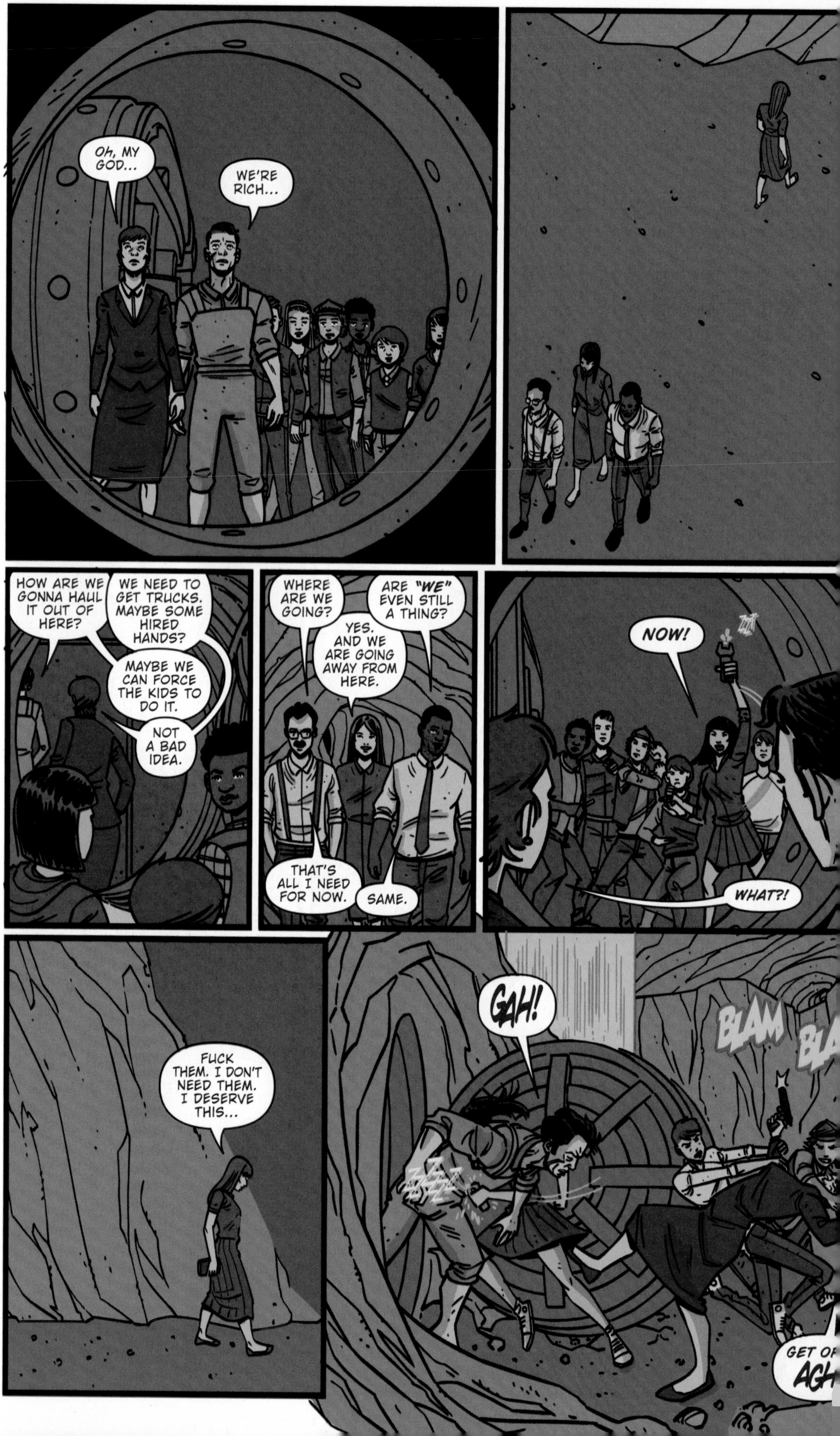

Oh, MY GOD...
WE'RE RICH...
HOW ARE WE GONNA HAUL IT OUT OF HERE?
WE NEED TO GET TRUCKS. MAYBE SOME HIRED HANDS?
MAYBE WE CAN FORCE THE KIDS TO DO IT.
NOT A BAD IDEA.
WHERE ARE WE GOING?
ARE "WE" EVEN STILL A THING?
YES. AND WE ARE GOING AWAY FROM HERE.
THAT'S ALL I NEED FOR NOW.
SAME.
NOW!
WHAT?!
FUCK THEM. I DON'T NEED THEM. I DESERVE THIS...
GAH!
BLAM

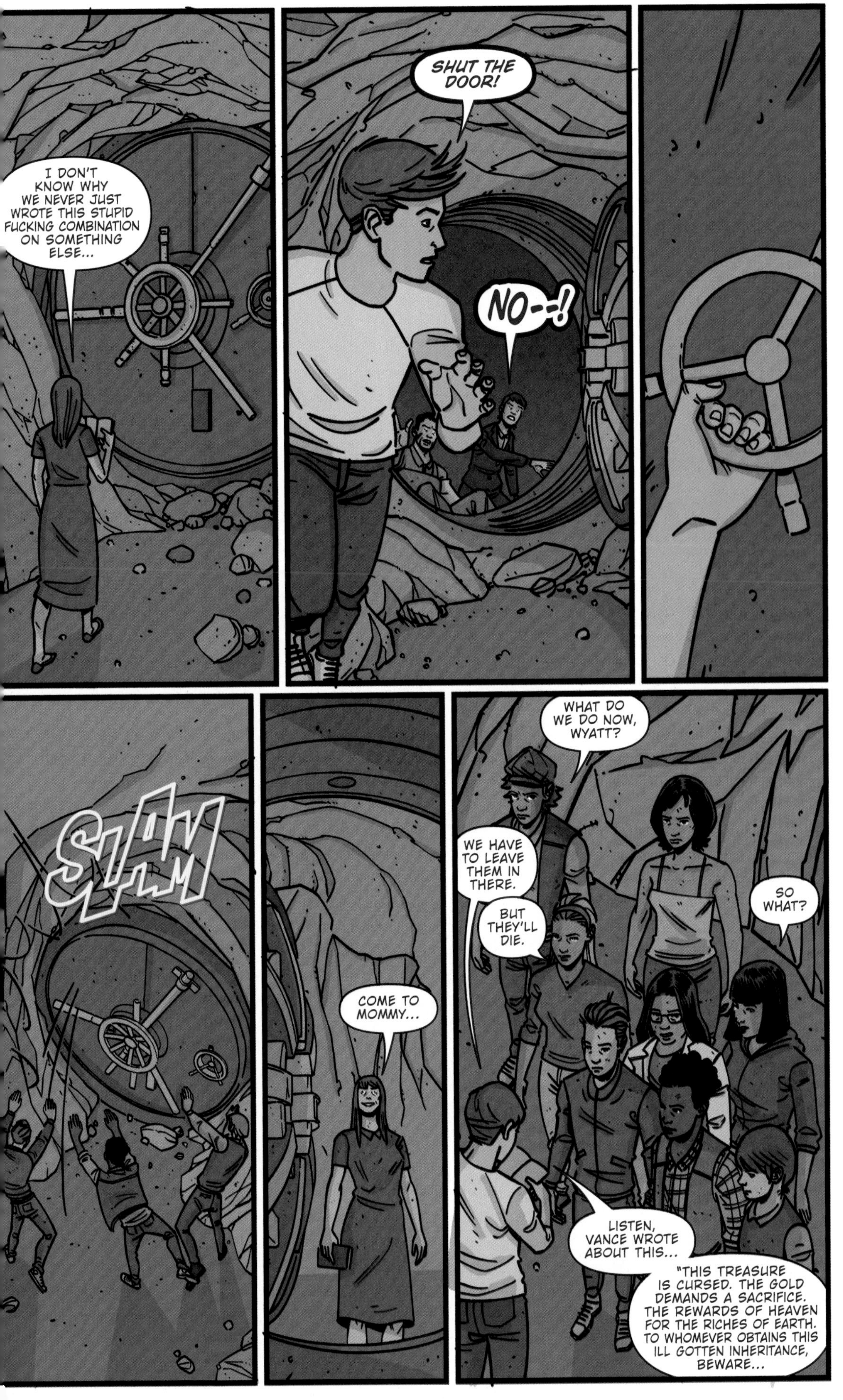
I DON'T KNOW WHY WE NEVER JUST WROTE THIS STUPID FUCKING COMBINATION ON SOMETHING ELSE...
SHUT THE DOOR!
NO--!
SLAM
COME TO MOMMY...
WHAT DO WE DO NOW, WYATT?
WE HAVE TO LEAVE THEM IN THERE.
BUT THEY'LL DIE.
SO WHAT?
LISTEN, VANCE WROTE ABOUT THIS...
"THIS TREASURE IS CURSED. THE GOLD DEMANDS A SACRIFICE. THE REWARDS OF HEAVEN FOR THE RICHES OF EARTH. TO WHOMEVER OBTAINS THIS ILL GOTTEN INHERITANCE, BEWARE...

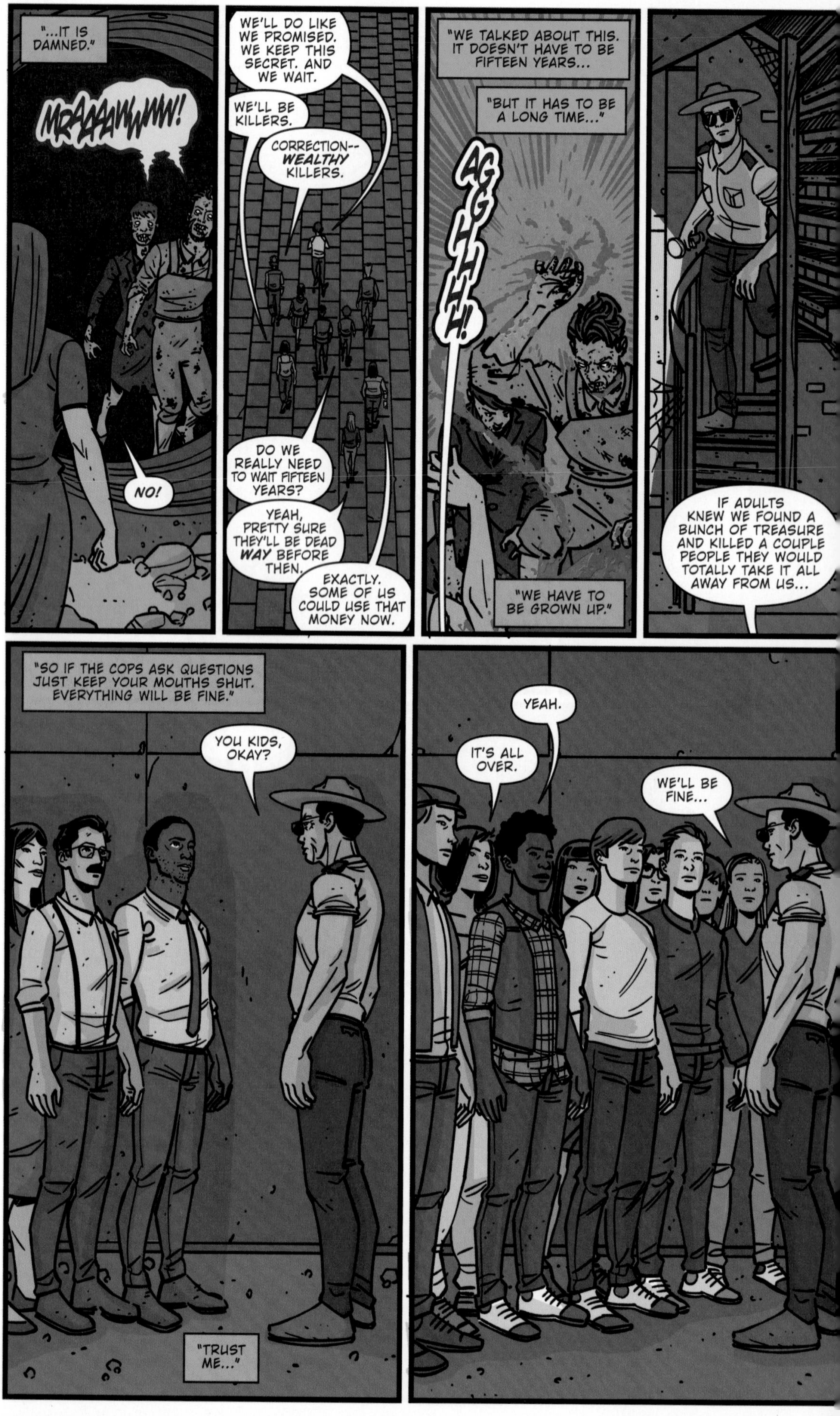
"...IT IS DAMNED."
MRAAAAWWWW!
NO!
WE'LL DO LIKE WE PROMISED. WE KEEP THIS SECRET. AND WE WAIT.
WE'LL BE KILLERS.
CORRECTION-- *WEALTHY* KILLERS.
DO WE REALLY NEED TO WAIT FIFTEEN YEARS?
YEAH, PRETTY SURE THEY'LL BE DEAD *WAY* BEFORE THEN.
EXACTLY. SOME OF US COULD USE THAT MONEY NOW.
"WE TALKED ABOUT THIS. IT DOESN'T HAVE TO BE FIFTEEN YEARS...
"BUT IT HAS TO BE A LONG TIME..."
AGGHHHH!
"WE HAVE TO BE GROWN UP."
IF ADULTS KNEW WE FOUND A BUNCH OF TREASURE AND KILLED A COUPLE PEOPLE THEY WOULD TOTALLY TAKE IT ALL AWAY FROM US...
"SO IF THE COPS ASK QUESTIONS JUST KEEP YOUR MOUTHS SHUT. EVERYTHING WILL BE FINE."
YOU KIDS, OKAY?
"TRUST ME..."
YEAH.
IT'S ALL OVER.
WE'LL BE FINE...

CULT CLASSIC

COVER GALLERY

FEATURING FELIPE CUNHA & IRENE KOH

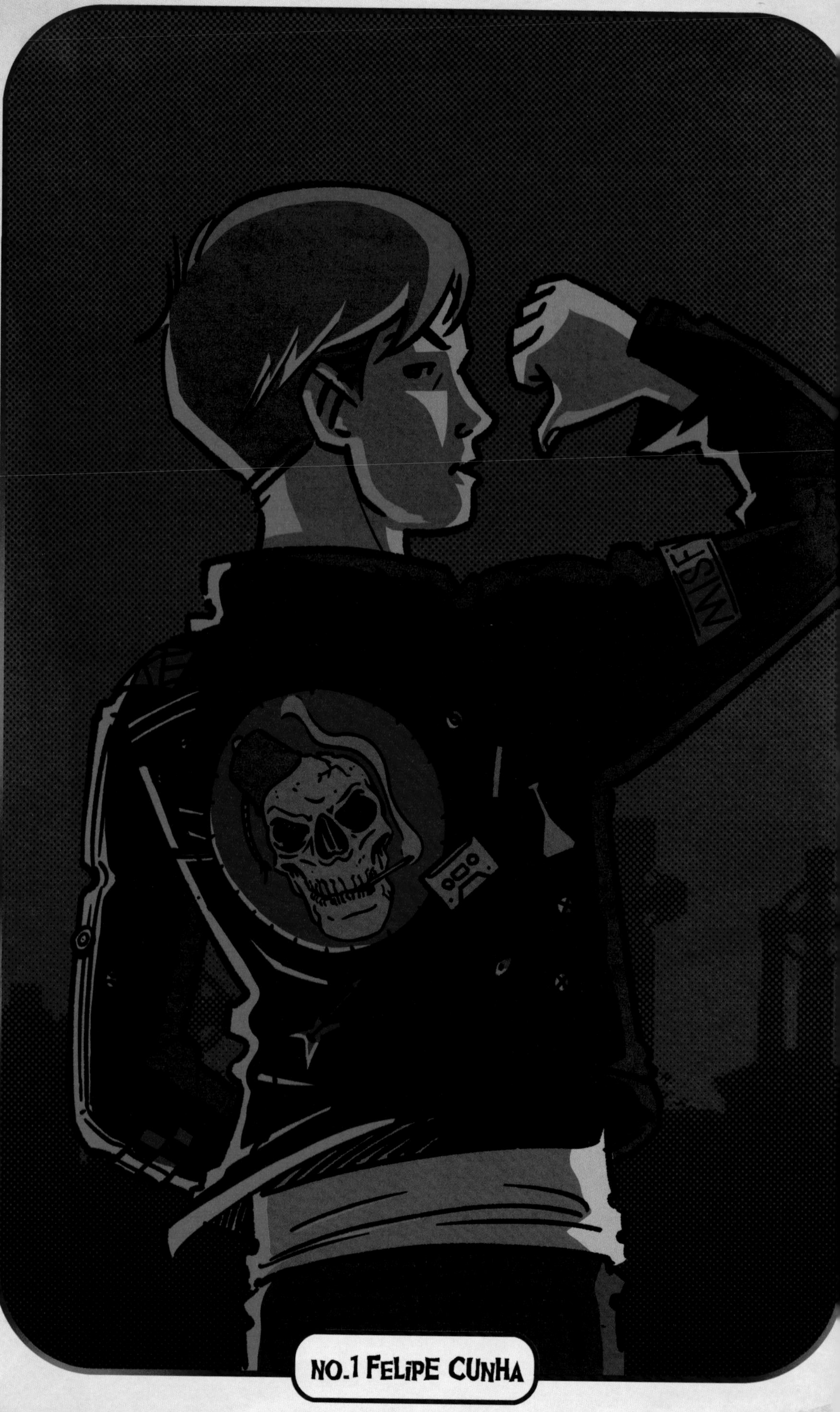
MISF

NO.1 FELIPE CUNHA

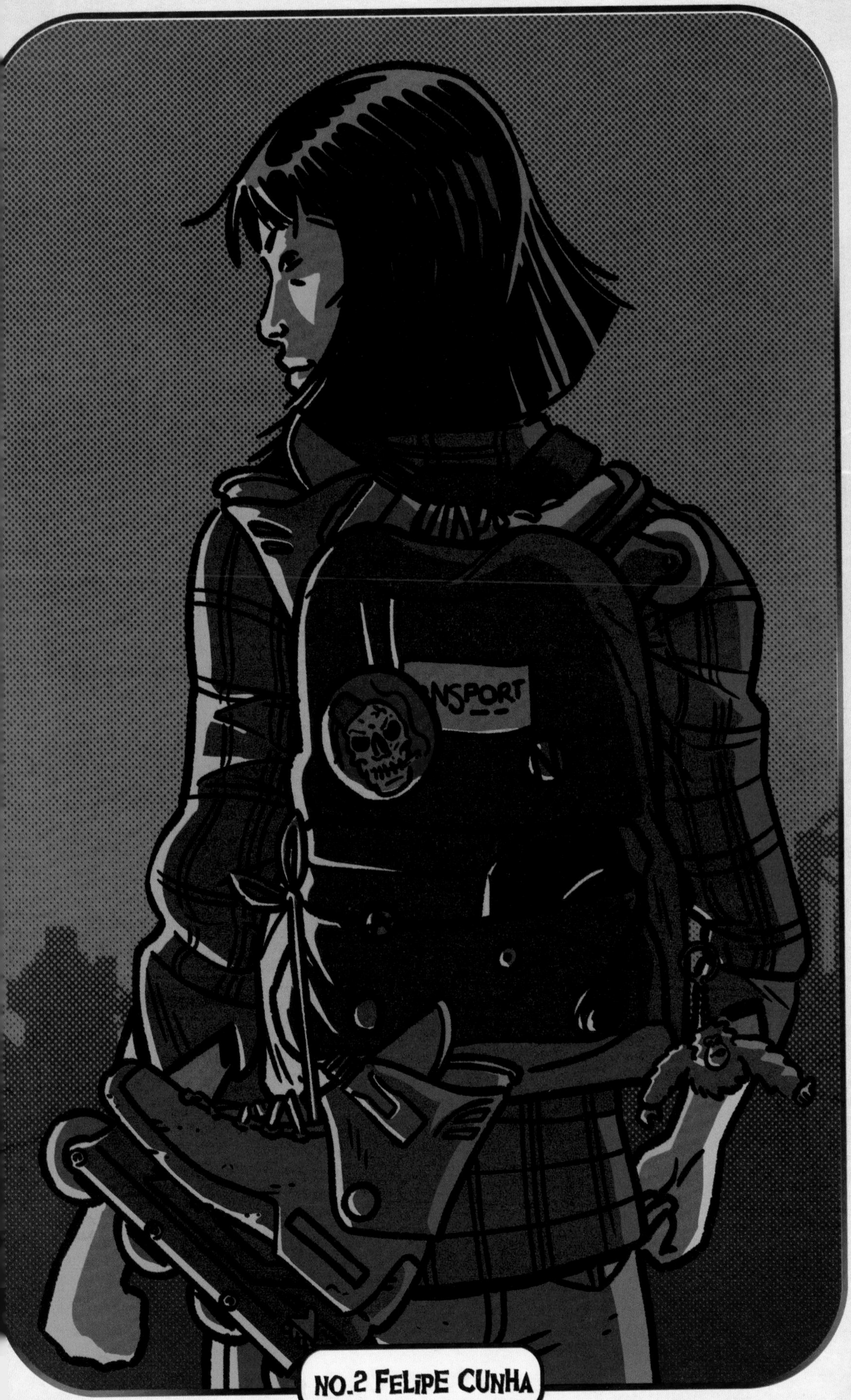
NSPORT

NO.2 FELIPE CUNHA

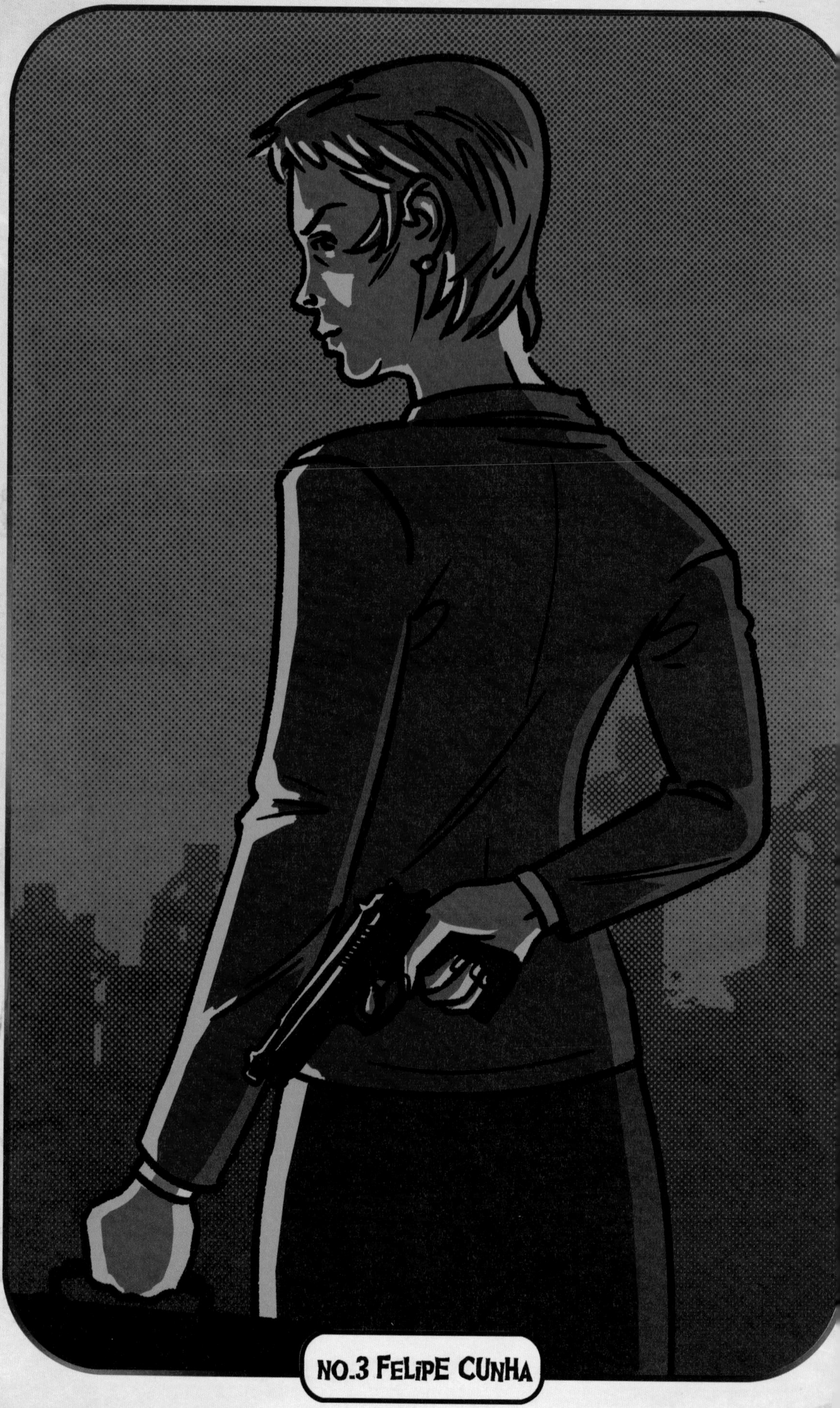
NO.3 FELIPE CUNHA

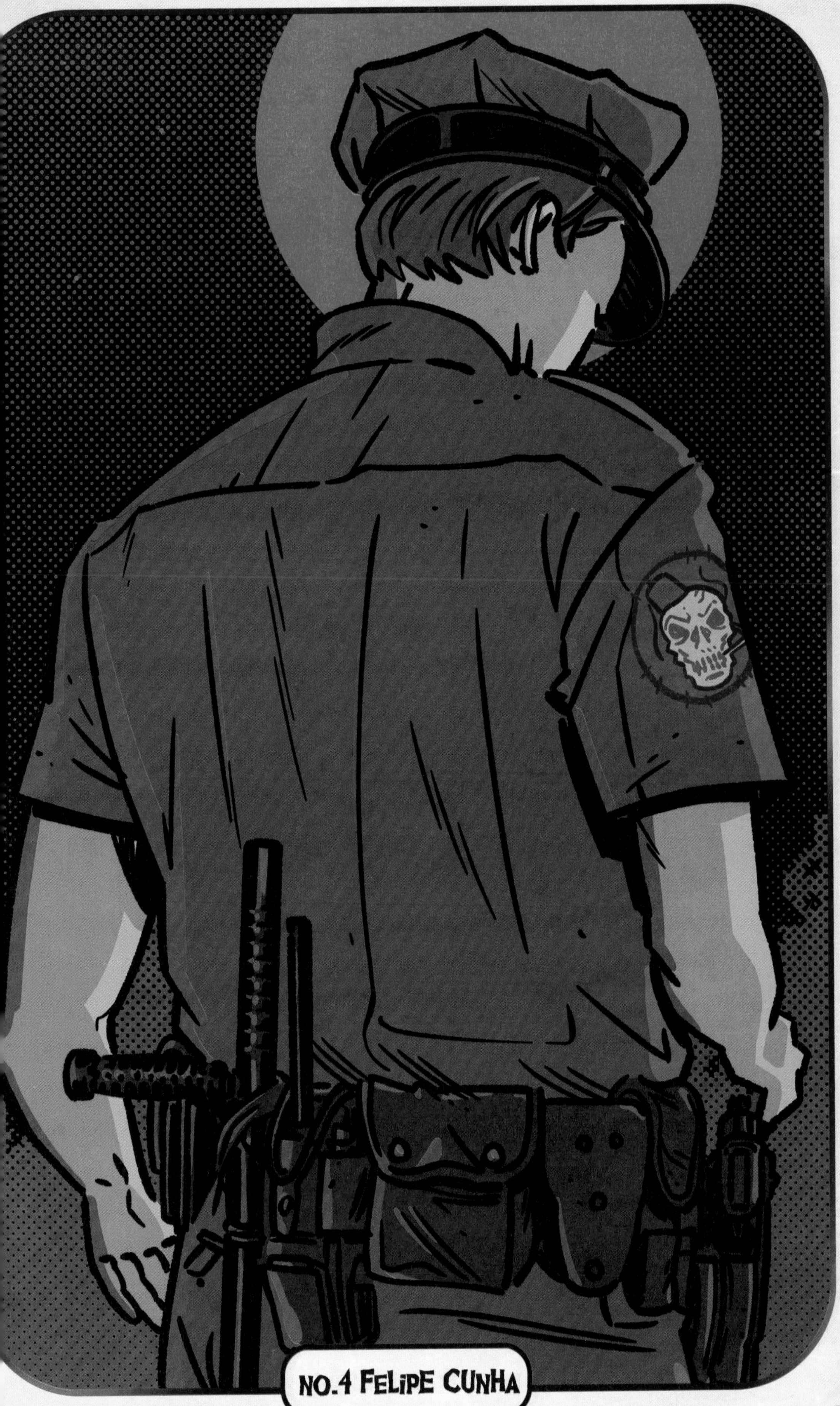
NO.4 FELIPE CUNHA

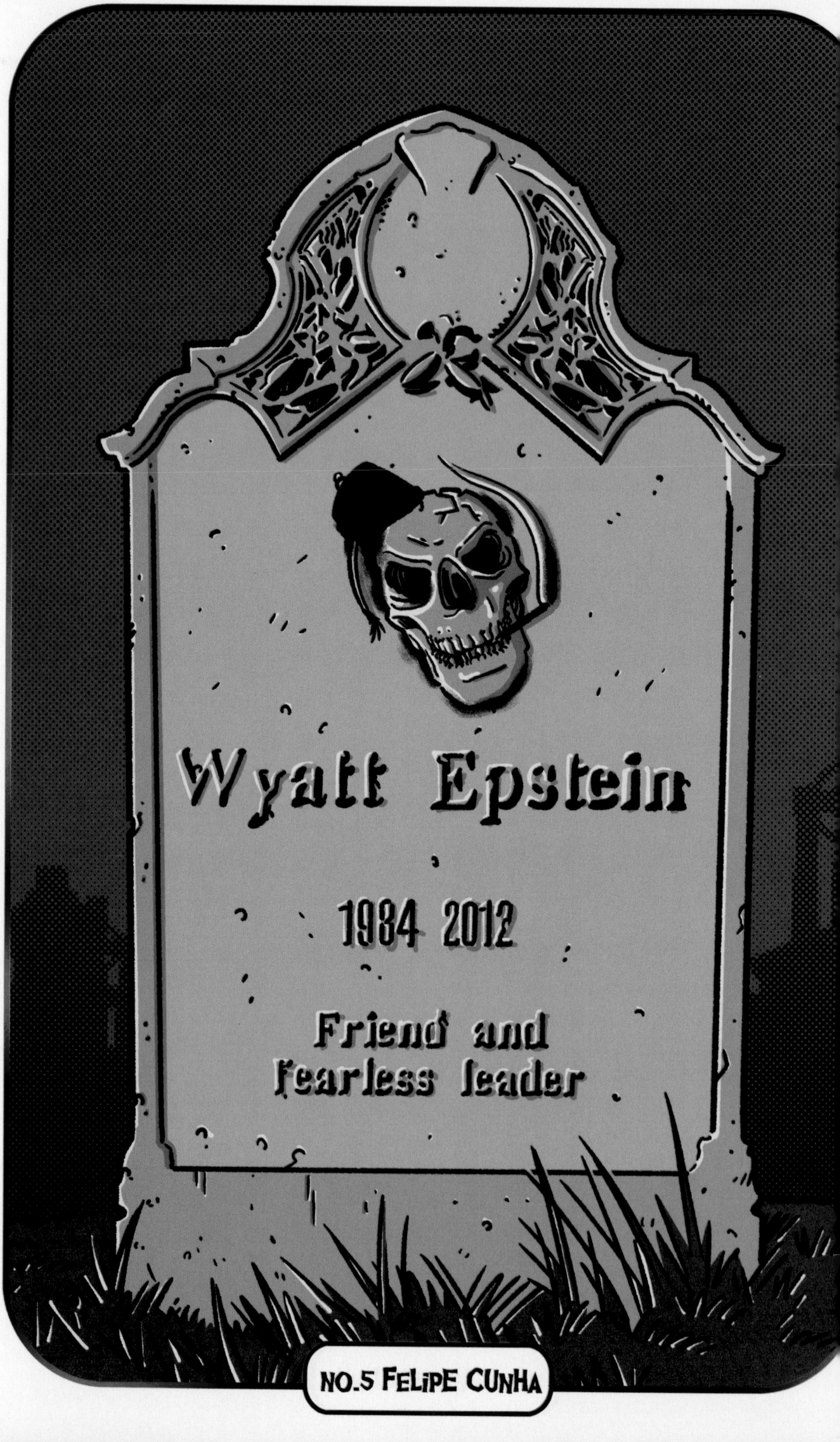
Wyatt Epstein
1984 2012
Friend and
fearless leader
NO.5 FELIPE CUNHA

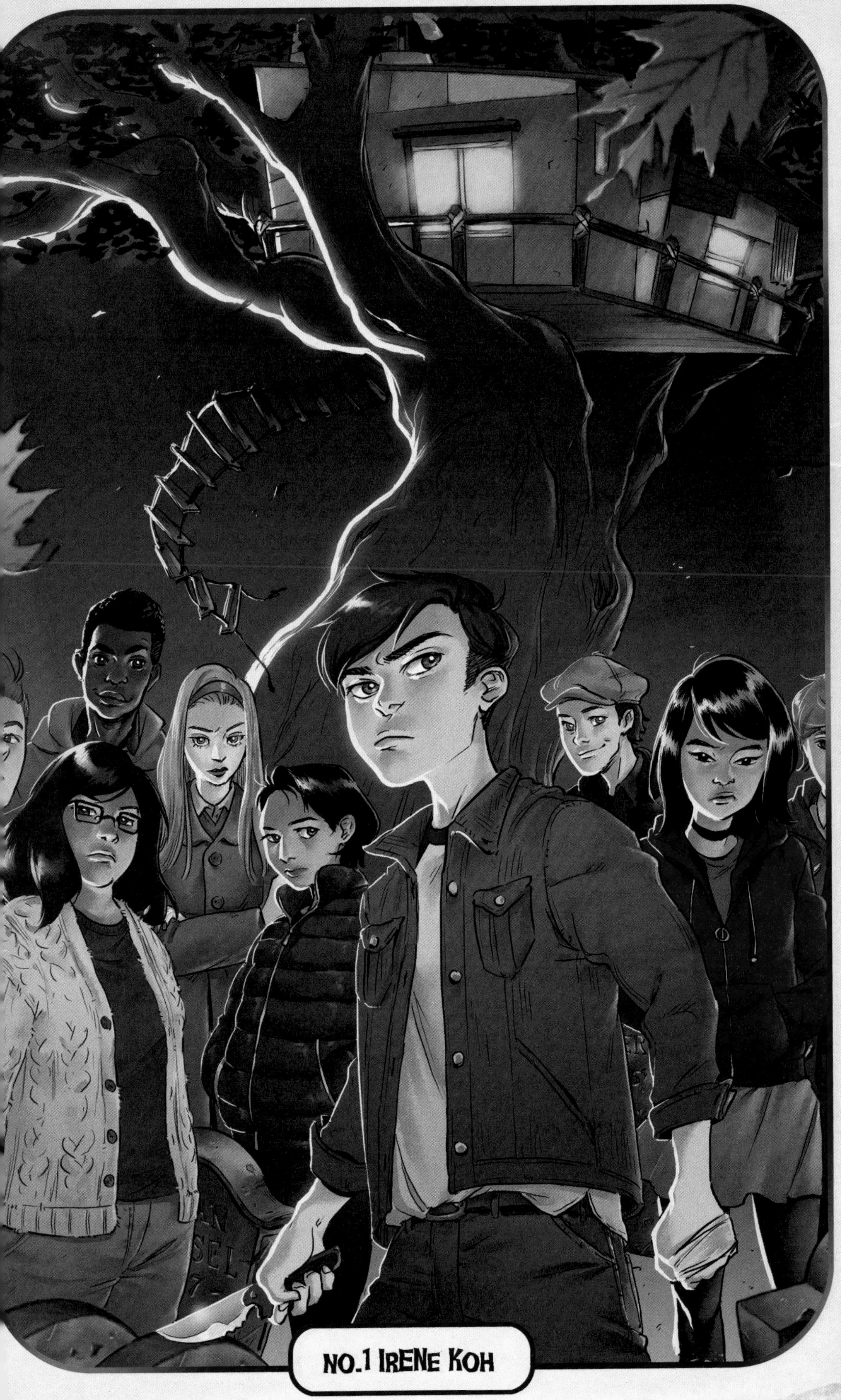
NO.1 IRENE KOH

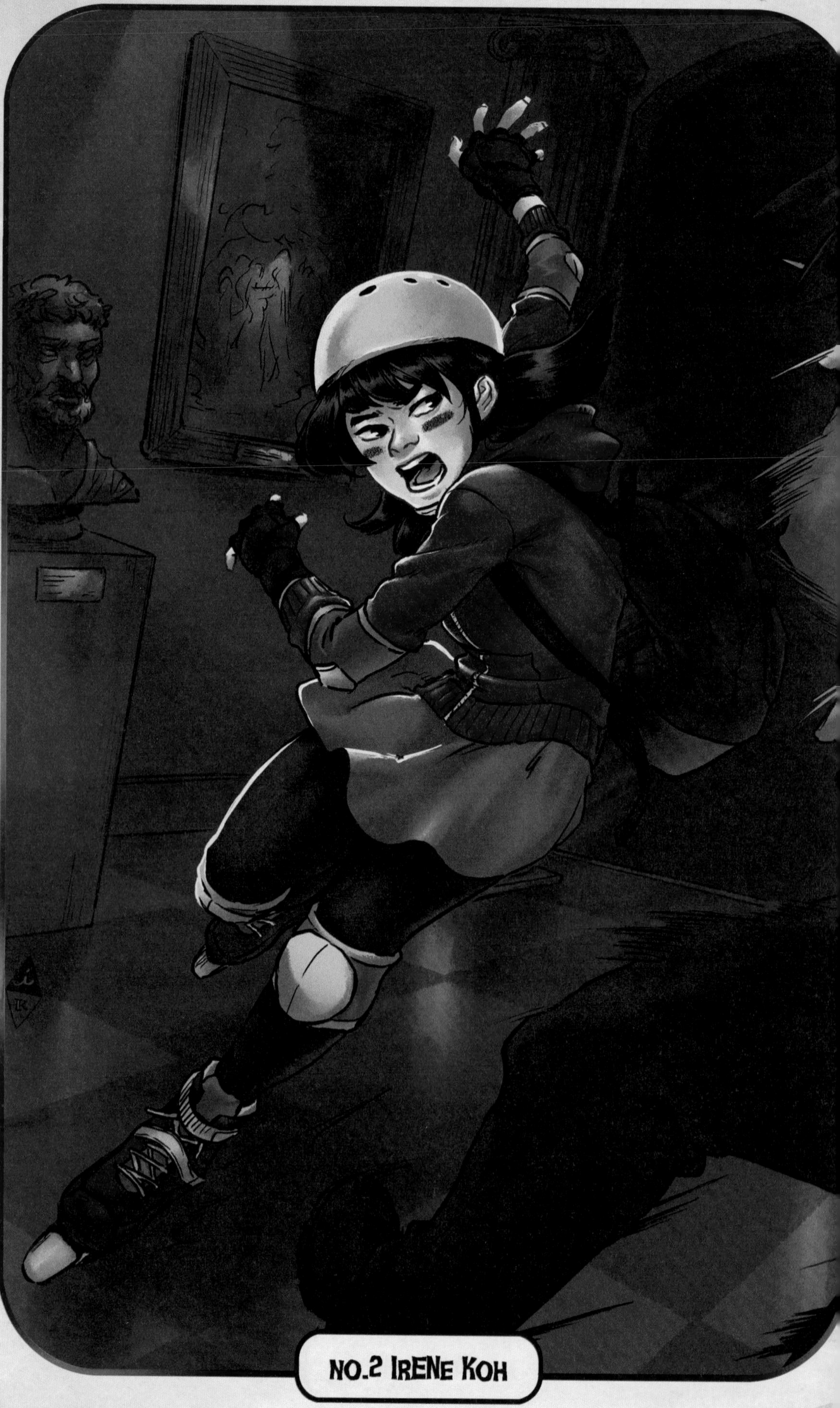

NO.2 IRENE KOH

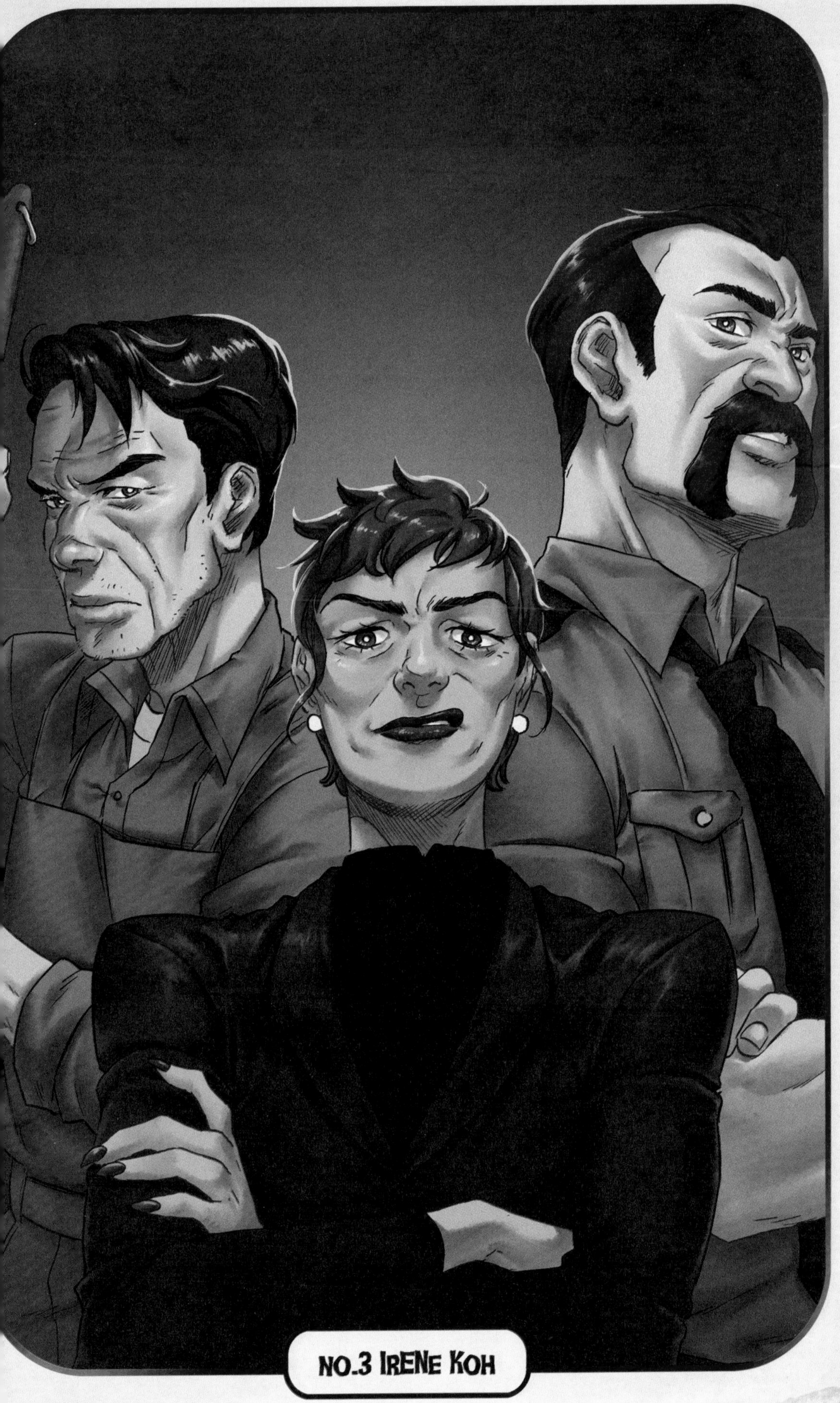
NO.3 IRENE KOH

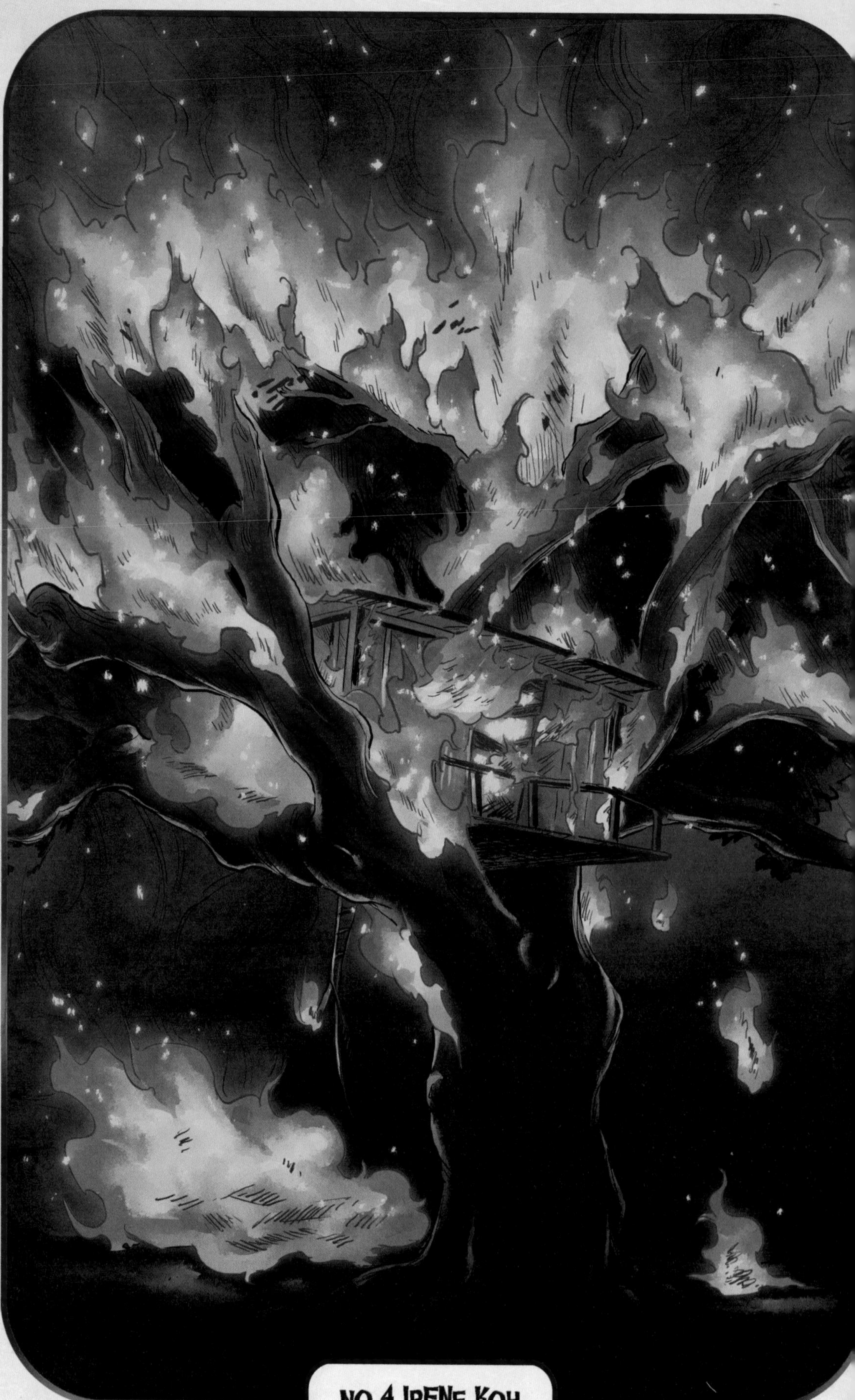

NO.4 IRENE KOH

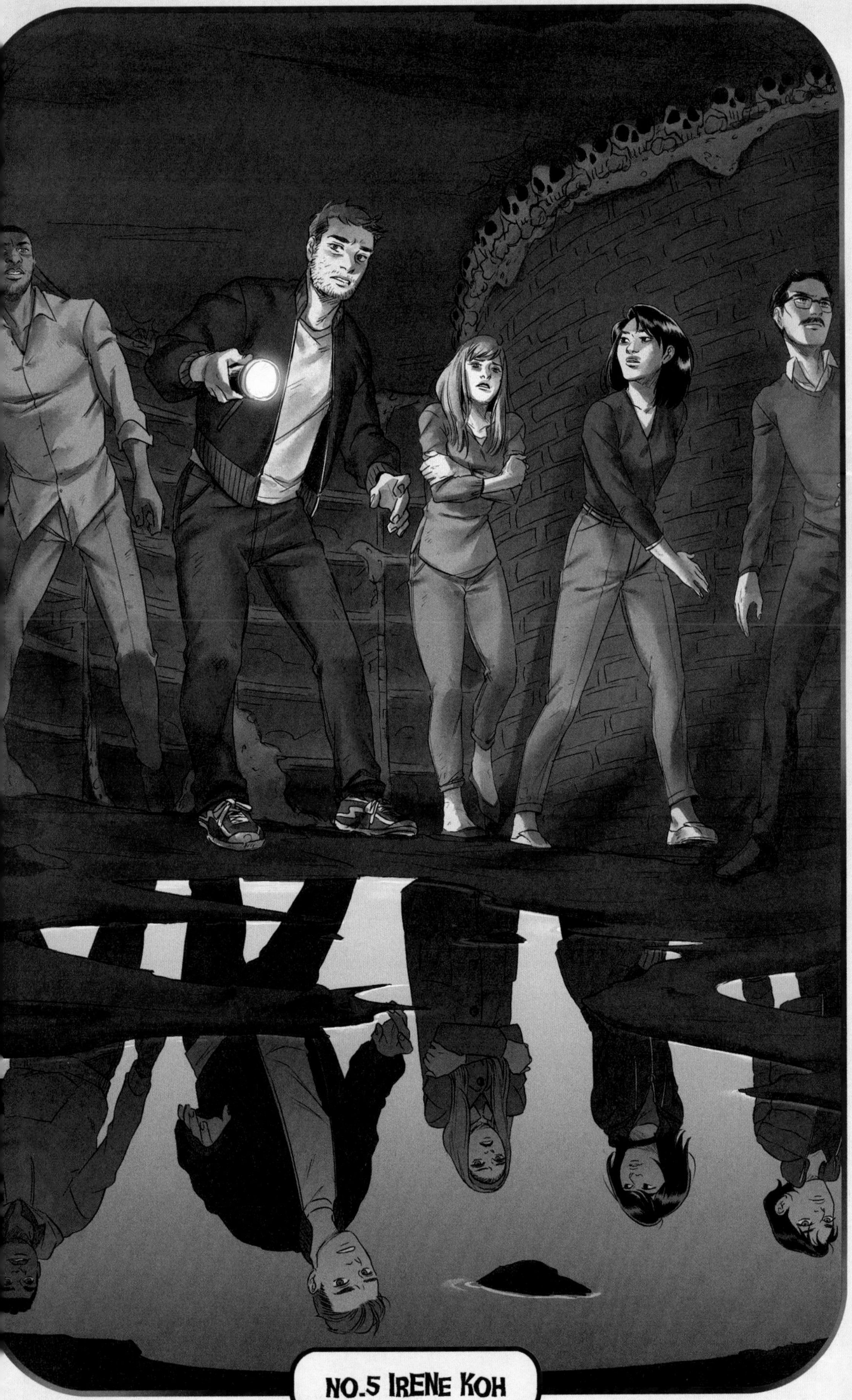

NO.5 IRENE KOH

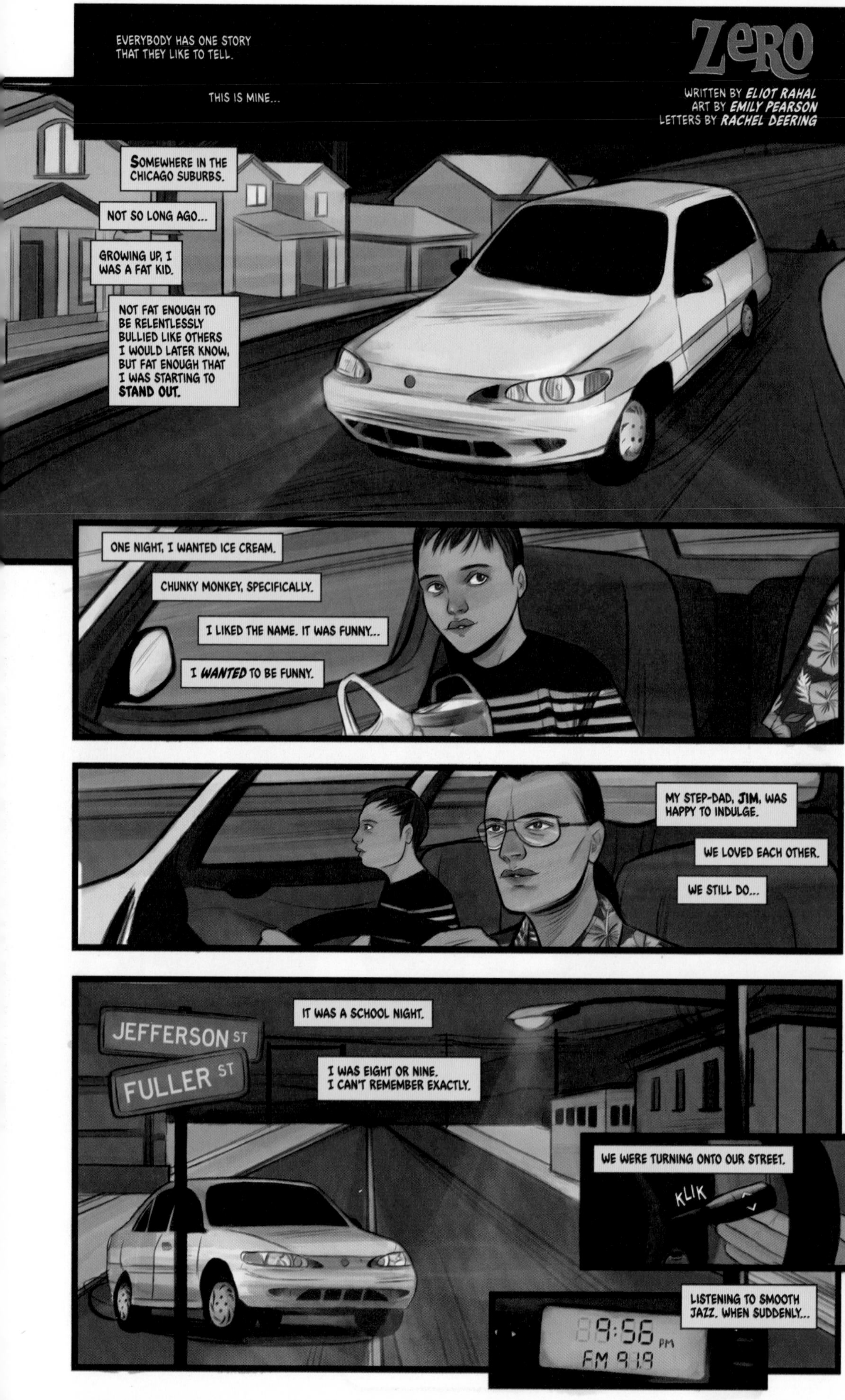
EVERYBODY HAS ONE STORY THAT THEY LIKE TO TELL.
THIS IS MINE...
ZERO
WRITTEN BY ELIOT RAHAL
ART BY EMILY PEARSON
LETTERS BY RACHEL DEERING
SOMEWHERE IN THE CHICAGO SUBURBS.
NOT SO LONG AGO...
GROWING UP, I WAS A FAT KID.
NOT FAT ENOUGH TO BE RELENTLESSLY BULLIED LIKE OTHERS I WOULD LATER KNOW, BUT FAT ENOUGH THAT I WAS STARTING TO STAND OUT.
ONE NIGHT, I WANTED ICE CREAM.
CHUNKY MONKEY, SPECIFICALLY.
I LIKED THE NAME. IT WAS FUNNY...
I WANTED TO BE FUNNY.
MY STEP-DAD, JIM, WAS HAPPY TO INDULGE.
WE LOVED EACH OTHER.
WE STILL DO...
JEFFERSON ST
FULLER ST
IT WAS A SCHOOL NIGHT.
I WAS EIGHT OR NINE. I CAN'T REMEMBER EXACTLY.
WE WERE TURNING ONTO OUR STREET.
KLIK
LISTENING TO SMOOTH JAZZ. WHEN SUDDENLY...
9:56 PM
FM 91.9

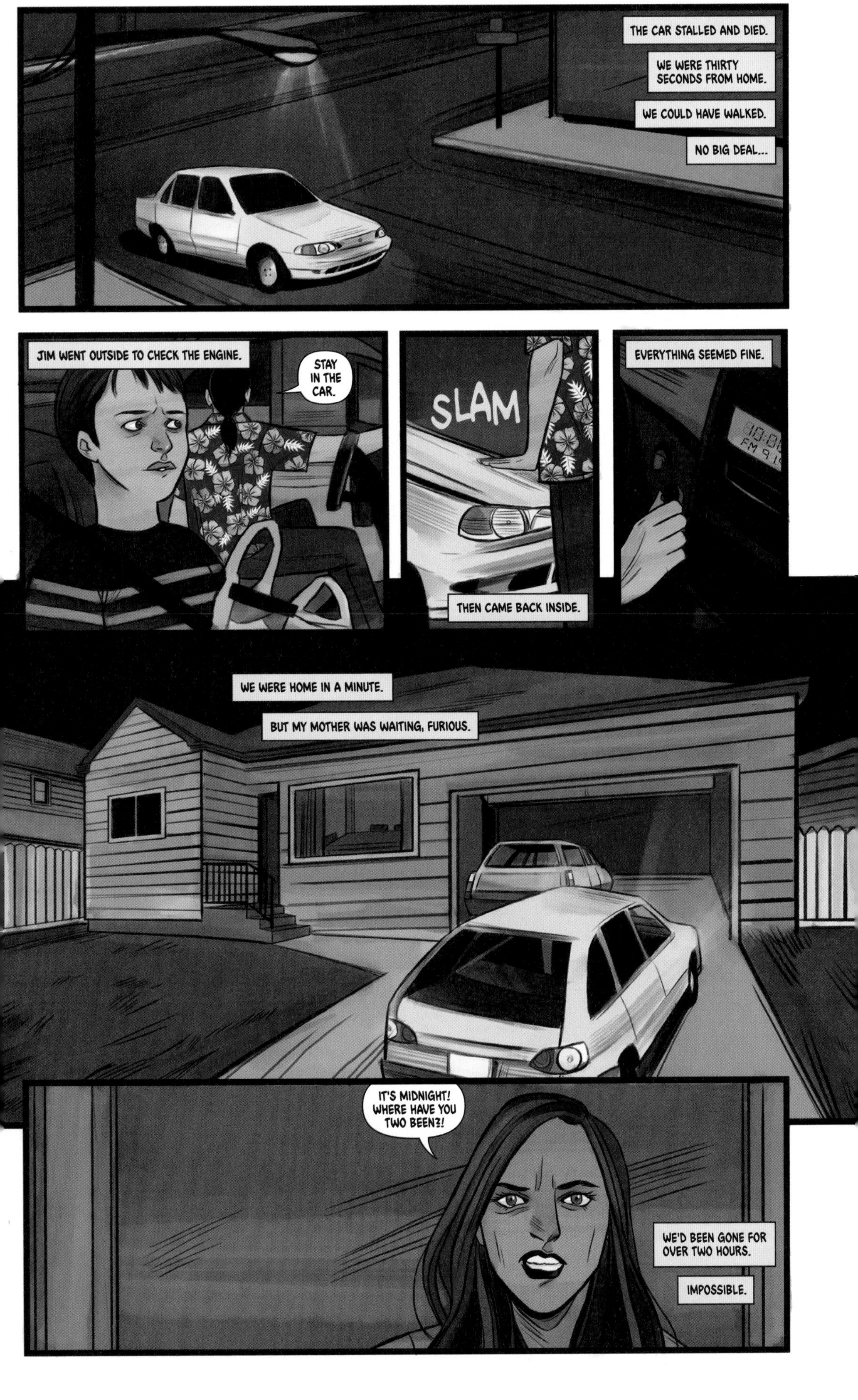

THE CAR STALLED AND DIED.
WE WERE THIRTY SECONDS FROM HOME.
WE COULD HAVE WALKED.
NO BIG DEAL...
JIM WENT OUTSIDE TO CHECK THE ENGINE.
STAY IN THE CAR.
SLAM
THEN CAME BACK INSIDE.
EVERYTHING SEEMED FINE.
WE WERE HOME IN A MINUTE.
BUT MY MOTHER WAS WAITING, FURIOUS.
IT'S MIDNIGHT! WHERE HAVE YOU TWO BEEN?!
WE'D BEEN GONE FOR OVER TWO HOURS.
IMPOSSIBLE.

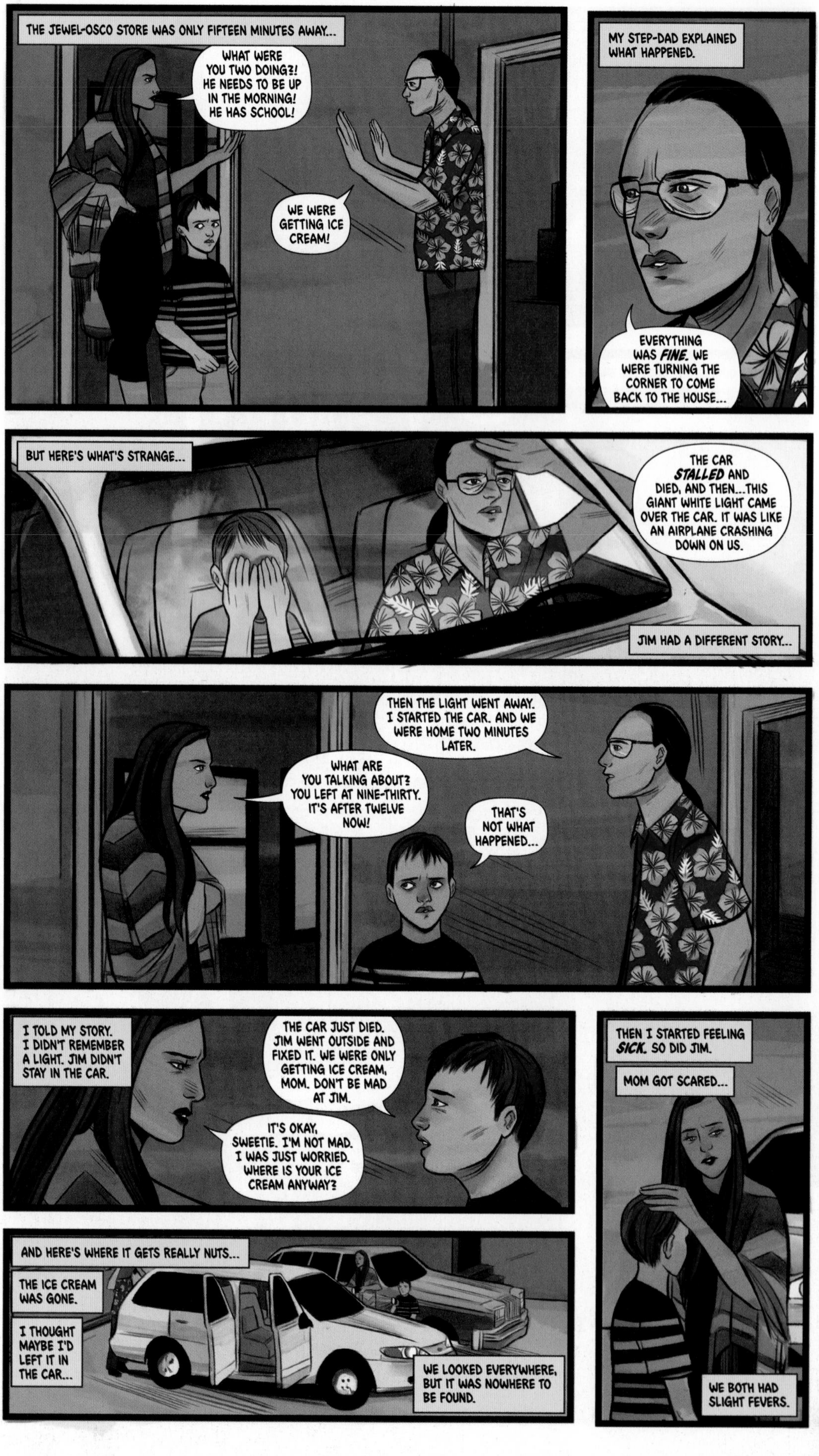
THE JEWEL-OSCO STORE WAS ONLY FIFTEEN MINUTES AWAY...
WHAT WERE YOU TWO DOING?! HE NEEDS TO BE UP IN THE MORNING! HE HAS SCHOOL!
WE WERE GETTING ICE CREAM!
MY STEP-DAD EXPLAINED WHAT HAPPENED.
EVERYTHING WAS FINE. WE WERE TURNING THE CORNER TO COME BACK TO THE HOUSE...
BUT HERE'S WHAT'S STRANGE...
THE CAR STALLED AND DIED, AND THEN...THIS GIANT WHITE LIGHT CAME OVER THE CAR. IT WAS LIKE AN AIRPLANE CRASHING DOWN ON US.
JIM HAD A DIFFERENT STORY...
THEN THE LIGHT WENT AWAY. I STARTED THE CAR. AND WE WERE HOME TWO MINUTES LATER.
WHAT ARE YOU TALKING ABOUT? YOU LEFT AT NINE-THIRTY. IT'S AFTER TWELVE NOW!
THAT'S NOT WHAT HAPPENED...
I TOLD MY STORY. I DIDN'T REMEMBER A LIGHT. JIM DIDN'T STAY IN THE CAR.
THE CAR JUST DIED. JIM WENT OUTSIDE AND FIXED IT. WE WERE ONLY GETTING ICE CREAM, MOM. DON'T BE MAD AT JIM.
IT'S OKAY, SWEETIE. I'M NOT MAD. I WAS JUST WORRIED. WHERE IS YOUR ICE CREAM ANYWAY?
AND HERE'S WHERE IT GETS REALLY NUTS...
THE ICE CREAM WAS GONE.
I THOUGHT MAYBE I'D LEFT IT IN THE CAR...
WE LOOKED EVERYWHERE, BUT IT WAS NOWHERE TO BE FOUND.
THEN I STARTED FEELING SICK. SO DID JIM.
MOM GOT SCARED...
WE BOTH HAD SLIGHT FEVERS.

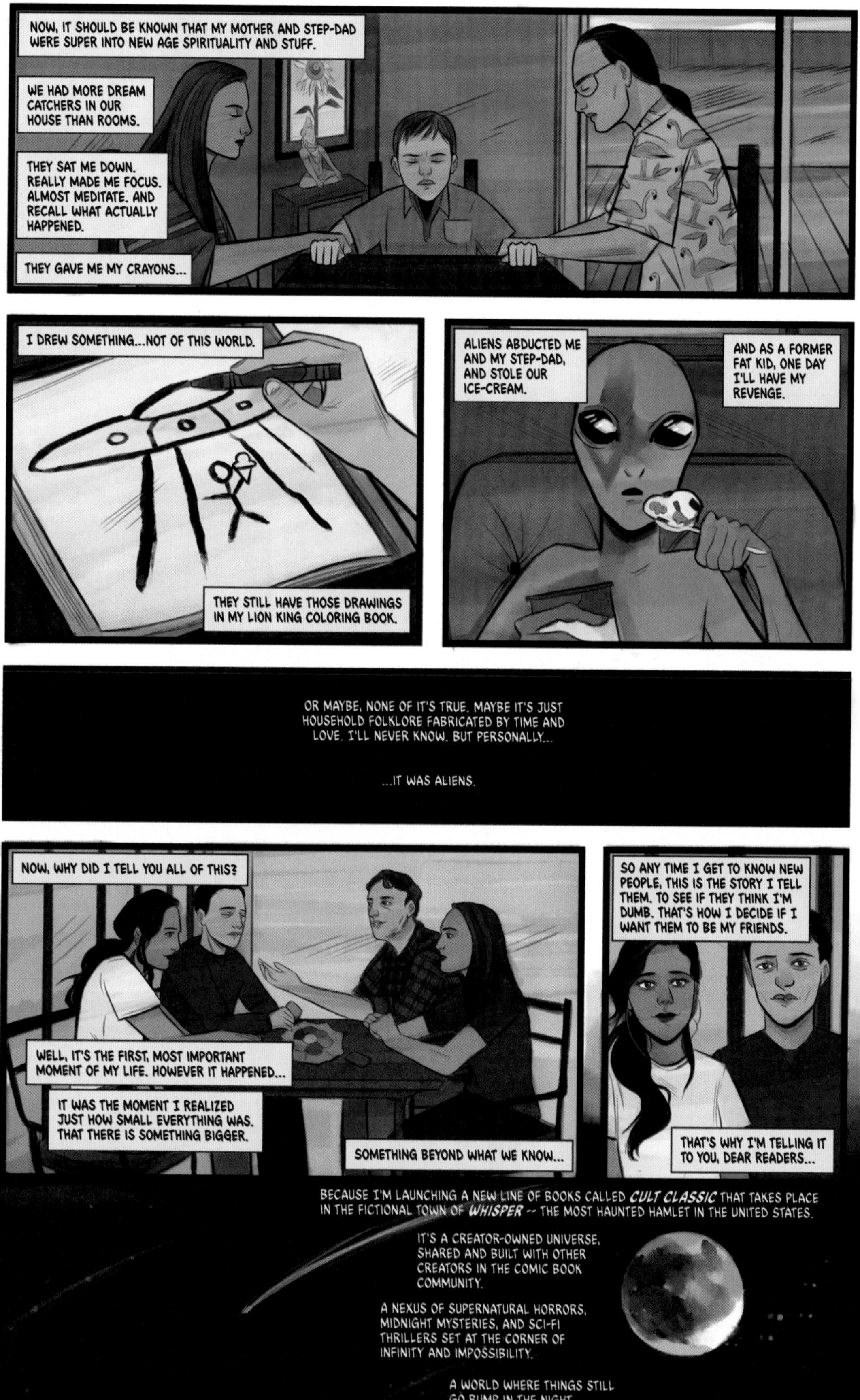
NOW, IT SHOULD BE KNOWN THAT MY MOTHER AND STEP-DAD WERE SUPER INTO NEW AGE SPIRITUALITY AND STUFF.
WE HAD MORE DREAM CATCHERS IN OUR HOUSE THAN ROOMS.
THEY SAT ME DOWN. REALLY MADE ME FOCUS. ALMOST MEDITATE. AND RECALL WHAT ACTUALLY HAPPENED.
THEY GAVE ME MY CRAYONS...
I DREW SOMETHING...NOT OF THIS WORLD.
THEY STILL HAVE THOSE DRAWINGS IN MY LION KING COLORING BOOK.
ALIENS ABDUCTED ME AND MY STEP-DAD, AND STOLE OUR ICE-CREAM.
AND AS A FORMER FAT KID, ONE DAY I'LL HAVE MY REVENGE.
OR MAYBE, NONE OF IT'S TRUE. MAYBE IT'S JUST HOUSEHOLD FOLKLORE FABRICATED BY TIME AND LOVE. I'LL NEVER KNOW. BUT PERSONALLY...
...IT WAS ALIENS.
NOW, WHY DID I TELL YOU ALL OF THIS?
WELL, IT'S THE FIRST, MOST IMPORTANT MOMENT OF MY LIFE. HOWEVER IT HAPPENED...
IT WAS THE MOMENT I REALIZED JUST HOW SMALL EVERYTHING WAS. THAT THERE IS SOMETHING BIGGER.
SOMETHING BEYOND WHAT WE KNOW...
SO ANY TIME I GET TO KNOW NEW PEOPLE, THIS IS THE STORY I TELL THEM. TO SEE IF THEY THINK I'M DUMB. THAT'S HOW I DECIDE IF I WANT THEM TO BE MY FRIENDS.
THAT'S WHY I'M TELLING IT TO YOU, DEAR READERS...
BECAUSE I'M LAUNCHING A NEW LINE OF BOOKS CALLED CULT CLASSIC THAT TAKES PLACE IN THE FICTIONAL TOWN OF WHISPER -- THE MOST HAUNTED HAMLET IN THE UNITED STATES.
IT'S A CREATOR-OWNED UNIVERSE, SHARED AND BUILT WITH OTHER CREATORS IN THE COMIC BOOK COMMUNITY.
A NEXUS OF SUPERNATURAL HORRORS, MIDNIGHT MYSTERIES, AND SCI-FI THRILLERS SET AT THE CORNER OF INFINITY AND IMPOSSIBILITY.
A WORLD WHERE THINGS STILL

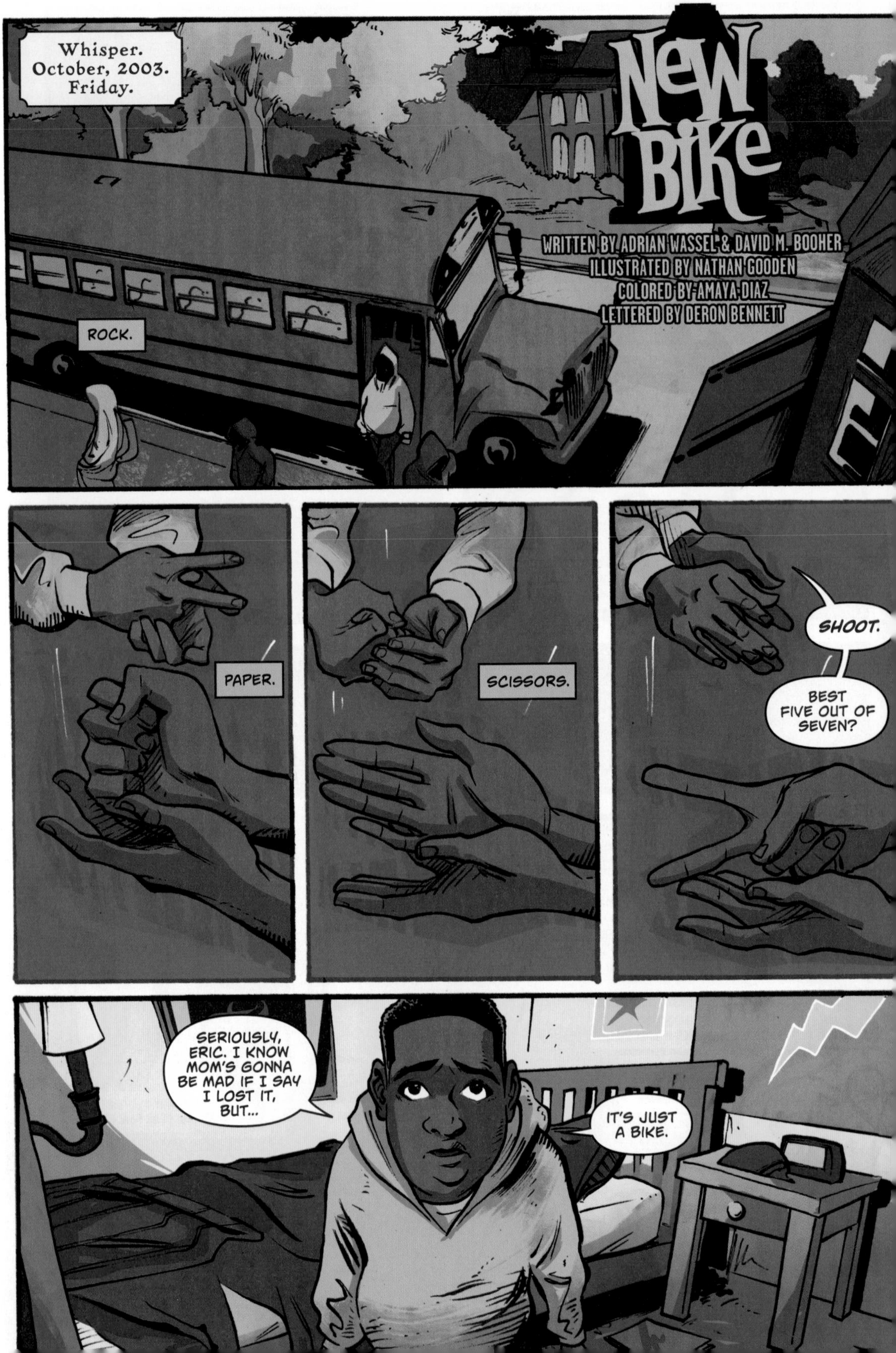
Whisper.
October, 2003.
Friday.
NEW BIKE
WRITTEN BY ADRIAN WASSEL & DAVID M. BOOHER
ILLUSTRATED BY NATHAN GOODEN
COLORED BY AMAYA DIAZ
LETTERED BY DERON BENNETT
ROCK.
PAPER.
SCISSORS.
SHOOT.
BEST FIVE OUT OF SEVEN?
SERIOUSLY, ERIC. I KNOW MOM'S GONNA BE MAD IF I SAY I LOST IT, BUT...
IT'S JUST A BIKE.

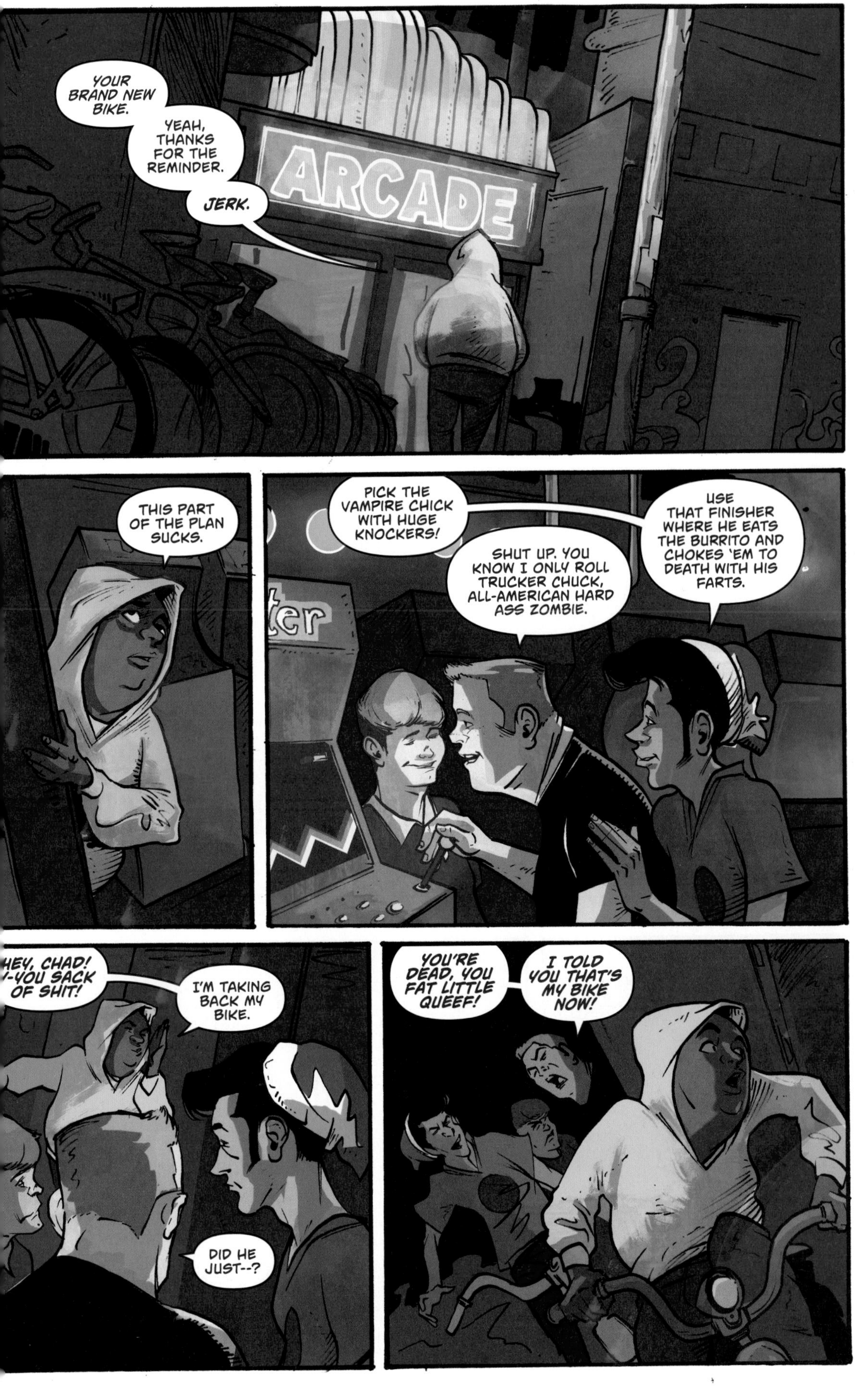
YOUR BRAND NEW BIKE.
YEAH, THANKS FOR THE REMINDER.
JERK.
ARCADE
THIS PART OF THE PLAN SUCKS.
PICK THE VAMPIRE CHICK WITH HUGE KNOCKERS!
USE THAT FINISHER WHERE HE EATS THE BURRITO AND CHOKES 'EM TO DEATH WITH HIS FARTS.
SHUT UP. YOU KNOW I ONLY ROLL TRUCKER CHUCK, ALL-AMERICAN HARD ASS ZOMBIE.
HEY, CHAD! -YOU SACK OF SHIT!
I'M TAKING BACK MY BIKE.
DID HE JUST--?
YOU'RE DEAD, YOU FAT LITTLE QUEEF!
I TOLD YOU THAT'S MY BIKE NOW!

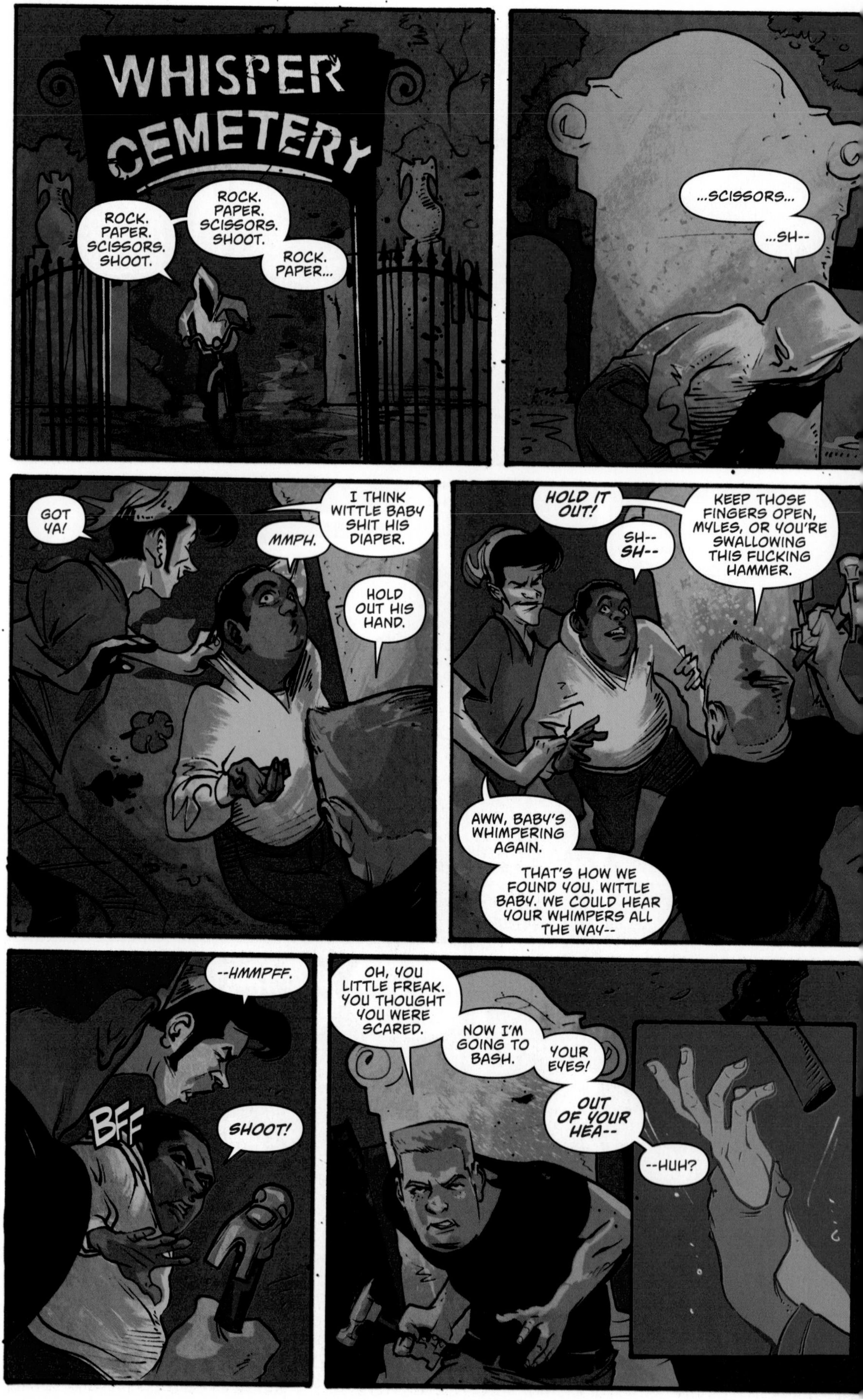
WHISPER CEMETERY
ROCK. PAPER. SCISSORS. SHOOT.
ROCK. PAPER. SCISSORS. SHOOT.
ROCK. PAPER...
...SCISSORS...
...SH--
GOT YA!
I THINK WITTLE BABY SHIT HIS DIAPER.
MMPH.
HOLD OUT HIS HAND.
HOLD IT OUT!
SH-- SH--
KEEP THOSE FINGERS OPEN, MYLES, OR YOU'RE SWALLOWING THIS FUCKING HAMMER.
AWW, BABY'S WHIMPERING AGAIN.
THAT'S HOW WE FOUND YOU, WITTLE BABY. WE COULD HEAR YOUR WHIMPERS ALL THE WAY--
--HMMPFF.
BFF
SHOOT!
OH, YOU LITTLE FREAK. YOU THOUGHT YOU WERE SCARED.
NOW I'M GOING TO BASH.
YOUR EYES!
OUT OF YOUR HEA--
--HUH?

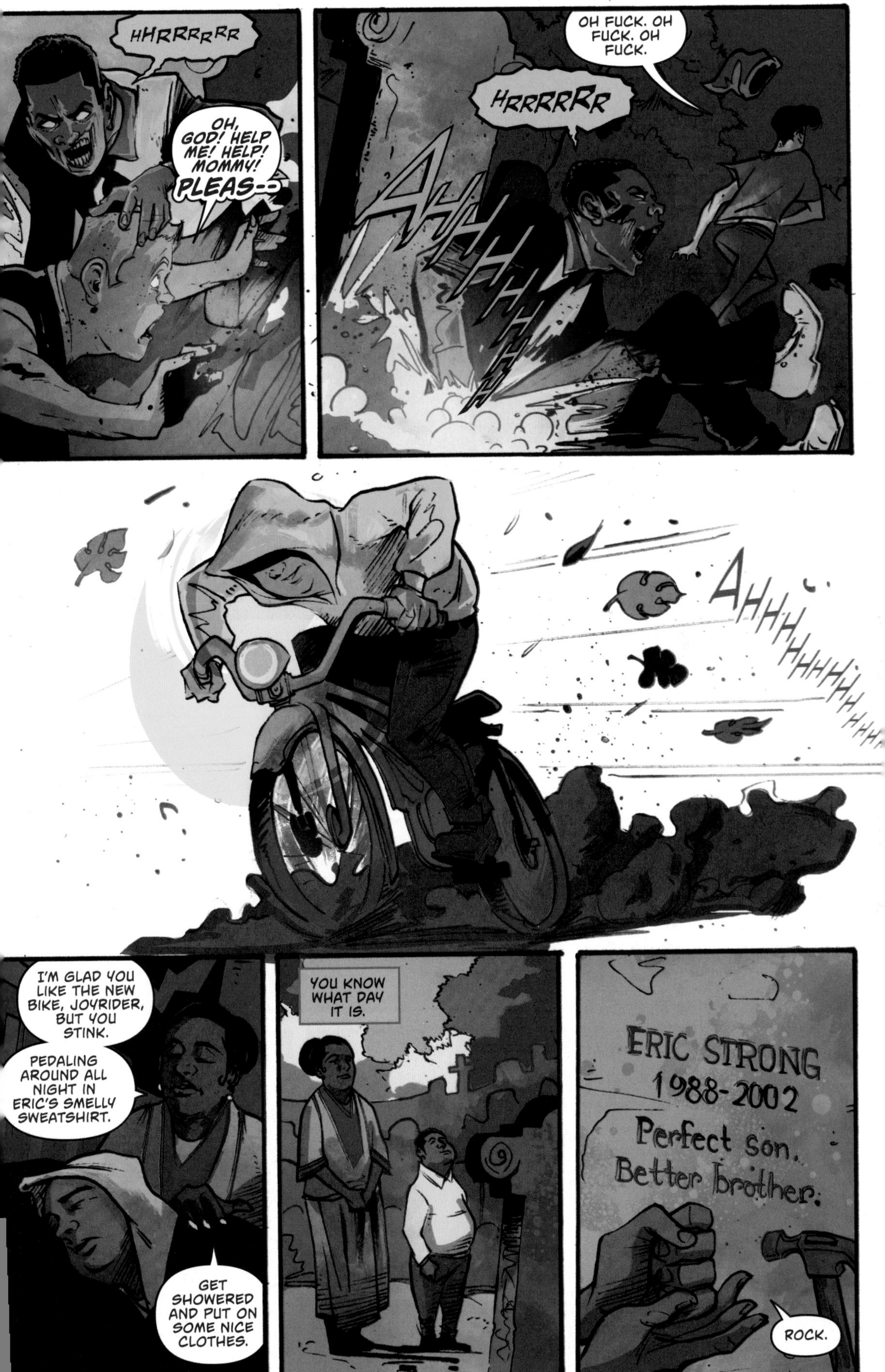
HHRRRRRR
OH, GOD! HELP ME! HELP! MOMMY! PLEAS--
OH FUCK. OH FUCK. OH FUCK.
HRRRRRR
AHHHHHHHH
AHHHHHHHHHHHH
I'M GLAD YOU LIKE THE NEW BIKE, JOYRIDER, BUT YOU STINK.
PEDALING AROUND ALL NIGHT IN ERIC'S SMELLY SWEATSHIRT.
GET SHOWERED AND PUT ON SOME NICE CLOTHES.
YOU KNOW WHAT DAY IT IS.
ERIC STRONG
1988-2002
Perfect son.
Better brother.
ROCK.

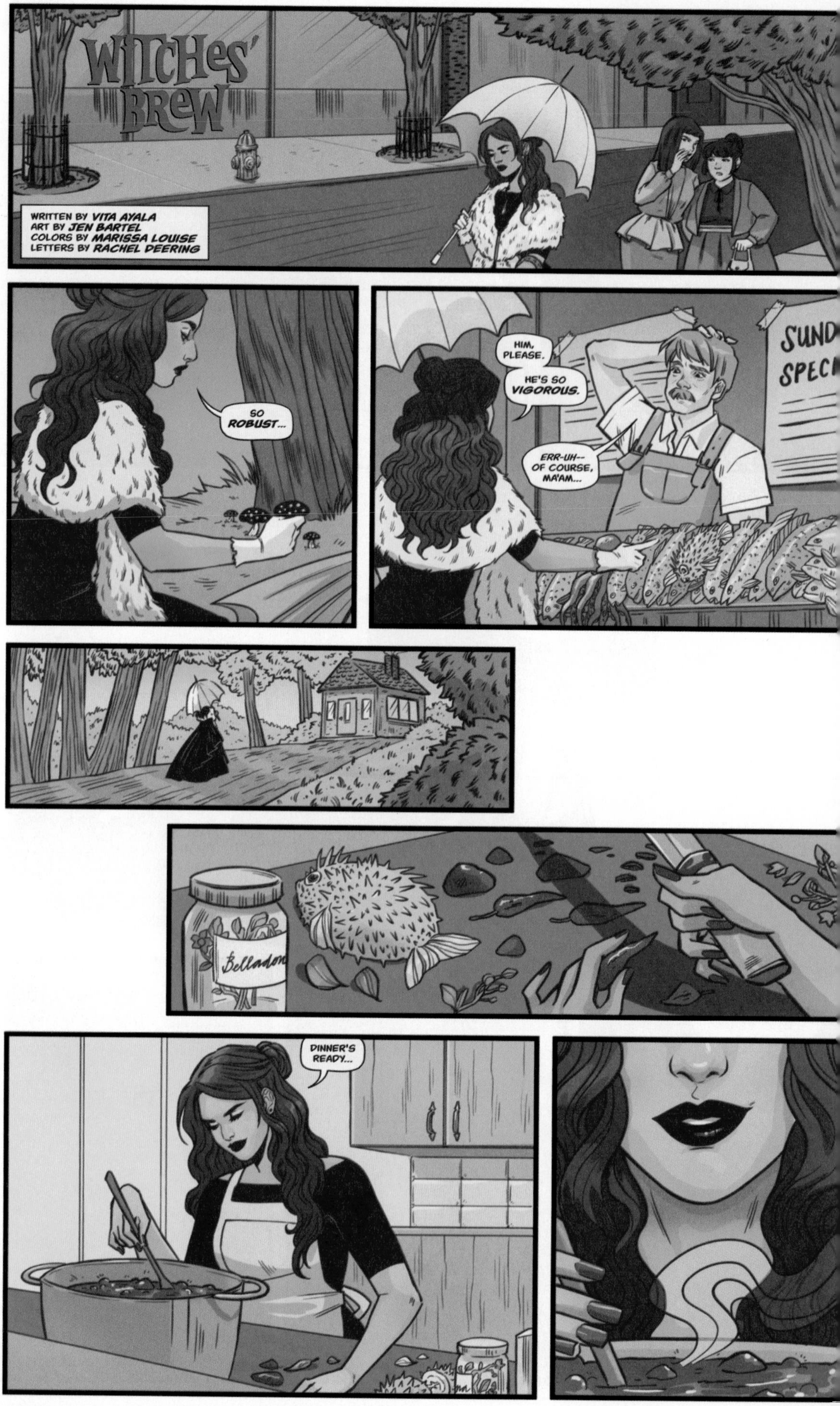
WITCHES' BREW
WRITTEN BY VITA AYALA
ART BY JEN BARTEL
COLORS BY MARISSA LOUISE
LETTERS BY RACHEL DEERING
SO ROBUST...
HIM, PLEASE.
HE'S SO VIGOROUS.
ERR-UH-- OF COURSE, MA'AM...
Belladon
DINNER'S READY...

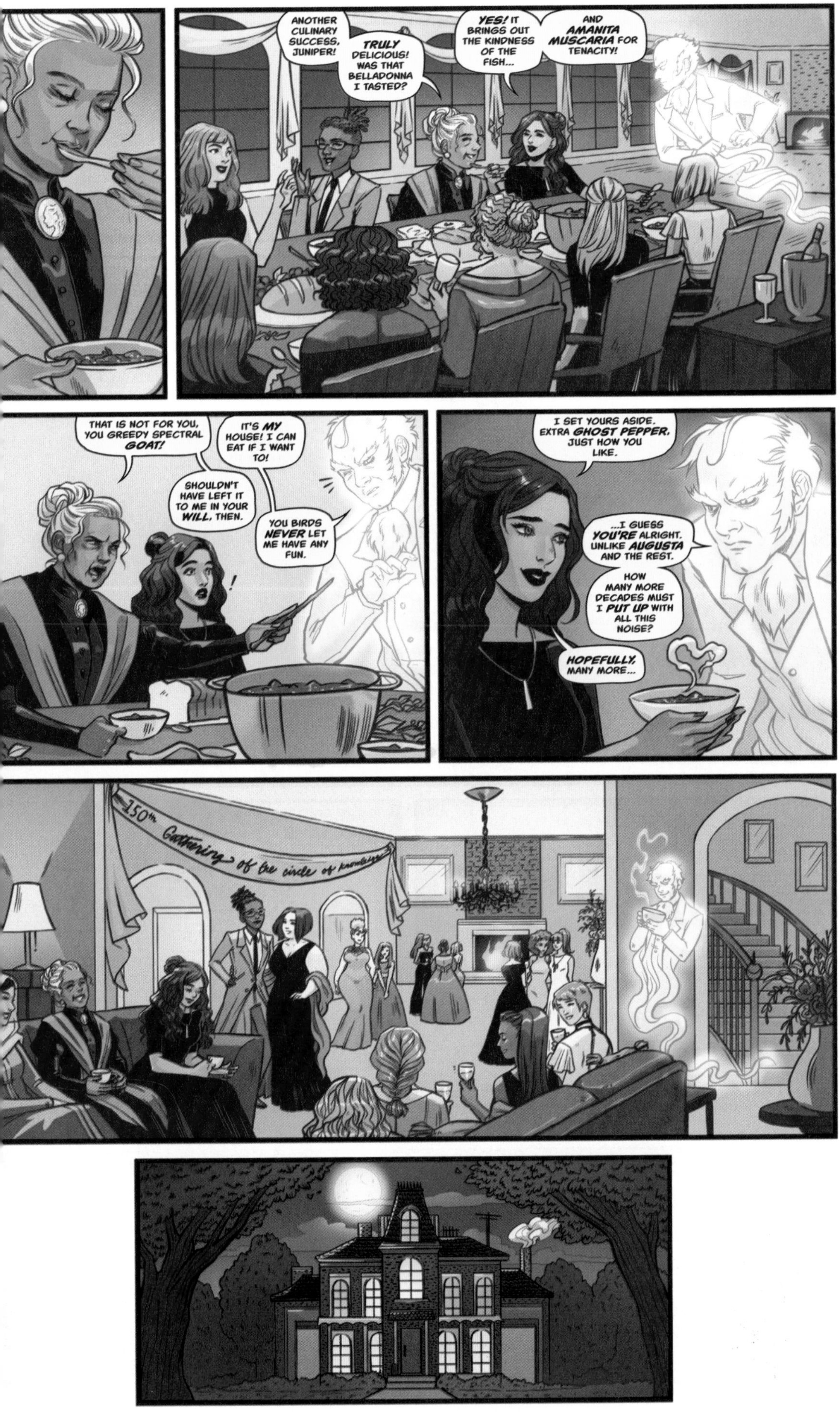
ANOTHER CULINARY SUCCESS, JUNIPER!
TRULY DELICIOUS! WAS THAT BELLADONNA I TASTED?
YES! IT BRINGS OUT THE KINDNESS OF THE FISH...
AND AMANITA MUSCARIA FOR TENACITY!
THAT IS NOT FOR YOU, YOU GREEDY SPECTRAL GOAT!
IT'S MY HOUSE! I CAN EAT IF I WANT TO!
SHOULDN'T HAVE LEFT IT TO ME IN YOUR WILL, THEN.
YOU BIRDS NEVER LET ME HAVE ANY FUN.
!
I SET YOURS ASIDE. EXTRA GHOST PEPPER, JUST HOW YOU LIKE.
...I GUESS YOU'RE ALRIGHT. UNLIKE AUGUSTA AND THE REST.
HOW MANY MORE DECADES MUST I PUT UP WITH ALL THIS NOISE?
HOPEFULLY, MANY MORE...
150th Gathering of the circle of

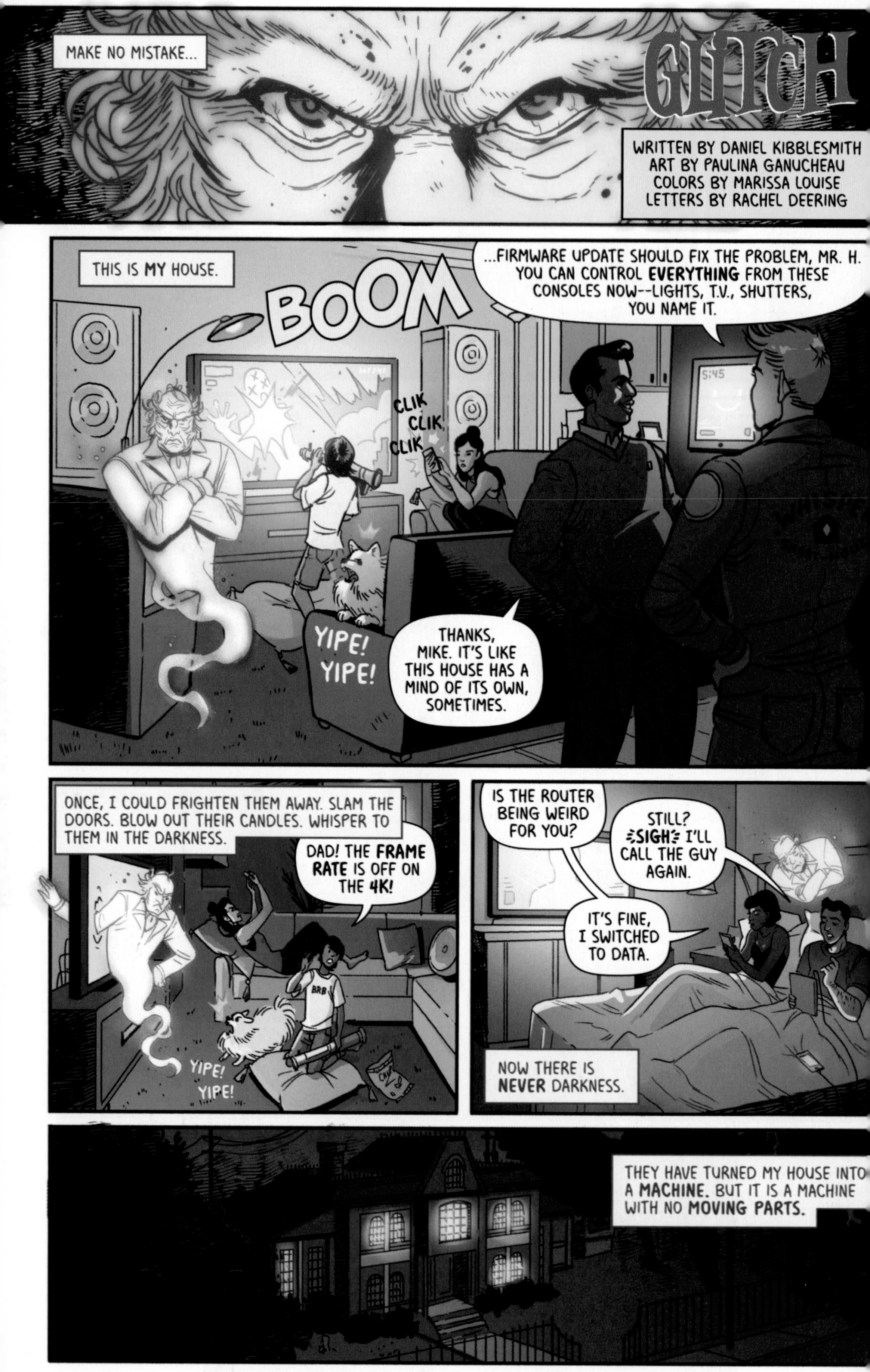
MAKE NO MISTAKE...
GLITCH
WRITTEN BY DANIEL KIBBLESMITH
ART BY PAULINA GANUCHEAU
COLORS BY MARISSA LOUISE
LETTERS BY RACHEL DEERING
THIS IS MY HOUSE.
BOOM
...FIRMWARE UPDATE SHOULD FIX THE PROBLEM, MR. H. YOU CAN CONTROL EVERYTHING FROM THESE CONSOLES NOW--LIGHTS, T.V., SHUTTERS, YOU NAME IT.
5:45
CLIK CLIK CLIK
YIPE! YIPE!
THANKS, MIKE. IT'S LIKE THIS HOUSE HAS A MIND OF ITS OWN, SOMETIMES.
ONCE, I COULD FRIGHTEN THEM AWAY. SLAM THE DOORS. BLOW OUT THEIR CANDLES. WHISPER TO THEM IN THE DARKNESS.
DAD! THE FRAME RATE IS OFF ON THE 4K!
BRB
YIPE! YIPE!
IS THE ROUTER BEING WEIRD FOR YOU?
STILL? *SIGH* I'LL CALL THE GUY AGAIN.
IT'S FINE, I SWITCHED TO DATA.
NOW THERE IS NEVER DARKNESS.
THEY HAVE TURNED MY HOUSE INTO A MACHINE. BUT IT IS A MACHINE WITH NO MOVING PARTS.

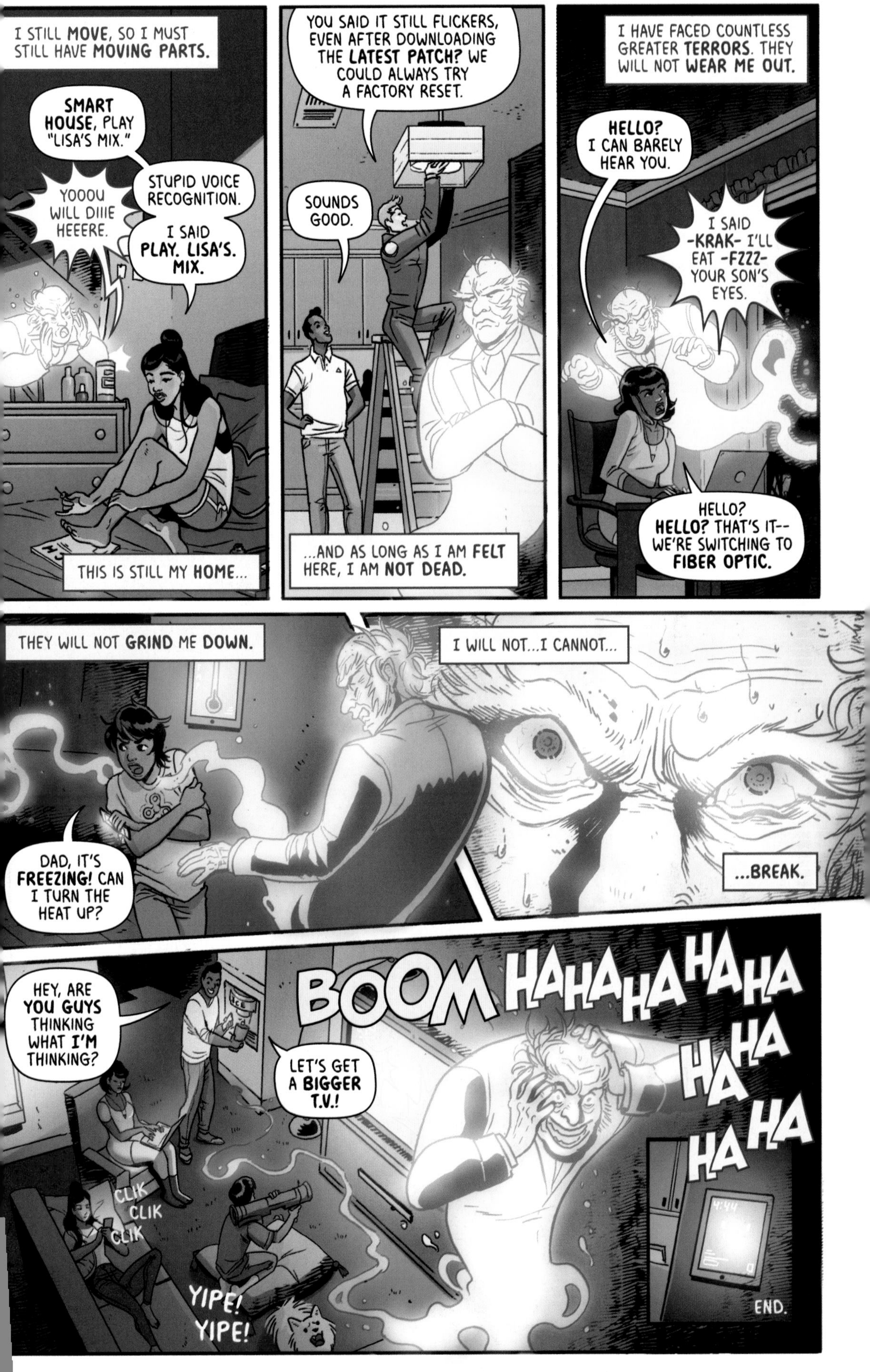

I STILL MOVE, SO I MUST STILL HAVE MOVING PARTS.
SMART HOUSE, PLAY "LISA'S MIX."
YOOOU WILL DIIIE HEEERE.
STUPID VOICE RECOGNITION.
I SAID PLAY. LISA'S. MIX.
THIS IS STILL MY HOME...
YOU SAID IT STILL FLICKERS, EVEN AFTER DOWNLOADING THE LATEST PATCH? WE COULD ALWAYS TRY A FACTORY RESET.
SOUNDS GOOD.
...AND AS LONG AS I AM FELT HERE, I AM NOT DEAD.
I HAVE FACED COUNTLESS GREATER TERRORS. THEY WILL NOT WEAR ME OUT.
HELLO? I CAN BARELY HEAR YOU.
I SAID -KRAK- I'LL EAT -FZZZ- YOUR SON'S EYES.
HELLO? HELLO? THAT'S IT-- WE'RE SWITCHING TO FIBER OPTIC.
THEY WILL NOT GRIND ME DOWN.
I WILL NOT...I CANNOT...
DAD, IT'S FREEZING! CAN I TURN THE HEAT UP?
...BREAK.
HEY, ARE YOU GUYS THINKING WHAT I'M THINKING?
LET'S GET A BIGGER T.V.!
BOOM
HAHAHAHAHAHA
HAHA
HA
HAHA
CLIK
CLIK
CLIK
YIPE! YIPE!
END.

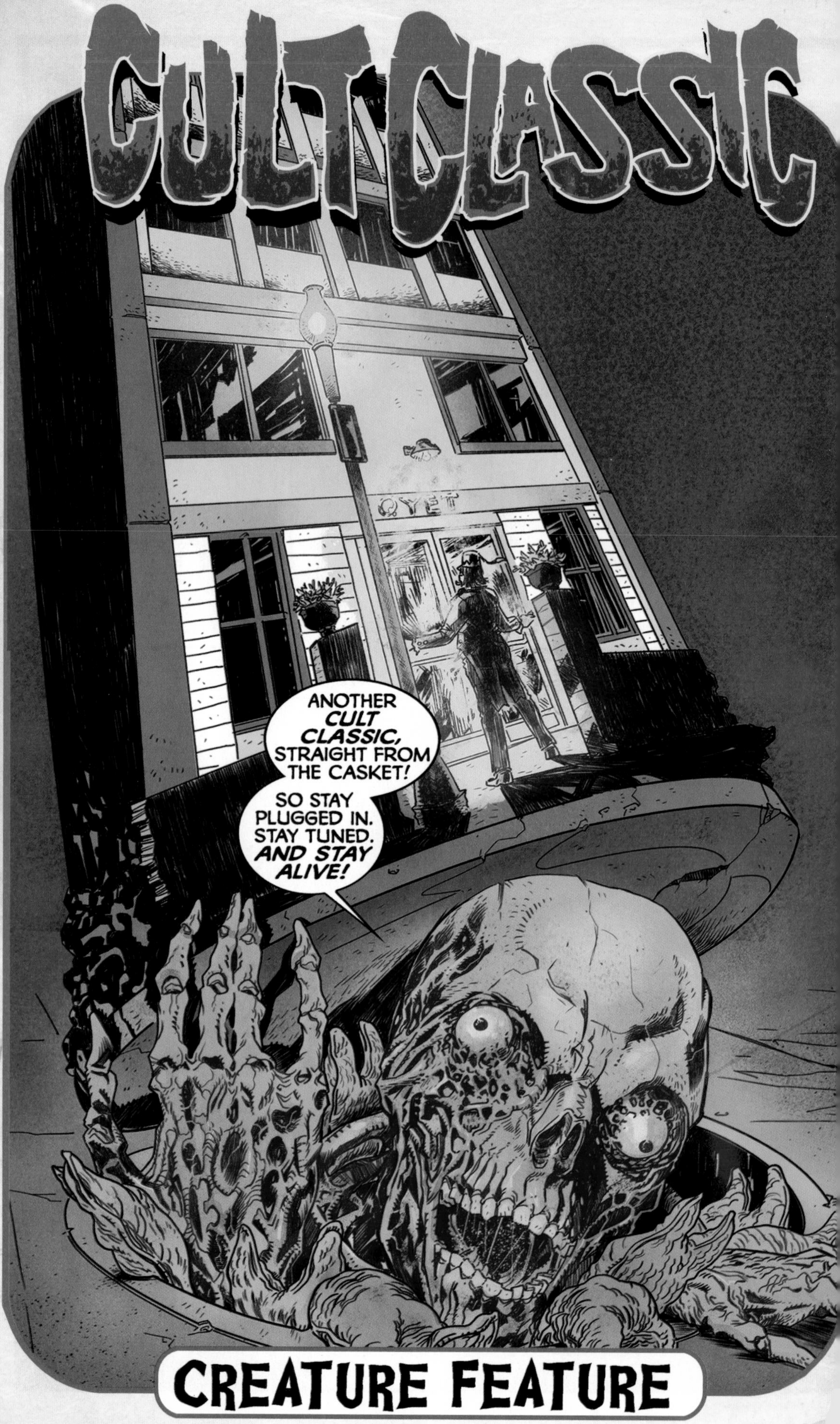
CULT CLASSIC
OYET
ANOTHER CULT CLASSIC, STRAIGHT FROM THE CASKET!
SO STAY PLUGGED IN. STAY TUNED. AND STAY ALIVE!
CREATURE FEATURE